ADAPTIVE

Building Workforce Systems for an (Unpredictable) Future

A Field Guide for the Collaborative Intelligence Era

Ted Lango

Founder, WFM Labs

Published by:
Specialty Directories LLC
d/b/a Kyodo Solutions
6278 N Federal Hwy, Suite 41
Fort Lauderdale, FL 33308
https://www.kyodosolutions.com

ISBN 979-8-9934867-0-3 *(paperback)*

Dedicated to all the workforce management professionals navigating seemingly impossible trade-offs between service, cost, and people— who know their work deserves to be strategic, not just tactical.

Let's build that future together.

Contents

Foreword

Over the course of my career, I've met only a handful of people who could look at a complex operational problem—one that most of us had long accepted as "just the way it is"—and see a new, better way forward. Ted Lango is one of those rare people. Brilliant, creative, and genuinely passionate about his field, Ted has spent his career tackling one of the most stubborn challenges in modern business: how to effectively match customer service supply with unpredictable customer demand.

I first met Ted when he was a customer of Intradiem, a company I founded and where I serve as Co–CEO. Even then, it was clear he wasn't content to operate within the boundaries of existing tools or conventions. He questioned assumptions most people didn't even realize they were making, and he used Intradiem's product to push the boundaries and to achieve the previously unachievable.

Later, I was able to convince Ted to join Intradiem. He had lived the reality of managing some of the world's largest and most complex customer service operations, and he understood—deeply—the limitations of the systems the whole industry relied on. What he brought to the table was not just technical insight, but vision: an ability to connect the dots between mathematics, human behavior, and emerging technology to reimagine what workforce management could be.

Ted and I share a conviction that the future of work is not about replacing people with machines but about building systems that make people better at what only people can do. For both of us, that belief became the foundation of our life's work. At Intradiem, we've spent decades developing technology that allows enterprises to respond dynamically to the unpredictable rhythm of real life—to harvest variance rather than fight it. Ted's thinking, captured so clearly in these pages, extends that same principle into a larger framework for what he calls the Collaborative Intelligence Era.

He's right to frame this moment as a turning point. In the developed world, the average person will spend more than 120 days of their lives waiting—on hold, in line, or for a service technician to arrive. That is absurd in an age when you can order almost any product imaginable and have it delivered to your door within hours. The challenge of delivering that product to you is far more complex than the challenge of providing service for it, and yet our service systems lag decades behind. Fixing that gap is long overdue.

The solution won't come from another round of incremental efficiency improvements. It requires new thinking and new tools—systems that sense, learn, and adapt in real time. That's exactly what Ted delivers in *Adaptive*. This book is both a history and a field guide. It traces how we arrived here, through generations of increasingly sophisticated but rigid workforce systems, and it lays out a clear, actionable path toward the next evolution—one where humans and AI work together fluidly to meet customers where they are, when they need it, with empathy and precision.

What I admire most about Ted's work is that it never loses sight of the human element. He understands that algorithms alone don't create great experiences—people do. His frameworks don't reduce workers to variables; they elevate them to partners in a continuously learning system. In that sense, this isn't just a book about technology. It's a book about possibility—about building a future of work that is more responsive, more intelligent, and ultimately more human.

I have tremendous respect for Ted, both as a professional and as a friend. He has taken everything he's learned—the frustrations, the breakthroughs, the years of trial and error—and distilled it into a body of work that will challenge and inspire anyone who cares about the intersection of people, process, and technology.

If you lead teams, design systems, or simply believe the way we work can be better, you're in the right hands. The journey Ted outlines here is ambitious but achievable—and, as he makes clear, urgently necessary. The time to build adaptive systems is now.

Matt McConnell
Chief Executive Officer, Intradiem

Preface

In 2008, in Comcast's Southern Division, I saw a simple mistake with big consequences: we were deploying the same WFM platform in different ways. Each contact center had unique settings, standards, and rituals. That fragmentation killed the very thing we needed most—*shared capacity* and *coordinated response*. I raised my hand, and the critique became a mandate: lead the deployment, standardize the work, and make the centers operate as one system.

That experience taught me that workforce management is not software—it is *system design*. A year later we proved it by launching the first Resource Optimization Center (ROC): a centralized function that unified real-time operations, routing oversight, and third-party management. In ninety days we stood the ROC up; in another thirty we were fully live. The lesson was enduring: real-time intelligence, when orchestrated across sites, turns contact centers from cost centers into strategic assets. That capability is now amplified by AI.

We are entering the era of Collaborative Intelligence: humans and AI amplifying each other to deliver better service at lower cost. This shift makes building adaptive systems both possible and necessary—AI amplifies our capacity to sense and respond while simultaneously accelerating the unpredictability we must manage. That journey—from reactive silos to *Adaptive Orchestration*—frames this book. Across two decades and multiple organizations, I witnessed one pattern: the winners don't fight variance with perfect plans; they build systems that turn unpredictability into advantage.

Why Change Meets Resistance

Innovation friction follows predictable patterns. Roughly 2.5% are innovators and 13.5% are early adopters; the early and late majorities (34% + 34%) wait for proof; the final 16% move only when forced [1, 2]. The same pattern shows up in WFM. A small set of organizations already operate as human–AI teams and treat contact centers as differentiators. Most remain at "Level 2": solid forecasts, static schedules, and the comforting illusion that a perfect plan can tame an unpredictable day. They measure efficiency while missing the strategic upside hiding in plain sight.

Who This Book Is For

This is not a book to convince skeptics. It is a field guide for early adopters: leaders who sense that WFM must evolve even if the path is fuzzy. You might run a contact center that delivers cost savings but not strategic lift; you might be a CEO watching competitors gain ground; you might be a WFM professional frustrated that your capabilities outstrip your remit. If you believe humans and AI can achieve more together than either can alone, you are the audience.

The Tipping Point

Markets tip when adoption passes 15–18%. We are close. Early adopters are already demonstrating that adaptive systems deliver measurable returns—transforming WFM from tactical forecasting and scheduling into strategic orchestration. As adoption accelerates, first-mover advantage narrows. Moving now matters.

The Choice

The Collaborative Intelligence Era is not a choice—it is the transformation already underway. AI capability, customer expectations, and volatility will increase with or without you. The only choice is how you respond.

You can cling to rigid systems built for predictability and let variance punish you. Or you can build adaptive capability—workforce systems that sense, learn, and respond; systems where humans and AI amplify each other to deliver better service at lower cost.

Adaptive is not a methodology. It is the mindset and discipline required to thrive in this era—the capability that separates leaders from followers, those who shape transformation from those who endure it.

This book is for leaders who choose to lead—who will turn their workforce from the largest expense line into the greatest advantage.

Ted Lango
November 2025

Acknowledgments

I am genuinely grateful to the hundreds of people and teams I have worked alongside over the past two decades. The learnings and lessons that shaped this book came from seeing whole ecosystems at work—how strategy, policy, technology, process, and people link across functions to deliver outcomes. Beyond the contact center, I learned with IT, HR, Finance, Marketing, Sales, Legal, Product, and Operations. Thank you to colleagues at Cleartel Communications, Comcast, MetLife, and Intradiem, and to the partners and vendors whose collaboration and healthy pushback sharpened my thinking.

While it is impractical to acknowledge every person who influenced these ideas, I want to extend special gratitude to leaders who gave me room to learn by building: Jeff Brown, Mike DeCandido, Matt McConnell, Kristine Poznanski, and David Rodrigue.

To Nate Brown, thank you for the clarity and rigor you brought to workforce management in contact centers; your example raised the standard for my work.

To Jim Simmons, co-founder of WFM Labs, thank you for helping build a community dedicated to better ways of working.

And finally, to the WFM Labs community—members, contributors, and peers—thank you. The most durable ideas in this book were strengthened by community practice: engaging in conferences, workshops, and seminars, and by joining other communities where we could share, test, and refine together, along with the day-to-day work with colleagues. For living resources, see Appendix A. This book is an invitation to keep building the next generation of workforce management together.

Part I

Adaptive Foundations:
Context, Drivers, and Frameworks

1 The Evolution of Work and Modern Business Models

Your workforce is anxious. Across boardrooms and break rooms worldwide, the same questions echo: Will AI replace my job? How do I stay relevant? What skills will matter tomorrow? These are not idle concerns—they define today's workforce. Yet while fear dominates headlines, the real story is more nuanced and ultimately hopeful. We stand at the threshold of the **Collaborative Intelligence Era**, where winners will not be those who replace humans with machines, but those who amplify human potential through intelligent partnership.

The anxiety stems from uncertainty about AI's trajectory. Some experts view AI as normal technology—powerful but controllable, like electricity or the internet[3]. Others forecast superhuman AI within years[4], which AI 2027 argues could fundamentally transform society. This uncertainty creates a strategic imperative: organizations must build workforce systems that deliver value today while remaining adaptable for multiple possible futures.

What follows is a guide to navigating that transformation—not through speculation about distant futures, but through practical frameworks proven in real organizations. Across industries, the right approach turns anxiety into opportunity, shifting Workforce Management (WFM) from a cost center to a strategic advantage.

In this opening chapter, we trace the evolution of work from survival to sophistication, examine how the fundamental business model endures despite technological upheaval, and show why understanding labor's strategic role across industries is essential for building workforce systems that are more efficient, more resilient, and more human.

The Evolution of Work

For as long as humans have existed, our relationship with labor has defined us. In the earliest days, work was survival—hunting, foraging, and building shelter to protect ourselves from the elements. Slowly, we began to innovate, creating tools and systems that extended our capabilities, from the first sharpened stones to fire-hardened spears. These simple yet transformative advancements laid the groundwork for every major leap forward. Over time, labor evolved, shaped by new tools, techniques, and the demands of growing societies. Each shift—from physical survival to cognitive problem-solving—has marked the dawn of a new era, with profound implications for how we live, work, and grow.

Today, we're at another monumental shift: the Collaborative Intelligence Era, defined as the deliberate design of human–AI teams that amplify one another's strengths. It acknowledges both the incremental reality of most AI deployments today and prepares for potential acceleration. As Narayanan and Kapoor argue, AI remains fundamentally a tool under human control[3], yet as scenarios like Kokotajlo et al.'s "AI 2027" remind us, the pace of capability advancement may surprise[4]. Workforce systems must therefore be robust enough for steady progress and flexible enough for rapid change.

This is not merely an extension of the Information Age but a new paradigm. Tasks once reliant on physical strength or cognitive repetition are increasingly handled by machines, leaving us to focus on uniquely human traits: creativity, ethical reasoning, and emotional connection. Humans will also remain critical where deep expertise meets judgment—situations requiring ethical discernment, contextual understanding, and attention to long-term consequences.

Furthermore, humans excel at prediction in ways AI cannot yet match. We imagine future outcomes based on incomplete information, cultural context, and intuitive leaps. While AI systems are advancing in predictive mechanisms—like real-time traffic optimization or demand forecasting—they are still limited by gaps in connectivity and data ingestion. Vast portions of our world are not yet "wired" for continuous, real-time feedback, leaving room for human foresight where AI cannot yet operate.

The trajectory of this evolution reveals enduring patterns that guide us today. In the Stone Age, labor was physical and rooted in survival. As humanity progressed into the Bronze and Iron Ages, specialization and coordination emerged through metallurgy, agriculture, and craftsmanship, enabling trade networks and early economies. The Industrial Age transformed productivity via mechanization and assembly lines—but also introduced the modern tension between efficiency and humanity. The Information Age shifted value to knowledge and connectivity, making continuous learning a survival skill.

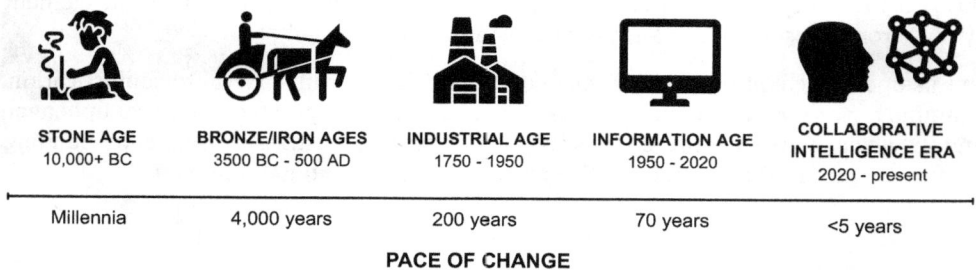

STONE AGE	BRONZE/IRON AGES	INDUSTRIAL AGE	INFORMATION AGE	COLLABORATIVE INTELLIGENCE ERA
10,000+ BC	3500 BC - 500 AD	1750 - 1950	1950 - 2020	2020 - present
Millennia	4,000 years	200 years	70 years	<5 years

PACE OF CHANGE

Figure 1.1: The accelerating pace of change across time

Now, in the Collaborative Intelligence Era, those lessons converge. The core human elements that drove success in every previous era—creativity, judgment, relationships, and adaptability—remain irreplaceable even as the *pace* of change accelerates. Building adaptive systems translates those elements into operating practice. Changes that once unfolded over generations now occur in years or months, demanding workforce management approaches that match the pace while maintaining human well-being.

1.1 The Standard Business Model and AI's Reinforcing Role

Understanding how work has evolved sets the stage for a crucial insight: while the nature of work transforms, the fundamental engine of business remains remarkably stable. At its core, most businesses operate with a simple equation: **Revenue minus Expense equals Profit**. This formula drives decisions at every level. While it is tempting to speculate about radical changes in economic structures as AI advances, the practical reality for business leaders is clear: this fundamental model will guide decisions for the foreseeable future.

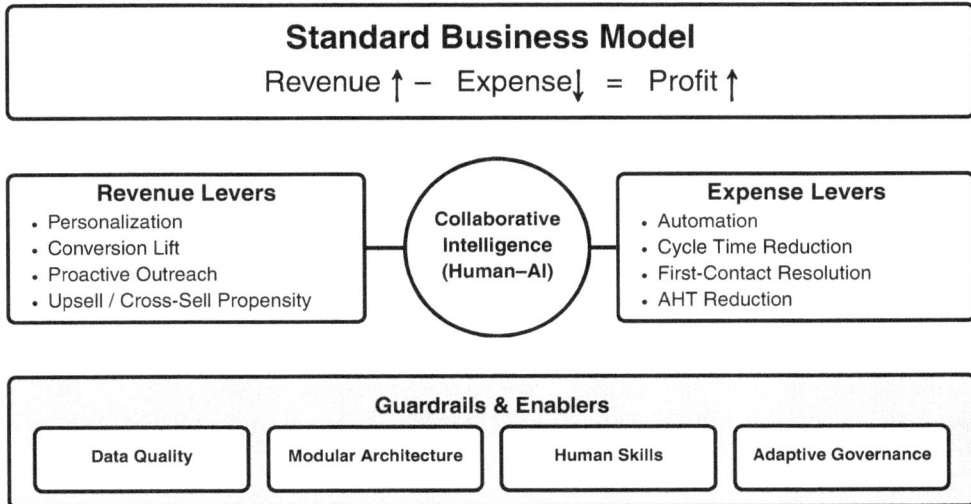

Figure 1.2: AI reinforces the standard business model by lifting revenue and optimizing expense in a human–AI system. *Collaborative Intelligence* is the driver; *Adaptive Orchestration*—data quality, modular architecture, durable human skills, and feedback-driven workflows—makes the gains repeatable.

Recent academic research reinforces this stability. Analysis of Fortune 100 companies from 1955–2020 suggests that despite decades of technological disruption, average company age has increased from 63 to 100 years[5], challenging the popular narrative of rapid creative destruction. This indicates that established business models possess adaptation mechanisms that enable continuity within change.

This persistence stems from what economists term *institutional confluence*—the convergence of legal, financial, cultural, and psychological factors that resist business model change. Even firms that publicly embrace alternatives like stakeholder capitalism typically maintain traditional profit structures privately, underscoring the entrenchment of the revenue–expense–profit equation.

Since the release of ChatGPT 3.5 in November 2022, AI capabilities have advanced rapidly, yet integration patterns remain practical: AI largely reinforces existing structures rather than replacing them. MIT research finds that despite widespread assumptions about disruption, AI primarily functions as a *sustaining technology*, enhancing incumbents more than enabling model disruption[6]. McKinsey reports that while 78% of organizations use AI in at least one function, deployments concentrate on efficiency improvements within current frameworks rather than wholesale transformation[7].

AI's development exhibits a "productive tension" that should shape workforce strategy:

Evolutionary Adoption: For most organizations, AI is an incremental enhancer of existing processes, following familiar diffusion curves—gradual implementation, integration work, and learning cycles.

Exponential Capabilities: Simultaneously, specific AI capabilities improve quickly. The time horizon for long, multi-step tasks has expanded rapidly (doubling roughly every seven months since 2019)[8], shifting feasibility boundaries.

Rather than choosing between these perspectives, successful workforce transformation requires adaptive resilience—systems that deliver value today while maintaining flexibility for multiple futures. Practically, this means:

- Investing in foundational capabilities (data quality, process documentation) that pay off regardless of AI's pace
- Developing modular systems that can absorb new AI components without wholesale reconstruction
- Fostering human skills that remain valuable across scenarios—creativity, judgment, relationship building
- Creating governance structures that evolve with technological capabilities

For forward-looking organizations, AI is an extraordinary opportunity within the existing revenue–expense–profit model. The question is not whether AI will eliminate jobs or invent an entirely new economy, but how it can enhance revenue and optimize cost while creating new categories of human–AI collaborative work.

1.2 Labor as Strategic Differentiator—and Its Limits

Within this enduring framework, labor is often both the largest cost and the greatest source of competitive advantage. Understanding how industries leverage their workforce reveals why *workforce transformation*—not business model revolution—is the key to thriving in the Collaborative Intelligence Era. Advantage increasingly flows to organizations that combine human capability with AI via *Adaptive Orchestration* inside existing structures.

This makes human–AI collaboration a strategic imperative. The question is less "Will our business model change?" and more "Will our workforce strategy evolve fast enough to capture the advantage?"

Labor as Strategic Differentiator—Where AI Reinforces It
Human capability drives advantage; AI amplifies it inside existing operating models.

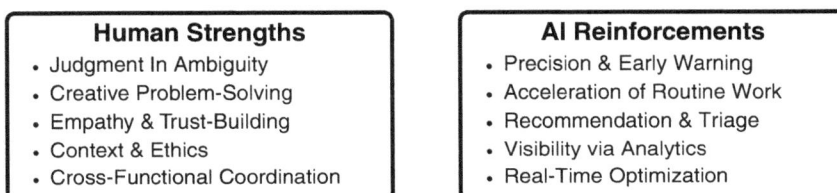

Human Strengths	AI Reinforcements
• Judgment In Ambiguity	• Precision & Early Warning
• Creative Problem-Solving	• Acceleration of Routine Work
• Empathy & Trust-Building	• Recommendation & Triage
• Context & Ethics	• Visibility via Analytics
• Cross-Functional Coordination	• Real-Time Optimization

Figure 1.3: Examples: manufacturing (quality + failure prediction) • healthcare (empathy + decision support) • retail (service + recommendation) • finance (advice + risk scoring).

Labor plays a multifaceted role across industries:

In **manufacturing**, despite extensive automation, human expertise remains essential for quality, exception handling, and continuous improvement. The opportunity: AI-augmented workers who predict failures, optimize schedules in real time, and make quality decisions with better visibility.

The **healthcare** sector showcases labor's irreplaceable value. With labor costs at 50–60% of operations, care quality depends on technical skill plus empathy and judgment under uncertainty. AI enhances diagnosis and planning; clinicians provide trust, ethics, and context.

In **technology**, the very industry building AI depends on human creativity. AI accelerates development but does not substitute for the product sense and architectural judgment that drive innovation.

Education highlights the enduring value of human connection in learning. Platforms and AI tutors scale access, but mentorship, adaptive teaching, and inspiration remain decisive.

In **retail**, as shopping becomes experiential, frontline talent differentiates brands even as automation streamlines transactions.

Finance illustrates a shift from processing to advising: automation handles routine tasks while human expertise tackles trust, regulation, and nuanced risk decisions.

Across sectors, the highest-value work increasingly requires distinctly human capabilities—judgment in ambiguity, creative problem-solving, emotional intelligence, and trust-building. This has profound implications for how we manage and develop the workforce, and why traditional workforce management approaches are failing.

How Labor is Managed

Given labor's centrality, how organizations manage their workforce becomes a strategic differentiator, yet sophistication varies widely.

In **manufacturing**, labor management evolved from Taylor's scientific management and Ford's assembly innovations—foundational steps toward data-driven optimization. **Healthcare** faces acuity, skills, regulation, and layout constraints that defy simple ratios. **Retail** manages extreme variability across hours, days, and seasons, with omnichannel complexity challenging simplified models. Knowledge work introduced further ambiguity; many organizations rely on rough headcount ratios rather than true optimization.

One domain, however, has matured a precise discipline: the **contact center**. WFM in contact centers combines forecasting, scheduling, and real-time optimization to align labor supply and demand:

- Forecast demand at fine intervals using sophisticated algorithms
- Create optimized schedules balancing service levels, costs, and employee preferences
- Adjust in real time as conditions change
- Measure performance across multiple dimensions simultaneously

This sophistication stems from necessity: the impact of being over- or under-staffed is immediately visible in outcomes, creating rapid feedback loops and strong incentives to improve. *Accordingly, this book uses contact centers as the primary case study and laboratory for workforce transformation.* The rationale, implications for AI augmentation (versus replacement), and the detailed business case are developed fully in Chapter 6; here, the contact center serves as a practical lens for principles that generalize across operations.

Seen through this lens, methods that once defined excellence also reveal their limits—especially as volatility, skill heterogeneity, and AI augmentation rise.

Shortfalls of Traditional Staffing Models

What made traditional workforce management successful now constrains its potential. The rigid precision and mathematical elegance that once set contact centers apart have become weaknesses. These limitations are not unique to contact centers; they are universal challenges in the Collaborative Intelligence Era.

Traditional staffing models, even advanced ones, rest on assumptions that no longer hold:

The Predictability Assumption: Historical patterns will predict future demand. Increasingly false amid social media cascades, supply shocks, and shifting expectations.

The Interchangeability Assumption: Workers are fungible units of capacity. In complex service and knowledge work, individual capability and engagement drive outcomes.

The Efficiency-First Assumption: Optimize occupancy, handle time, and unit cost. Overemphasis can erode the human factors that sustain performance, fueling burnout and attrition.

The Stability Assumption: Operating conditions are steady enough for small adjustments. Events like COVID-19 exposed the fragility of finely tuned, low-resilience systems.

The Static Capability Assumption: Workforce capability changes slowly. AI augmentation can expand capability overnight, invalidating static plans.

These gaps show up in practice:

- Contact centers with triple-digit annual turnover despite "sophisticated" scheduling
- Hospitals scrambling during surges their ratios never anticipated
- Retailers missing revenue when viral demand overwhelms historical models
- Technology teams burning out as "always-on" expectations collide with static planning

This landscape calls for a **new, *Adaptive* maturity model**—one that reimagines workforce management as dynamic and employee-centric, integrating with AI while preserving human agency through intelligent orchestration. The journey is not only about better algorithms; it elevates WFM from back-office cost control to a strategic enabler.

1.3 Your Roadmap Forward

The challenges and opportunities highlighted in contact centers reflect broader patterns across people operations. Although this book focuses on contact centers as the primary case study, the underlying principles—understanding organizational context, managing uncertainty, and building adaptive capacity—apply across operational environments.

This book provides your roadmap in two complementary parts:

Part I: The Foundations of Operational Transformation

Part I establishes the core frameworks and principles for effective workforce transformation. Whether AI remains a powerful tool or evolves toward more autonomous capabilities, these principles help ensure your workforce systems remain effective and adaptable.

After Part I, you will be able to trace the evolution of workforce sophistication and why traditional approaches struggle; prioritize the ten change drivers that matter most; apply **STaRS**, the **Service-Profit Chain**, and **GRPIT** to guide action; design adaptive capacity plans that embrace variance; and assess your position on the **WFM Labs Maturity Model**™ to define a practical roadmap.

- **Historical Context** (Chapter 2): The evolution of contact center WFM across eras—from Erlang's formulas to digital PBXs, WFM software, multi-channel complexity, real-time adaptation, and today's AI moment.
- **Drivers of Change** (Chapter 3): Ten forces reshaping workforce requirements, from AI advancement to evolving employee expectations.
- **Frameworks and Tools** (Chapter 4): How to select and apply *STaRS*, the *Service-Profit Chain*, and *GRPIT*.
- **Variance and Volatility** (Chapter 5): Building resilience beyond precision forecasting through adaptive capacity management.
- **Maturity Models and Roadmaps** (Chapter 6): The *WFM Labs Maturity Model*™, a five-level progression from reactive manual planning to AI-powered workforce orchestration.

Part II: Transformation in Action

Part II brings these concepts to life through the maturity levels. Contact centers serve as a universal lens: nearly every large organization has one, and they concentrate workforce challenges in measurable form. Lessons translate directly to any operation where human capability drives value.

- **Level 1: Initial/Manual** (Chapter 7): From spreadsheet chaos to foundational WFM capabilities.
- **Level 2: Foundational** (Chapter 8): Traditional excellence—*and* its limits—in structured forecasting and scheduling.
- **Level 3: Progressive** (Chapter 9): Real-time automation that turns variance from enemy to asset.

- **Level 4: Advanced** (Chapter 10): Ecosystem thinking and probabilistic planning over deterministic models.
- **Level 5: Pioneering** (Chapter 11): Human–AI orchestration and autonomous optimization with safeguards.
- **The Journey Forward** (Chapter 12): Synthesis and path-setting across all levels.

Each chapter builds on the previous, moving from why transformation is necessary to how to achieve it.

Why This Transformation Cannot Wait

Three converging factors make workforce transformation urgent:

First, the capability gap is widening. Organizations using AI-augmented operations are showing material productivity gains[9, 10]. With specific capabilities doubling in months[8], gaps grow exponentially.

Second, the talent market has shifted. Workers increasingly value AI-enabled tools[11] and modern, autonomy-emphasizing ways of working[12]. Workforce strategy now directly shapes attraction and retention.

Third, the window for gradual transition is closing. Whether AI progresses incrementally or accelerates, foundational work must begin now. Organizations that build adaptive capacity today will surf the wave of change; those that wait risk being overwhelmed.

Your Journey Starts Now

The Collaborative Intelligence Era has arrived, though its ultimate form remains unwritten. We stand between two possible futures: one where AI remains a powerful, manageable tool enhancing human work; another where capabilities advance so rapidly that work itself must be redefined. The principles in this book prepare you for either scenario.

By building adaptive, human-centered workforce systems, you create value today while maintaining flexibility for tomorrow. By fostering collaboration between humans and AI, you develop capabilities that compound regardless of technology's pace. By prioritizing resilience over rigid optimization, you build organizations that thrive amid uncertainty.

Whether optimizing a small team or reshaping a global workforce—and whether AI progresses incrementally or exponentially—the journey toward *Adaptive Orchestration* begins with the same first step: understanding where you are and taking practical action toward where you need to be.

The future belongs to organizations that master human–AI collaboration in workforce management. Let's begin building that future together.

2 Historical Context

As artificial intelligence reshapes workplaces worldwide, workforce management professionals face familiar anxieties: Will automation eliminate jobs? How do we balance efficiency with employee wellbeing? Can we predict and control the future of work? These questions feel urgent and unprecedented, yet contact centers offer a surprising lesson—the industry now experiencing its greatest transformation has navigated similar disruptions four times before.

Each era believed it had discovered the perfect solution. Mathematical formulas would eliminate guesswork. Software would automate complexity. Real-time systems would adapt to any variance. AI would optimize everything autonomously. Each breakthrough delivered genuine improvements while planting the seeds of new challenges that demanded the next evolution.

The pattern reveals something profound: workforce management never reaches a final destination. Instead, it evolves continuously as technology capabilities, business requirements, and human expectations advance together. Understanding this historical rhythm provides both perspective and guidance for leaders navigating today's AI moment.

Contact centers didn't accidentally become laboratories for human-AI collaboration—they were forged by six decades of managing the tension between mathematical precision and operational reality. Every sophisticated algorithm, real-time dashboard, and optimization engine traces back to fundamental questions that remain as relevant today as they were in 1965: How do we balance predictability with flexibility? When does precision become brittleness? How do we optimize systems that depend on human judgment?

The four eras that follow chronicle not just technological progress, but the persistent human challenge of building systems that enhance rather than constrain our capabilities. As we stand at the threshold of the Collaborative Intelligence Era, these historical lessons illuminate both the opportunities ahead and the pitfalls to avoid.

2.1 Era 1: Mathematical Foundation (1960s–1985)

Before 1965, managing large-scale telephone operations meant managing organized chaos. Supervisors walked rows of operators manually connecting calls, estimating staffing needs based on yesterday's patterns and gut instinct. Call volumes fluctuated wildly throughout the day, but planning consisted of little more than 'add more people during busy times'. Structured and mathematically grounded practices that would later define workforce management in call centers simply did not exist. What we now recognize as the contact center had not yet emerged. Large telephone companies were struggling to keep up with demand using manual operations.

Then something remarkable happened: engineering precision met customer service operations, creating the foundation of modern workforce management. This convergence didn't occur by accident—it emerged from necessity as organizations recognized that customer service operations could be systematically optimized using scientific principles.

Birmingham's Revolution: The First Commercial Breakthrough

The transformation began with a 1965 installation at **Birmingham Press and Mail** in the UK. The **GEC PABX 4 ACD system** automated distribution of calls to available agents[13]. This seemingly simple innovation fundamentally changed workforce management. Supervisors could, for the first time, monitor call volumes, agent availability, and queue depths in real time. The classic contact center layout—rows of agents at individual terminals—emerged from this system's design, defining the industry's physical architecture for decades.

The Birmingham installation also demonstrated that customer service operations could be systematically measured and optimized. Supervisors discovered repeatable patterns—Monday mornings consistently generating higher call volumes, intraday peaks, and agent productivity varying by workload distribution. These insights laid the groundwork for scientific workforce planning.

Erlang's Century-Old Foundation

The mathematical basis for this revolution had been waiting for half a century. **Agner Krarup Erlang**, a Danish mathematician employed by Copenhagen Telephone Company, published "The Theory of Probabilities and Telephone Conversations" in 1909 [14]. This introduced what became known as the Erlang-B formula, describing the probability of call blocking in systems without waiting lines. In 1917, he extended this work in "Solution of some Problems in the Theory of Probabilities of Significance in Automatic Telephone Exchanges," introducing what is now called the Erlang-C formula, which modeled the probability of waiting in queue and established the fundamental relationship between arrival rates, service times, and staffing levels that remains essential to call center planning [15].

By the mid-1940s, the CCITT and national telephony bodies recognized the *erlang* as the unit of telephone traffic[16]. Erlang's rare honor as a mathematician reflected the operational impact of his work: his formulas did not merely describe systems, they enabled their optimization.

Digital Revolution: Northern Telecom's Game Changer

While Erlang provided the mathematical foundation and Birmingham demonstrated commercial viability, **Northern Telecom (Nortel)** introduced the SL-1 PBX, the world's first all-digital PBX aimed at medium-sized businesses[17]. The move from analog to digital increased data granularity, allowing supervisors to monitor queues and individual performance at short intervals and to identify improvement opportunities. The SL-1's success was decisive—by 1991, Nortel was the world's largest PBX supplier[18].

Digital platforms expanded capabilities with advanced reporting and, later, skill-based routing. The resulting continuous operational data streams underpinned modern workforce management, enabling statistical analysis and real-time optimization.

The Economic Imperative Driving Change

The move from manual to automated switching reflected broader labor and economic pressures. In 1910, the U.S. employed 88,000 female telephone operators, a figure that ballooned to 235,000 by 1930 [19]. Rising labor costs and wartime pressures made automation increasingly necessary. The last manual exchange in Enfield, North London, switched to automatic operation on October 5, 1960, symbolizing the end of the operator era [20].

Automation displaced hundreds of thousands of jobs globally, but simultaneously created new categories of employment, such as data entry, customer service, and system operation. More importantly, automation allowed supervisors to track metrics such as average call duration, peak patterns, and service level achievement—transforming workforce management from intuitive art to measurable science.

By the early 1980s, the foundation was solidly established. Erlang's mathematical principles provided the theoretical framework, digital PBX systems generated the operational data, and early commercial software began to emerge for systematic workforce planning.

The Seeds of Future Complexity

The Foundation Era's success contained the elements that would drive the next transformation. As organizations grew more sophisticated in their mathematical approach to workforce management, they began to demand more powerful tools to handle the computational complexity. The PC revolution of the early-to-mid 1980s was making computing power accessible to businesses of all sizes, creating the conditions for the software revolution that would follow.

Early vendors such as TCS Management Group were developing the *TeleCenter System* for workforce management, demonstrating early market demand for automated forecasting and scheduling solutions. By the mid-1980s, these pioneering efforts were gaining momentum as contact centers recognized that manual application of Erlang's formulas could not scale with their growing operational complexity.

The Seeds of Precision Obsession

By 1985, contact centers had achieved something unprecedented: systematic, mathematically grounded workforce optimization. Erlang's formulas made predictive staffing possible, digital PBXs produced streams of real-time data, and early software tools began turning theory into practice.

But the very success of these methods planted a seductive belief: that if staffing could be calculated precisely, operations could be managed precisely. This conviction of controllability would define the next two decades, even as rising operational complexity steadily exposed its limits.

The mathematical precision of the Foundation Era had created an intoxicating possibility: perfect control through perfect prediction. Armed with Erlang's formulas and increasingly accessible computing power, the contact center industry was about to embark on an ambitious quest that would transform reasonable pursuit of accuracy into an obsession with forecasting perfection.

2.2 Era 2: Software Sophistication (1985–2005)

The mid-1980s brought personal computing power to workforce management, promising to eliminate human guesswork through algorithmic precision. What began as a logical evolution of the Foundation Era's mathematical insights transformed into something more ambitious—and ultimately more constraining. The industry convinced itself that if mathematical formulas could optimize staffing, then software could optimize everything.

The seductive logic was undeniable: computers didn't forget patterns, didn't make calculation errors, and could process far more data than human planners. Vendors promised that sophisticated forecasting engines would turn workforce management from reactive art into predictive science. The promise proved both true and false—software did improve accuracy, but the pursuit of perfection created systems so rigid they broke when reality inevitably deviated from prediction.

The PC Revolution Enables Commercial WFM Software

The democratization of computing power in the mid-1980s transformed workforce management from a specialized discipline requiring mainframe access to a practical capability for any substantial contact center. **TCS Management Group**, which James R. Gordon had founded in 1975 with the *TeleCenter System*, found growing market demand as PC-based platforms made sophisticated workforce management accessible to organizations that could never have justified mainframe investments.

By the early 1990s, TCS software was widely adopted, illustrating the strong market appetite for automated scheduling and forecasting. The company's success demonstrated that contact centers were ready to move beyond manual application of Erlang's formulas toward systematic, software-driven optimization.

Pipkins Inc., founded in 1983 by Dr. James Pipkins, developed proprietary **Merlang algorithms** as modifications of Erlang's models. These innovations accounted for real-world effects such as abandons and multi-skill routing, enhancing forecast realism beyond the theoretical foundations [21]. By 2004, Pipkins supported over 100,000 agents in 300+ locations, demonstrating the scalability of PC-based workforce management platforms.

The transition to personal computers reached its culmination with **IEX Corporation**, founded in 1988. IEX leveraged PC architecture with its *TotalView* system, creating what became the template for modern workforce management platforms. By the mid-2000s, IEX's platform had achieved widespread global adoption. This represented a decisive shift from mainframe-batch forecasting to interactive, desktop-enabled workforce management that could respond to operational needs in near real-time.

The ARIMA Revolution: When Statistics Met Contact Centers

The 1990s witnessed a transformation in contact center planning through sophisticated time-series forecasting. Mabert's 1985 study on short-interval (e.g., 15-minute) workload forecasting for 911 centers demonstrated effective seasonal regression with event effects and showed clear advantages over manual techniques[22]. This work helped establish the feasibility of data-driven interval forecasting. By the mid-1990s, autoregressive integrated moving average (ARIMA) and transfer-function models had begun to see commercial use in contact centers[23].

In 1995, Andrews and Cunningham documented L.L. Bean's pioneering application of ARIMA and transfer-function modeling—incorporating promotions, catalogs, and holidays—to improve call-center forecasts and staffing decisions, reporting significant operational savings[23]. Their approach became an influential template for bringing formal time-series analysis into day-to-day workforce management practice.

Meanwhile, exponential-smoothing methods developed by Holt (1957) and Winters (1960) found broad commercial adoption because they were tractable, interpretable, and required limited statistical expertise[24, 25]. By the 1990s, **Holt–Winters** was a standard in many WFM platforms for capturing level, trend, and seasonality. Comparative studies showed that results depend on context: for some contact center workloads, intervention-capable ARIMA/transfer-function models outperformed Holt–Winters[26], yet Holt–Winters remained a workhorse due to its robustness and ease of implementation.

The Precision Obsession Takes Hold

As forecasting methods matured throughout the 1990s, forecast accuracy became the industry's holy grail. Vendors highlighted mean absolute percentage error (MAPE) improvements in their marketing materials, industry conferences centered on statistical techniques and model refinement, and professional certifications emphasized modeling expertise over operational insight. The implicit assumption driving this focus was clear: more accurate forecasts would solve workforce management challenges.

This mindset had profound operational consequences. Organizations optimized schedules with minimal buffer capacity, assuming forecasts would be precise enough to eliminate the need for flexibility. Real-time adjustments were increasingly stigmatized as forecast failures rather than expected operational variance that skilled managers should anticipate and accommodate. The result was sophisticated but brittle systems that delivered excellent results under normal conditions but became highly sensitive to any deviations from predicted patterns.

Seasonal Pattern Recognition: From Simple to Sophisticated

Early PC-based systems applied simple seasonal adjustments, recognizing patterns like "Mondays are typically 15% busier than average" before evolving toward sophisticated multi-seasonal decomposition. Operational experience consistently reflected intuitive patterns: in many industries, Mondays tend to produce the highest call volumes, while Fridays are typically lighter. Advanced methods like double seasonal ARIMA enabled simultaneous modeling of both intraday patterns (busy morning periods, lunch lulls, afternoon peaks) and weekly cycles.

Marketing campaigns introduced new layers of complexity that traditional statistical models struggled to capture effectively. Promotional activities created volume spikes that didn't follow historical seasonal patterns, product launches generated calls with unpredictable handling times that changed as customers became familiar with new offerings, and seasonal sales events compressed normal demand distribution curves into concentrated periods of intense activity. Each campaign became a forecasting challenge that required manual adjustments to statistical models, gradually undermining confidence in purely algorithmic approaches.

The Internet's Early Impact on Contact Centers

The emergence of the World Wide Web in the mid-1990s began to transform customer behavior in ways that existing workforce management systems struggled to accommodate. Early corporate websites provided basic information that might have previously required phone calls, creating the first hints of channel shifting that would later explode into full multi-channel complexity.

Email customer service, initially handled much like traditional correspondence, gradually developed into a more responsive channel that operated on different patterns than telephone demand. These early digital touchpoints were often managed separately from voice operations, but perceptive workforce managers began recognizing that customer interactions were becoming less predictable as alternative channels provided new options for problem resolution.

By the late 1990s, early web chat implementations and primitive self-service capabilities were beginning to affect traditional call patterns in ways that historical forecasting models couldn't easily capture. The precision that had seemed so achievable for voice-only operations became more elusive as customer behavior gained new dimensions of complexity.

When Technical Limitations Became Management Philosophy

Technical architecture defined more than system capabilities—it shaped fundamental management thinking about workforce optimization. Early PC-based workforce management systems were designed around batch processing cycles rather than real-time adaptation. Integration challenges, database storage constraints, and data transfer limitations meant forecasts were *often treated as "right the first time,"* because mid-course corrections were costly or technically constrained; *at the same time*, most operations staffed real-time WFM teams to adjust day-to-day realities within those constraints.

The industry adapted to these constraints by developing increasingly sophisticated planning rituals that emphasized front-end accuracy over operational flexibility. Organizations convinced themselves that perfect prediction was not only achievable but superior to building adaptive capacity into their operations. Technical limitations gradually became cultural orthodoxy: good forecasting would eliminate the need for variance management, and systems that required frequent manual interventions were *sometimes stigmatized* as failures rather than recognized as a normal characteristic of complex operations.

The Precision Paradox

By 2005, workforce management had achieved legitimate and measurable success. Statistical models consistently outperformed manual planning across *most* metrics that mattered to contact center operations. Commercial platforms had democratized sophisticated forecasting capabilities that had previously required specialized expertise. Service levels *often* stabilized while operational costs decreased, and the workforce management discipline had evolved into a data-driven profession with established career paths and professional recognition.

Yet this precision came with hidden costs that were becoming increasingly apparent. The industry had optimized brilliantly for predictable, single-channel voice operations just as customers were beginning to interact with organizations in fundamentally different ways. In many organizations the rhetoric around getting forecasts "right the first time" grew strong—but in practice *real-time WFM teams* existed precisely to manage day-to-day volatility, and schedule changes were relatively infrequent (e.g., *six-month rebids*), so a large share of effort went into *managing the live system* rather than endlessly reshaping schedules.

An important counterpoint: some apparent "variability" shrinks materially when teams improve model fidelity and *validate* both input distributions and outcomes—reducing "mystery variance" that is really modeling error.

The statistical tools that had successfully mastered the Foundation Era's operational chaos were about to encounter complexity they could not calculate away. Email volumes that did not follow voice patterns, web chat sessions with unpredictable duration, and emerging social media channels that operated on different rhythms would soon expose limitations of the precision-focused systems the industry had spent twenty years perfecting.

As the Software Sophistication Era reached its culmination around 2005, the seeds of the next transformation were already visible. The multichannel explosion would challenge assumptions about predictable customer behavior, demanding approaches that could manage complexity rather than simply calculating it away.

2.3 Era 3: Strategic Crossroads & Adaptive Evolution (2005–2020)

The mathematical precision that had defined workforce management for four decades faced its greatest challenge in the mid-2000s, as change accelerated across channels and customer expectations. Email, web chat, social media, and mobile apps transformed customer interactions from predictable single-channel conversations into complex multi-touchpoint journeys. The industry faced a fundamental question: extend existing deterministic methods or embrace entirely new approaches to planning and execution.

Two strategic crossroads emerged that would define modern workforce management. The choices organizations made during this fifteen-year period determined whether they would thrive or struggle when unprecedented disruption arrived in 2020.

Crossroads 1: Planning Philosophy – Deterministic Extension vs. Stochastic Planning

When traditional forecasting models struggled with multi-channel complexity, the industry split along philosophical lines about how to approach workforce planning fundamentally.

The Familiar Path: Extended Deterministic Planning

Most organizations chose to extend existing methods rather than abandon decades of investment in deterministic forecasting. Even those that had invested in sophisticated short-term planning engines from providers like NICE (IEX), Verint (Blue Pumpkin), and Aspect continued to rely heavily on manual processes for strategic decisions.

The reality was a "lift and load" approach to mid and long-term planning. Workforce management teams would extract data from their core WFM systems—pulling separate forecasts for different lines of business, voice channels, and digital channels—then manually combine this data in deterministic spreadsheets for critical business decisions. Annual budgeting cycles, hiring plans, and capacity sourcing strategies were built using Excel-based models that attempted to stitch together outputs from multiple sophisticated systems.

This approach involved applying "efficiency factors" to traditional Erlang-C results, using weighted average handle time calculations across channels, and developing complex rule-of-thumb adjustments for multi-skill environments. The irony was striking: organizations had invested in advanced workforce management platforms for operational execution while reverting to spreadsheet-based planning for the strategic decisions that determined their long-term success.

The Revolutionary Alternative: Stochastic Planning

Bay Bridge Decision Technologies, founded in 2000 by Ric Kosiba, represented a fundamental reimagining of workforce management mathematics. Instead of predicting one precise future, their approach used discrete-event simulation and stochastic modeling to evaluate how different staffing strategies would perform across multiple scenarios.

Bay Bridge's insight was mathematically profound: if multi-channel complexity made exact prediction impossible, stop trying to predict exactly. Instead, use simulation to model realistic contact center operations complete with caller abandons, complex routing rules, and multiple performance metrics. Their approach embraced uncertainty as a fundamental characteristic of complex systems rather than a problem to be solved.

The company secured notable enterprise clients across telecom, travel, healthcare, and financial services. Adoption patterns varied by *economics, packaging, and integration*: available compute and data readiness influenced pace and depth, and many organizations continued deterministic extensions for near-term needs given spreadsheet familiarity and licensing/change-management costs. Where deployed, results validated the approach and proved robust in practice.

Bay Bridge Decision Technologies was acquired by Interactive Intelligence in August 2012 [27], then absorbed into Genesys through their $1.4 billion acquisition in 2016 [28], preserving the technology for future application.

The Industry's Choice

Rather than a philosophical rejection of stochastic methods, adoption patterns largely tracked *economics and packaging*: platform seat adoption was broad *(hundreds of thousands of seats industry-wide)*, but many teams continued with spreadsheets because they were "free," familiar, and fit local workflows. As a result, deterministic extensions persisted alongside stochastic planning, with variability in depth by organization.

This choice would have profound consequences when organizations needed genuine adaptability rather than sophisticated rigidity.

Are we optimizing the right metric?

A recurring lesson from this period was to question inherited targets. The canonical service level (e.g., 80/20) often began as an *executive heuristic*. Mature teams reframed decisions in a decision-science mode: specify objectives and constraints, use simulation to evaluate outcomes under uncertainty, and *optimize* choices over ranges (hit-rate envelopes, cost/risk frontiers) rather than anchor on a single point target.

Crossroads 2: Execution Philosophy – Static Pre-Scheduling vs. Dynamic Variance Harvesting

While grappling with planning complexity, organizations simultaneously faced a fundamental choice about operational execution when reality inevitably deviated from forecasts.

The Traditional Response: Static Pre-Scheduling

The established model involved pre-scheduling training blocks, coaching sessions, breaks, lunches, and administrative activities weeks in advance, then scrambling to cancel or reschedule these activities when service levels were threatened. Schedule adherence metrics penalized agents whose calls ran into scheduled breaks or lunches, even when agents were doing the right thing by staying on the line to complete customer service rather than abruptly ending interactions. In many organizations, variance was treated as a problem to be corrected manually rather than a normal characteristic of complex operations.

This approach reflected the precision obsession inherited from previous eras. If forecasts were accurate enough, the thinking went, static schedules should work. Deviations were *sometimes* interpreted as planning failures; at the same time, most operations staffed real-time WFM teams to manage day-to-day volatility, and schedule changes were relatively infrequent (e.g., six-month rebids).

The Transformative Alternative: Dynamic Variance Harvesting

Intradiem, founded by Matt McConnell as Knowlagent in 1995, pioneered a revolutionary insight: operational variance could be harvested as opportunity rather than treated as a problem to be eliminated. This "variance harvesting" approach represented a fundamental philosophical shift from fighting unpredictability toward leveraging it strategically.

The approach evolved over two decades from simple e-learning delivery during idle periods to comprehensive intraday automation. By the 2010s, following the company's rebrand to Intradiem in 2013, the platform had become a sophisticated automation engine enabling workforce management professionals to build rules for dynamic operations. The system could automatically deliver training during agent availability windows, trigger coaching based on real-time conditions, dynamically adjust breaks and lunches forward or backward based on call completion rather than penalize agents for adherence violations, identify voluntary time-off opportunities within minutes of shift start, and manage administrative tasks—all while continuously adapting to actual demand rather than static forecasts.

Independent analysis documented significant hard returns on investment from this approach. A Forrester Total Economic Impact study found that organizations implementing dynamic variance harvesting achieved a 342% return on investment with substantial quantified benefits across training efficiency, agent productivity, voluntary time optimization, and reduced employee attrition [29].

The Gradual Recognition

Throughout the 2010s, forward-thinking organizations began recognizing that adaptive capacity outperformed rigid precision. The 2008 financial crisis had provided early evidence that historical patterns could become obsolete overnight, while growing operational complexity made manual intervention increasingly necessary regardless of forecasting sophistication.

Cultural barriers slowed adoption significantly. Many workforce management professionals had built careers on forecasting expertise and statistical modeling. Industry conferences continued emphasizing advanced mathematical techniques rather than variance-responsive capacity planning. Performance evaluations often rewarded forecast accuracy over operational flexibility, creating institutional resistance to approaches that explicitly embraced uncertainty.

The technology to support responsive management existed—real-time integration platforms, dynamic scheduling engines, and variance harvesting systems were commercially available. However, most organizations remained anchored to traditional approaches by cultural inertia, existing vendor relationships, and the significant change management required to shift from precision-focused to resilience-focused operations.

The innovators and early adopters who embraced dynamic variance harvesting were ready to challenge core workforce management philosophies. But the industry had not yet reached the tipping point where the majority would abandon the seductive myth of "getting the plan right" in favor of continuous planning under uncertainty. The early majority still believed that better forecasting could control uncertainty, rather than recognizing that systematic adaptation to uncertainty was the true competitive advantage. Until that fundamental philosophical shift occurred across the broader market, adaptive approaches would remain the advantage of the few rather than the standard of the many.

Foundations for Transformation

By 2020, Era 3 had established critical capabilities for the next evolution. Early adopter organizations had developed a self-adjusting infrastructure through real-time systems capable of continuous adjustment. They had gained expertise in variance management, recognizing that uncertainty could be systematically leveraged rather than fought. Most importantly, they had achieved cultural readiness, a growing acceptance that resilience trumped precision in complex environments.

The stochastic planning vision that Bay Bridge had pioneered two decades earlier was preserved through acquisitions, waiting for computational capabilities and organizational readiness to mature. The dynamic variance harvesting that Intradiem had proven effective was validated through rigorous economic analysis, demonstrating measurable business value from variance-responsive approaches.

As 2020 began, two massive disruptions were converging that would forever transform workforce management. A global pandemic would force overnight shifts to remote work while breaking every historical demand pattern, providing the ultimate test of adaptive versus rigid planning approaches. Simultaneously, advances in artificial intelligence were reaching the point where human-machine collaboration could fundamentally reshape the nature of work itself. The strategic choices made during Era 3 would determine which organizations were prepared to lead rather than merely survive the transformation ahead.

Author's note on examples. Looking back on Era 3's two crossroads, I name Bay Bridge Decision Technologies and Intradiem because they exemplify capabilities I've found essential to advancing workforce management: *probabilistic, simulation-based capacity planning* and *real-time variance harvesting (automation)*. I deployed Intradiem at MetLife and later worked at the company; those experiences shaped my perspective on variance as a critical operational lever (Chapter 5). As of 2025, Intradiem is the only platform I have personally seen deliver these capabilities consistently at enterprise scale; that said, the frameworks in this book are vendor-agnostic—adopt any stack that can demonstrably meet the same requirements.

2.4 Era 4: Collaborative Intelligence Emergence (2020–Present)

The period from 2020 onward is being defined by two developments that accelerate work-force management evolution. The first was the COVID-19 pandemic, which forced rapid shifts to remote work and broke historical demand patterns that had anchored forecast-ing models for decades. Contact center remote work adoption surged, with distributed workforce arrangements becoming commonplace by 2021. The second development is the emergence of artificial intelligence capabilities, marked by the public release of ChatGPT in November 2022 [30]. Despite early predictions of wholesale automation, implementation patterns reveal a clear preference for human augmentation, with many contact centers planning to use AI to support rather than replace agents.

Against this backdrop of accelerated change, organizations discover what I term Collabo-rative Intelligence—the strategic integration of human expertise with artificial intelligence capabilities to optimize workforce performance under conditions of increasing uncertainty; this is the *why* behind *Adaptive Orchestration* across workforce systems.

The Consequences of Era 3's Strategic Crossroads

The dual forces of pandemic disruption and AI emergence expose the consequences of strategic choices organizations made during Era 3's crossroads. Organizations with existing responsive capacity—those that had embraced dynamic variance harvesting over static pre-scheduling and stochastic thinking over deterministic extension—transition more successfully to distributed operations and AI collaboration.

The acceleration moment reveals why these choices matter significantly. MIT's Project NANDA (2025) reports that 95% of enterprise AI pilots fail to deliver measurable returns [31], with failure stemming not from technology limitations but from a "learning gap" between static systems and dynamic operational requirements. Success patterns validate this path: organizations that purchase specialized AI tools achieve 67% success rates compared to 33% for internal builds, while companies with adaptive cultures consistently outperform rigid, centralized approaches.

However, most organizations remain anchored in Era 2's precision-focused methods, having largely avoided Era 3's variance-responsive practices. Industry analysis suggests that major enterprise workforce management platforms continue to emphasize suite packaging and operational efficiency over the mathematical forecasting innovations that accelerating change requires. Leading comprehensive suite providers rely on deterministic forecasting models with incremental improvements rather than breakthrough innovation.

The New Operating Reality

Era 4 represents more than technological disruption—it marks continuous acceleration as the new operating environment. Organizations must adapt to multiple simultaneous changes at unprecedented speed, with transformation cycles that historically unfolded over decades now compressing into months.

Traditional workforce management assumptions prove inadequate under these conditions. Deterministic forecasting models assume stable patterns that no longer exist. Static capacity planning creates a fundamental mismatch with rapidly changing operational requirements, failing to acknowledge the continuous shifts in technology capabilities, customer expectations, and competitive dynamics. Annual planning cycles become obsolete when competitive conditions shift quarterly and technology capabilities advance monthly.

Organizations discover they need systems that can sense changes rapidly, adapt continuously, and learn from each adjustment—capabilities that traditional approaches were never designed to provide. The precision emphasis that served earlier eras becomes a constraint when flexibility and adaptability determine competitive advantage.

Bridge to Systematic Transformation

Era 4 establishes that workforce management evolution continues accelerating rather than reaching stable endpoints. The mathematical sophistication of Era 1, technological capabilities of Era 2, and adaptive insights of Era 3 provide foundation elements, but the acceleration reality demands integrated approaches that no previous era required.

The forces reshaping workforce management are not only more numerous but also deeply interconnected. A breakthrough in AI changes customer expectations overnight, which shifts workforce requirements, which alters competitive positioning, which pressures business models. Traditional linear thinking and sequential adaptation can no longer keep up with these cascading effects.

Organizations face transformation pressures that function as interconnected systems rather than isolated challenges. Digital acceleration forces—technological evolution, customer expectations, and employee preferences—amplify each other in self-reinforcing cycles. Operating environment shifts in market dynamics, regulatory requirements, and organizational culture reshape the competitive terrain. Macro pressure forces from economic volatility, demographic changes, and resource constraints create the broader context within which all workforce decisions must unfold.

The frameworks and methodologies required for thriving under continuous acceleration provide the foundation for systematic transformation. Organizations need approaches that can handle uncertainty as a normal operating condition, optimize across multiple objectives simultaneously, and adapt continuously without losing operational stability.

Era 4 does not represent a destination but an inflection point where the pace of change itself becomes the primary strategic challenge. Success requires moving beyond incremental improvements toward systematic assessment of which interconnected forces most powerfully impact organizational capability, followed by frameworks designed for continuous adaptation in environments where change acceleration is the only constant.

3 Change Drivers

If you're leading a workforce in 2025, you're likely feeling pressure from multiple directions at once. AI capabilities that seemed like science fiction just two years ago are now table stakes. Employee expectations shifted overnight during the pandemic and never shifted back. Customers demand personalized, instantaneous service across every channel. And just when you think you've adapted to one change, three more emerge.

This relentless pace of change isn't just overwhelming—it's fundamentally different from the disruptions our predecessors faced. Where the Industrial Revolution unfolded over decades and the Information Age over years, today's transformations happen in months or even weeks. Thriving in this environment requires dynamic capabilities—sensing emerging trends, seizing new opportunities, and reconfiguring resources to meet evolving demands. While these capabilities have always mattered, they must now operate at unprecedented speed and scale, often across multiple dimensions at once.

In this new era of Collaborative Intelligence, workforce pressures are multiplying and interlocking. A step-change in AI resets customer expectations, cascades into new workforce needs, reshapes competitive footing, and strains business models. Linear, sequential adaptation cannot keep up. Adaptive system design is required.

This chapter introduces a practical framework for navigating the ten most critical change drivers shaping workforce strategy today. These drivers don't operate in isolation—they function as four interconnected pressure systems, each generating cascading effects that demand integrated leadership responses:

- **Digital Acceleration Forces** form the most tightly woven and rapidly moving pressure system. This cluster includes three self-reinforcing drivers: technological evolution, shifting customer expectations, and the revolution in what employees expect from work. Each accelerates the others, creating an amplification loop at the heart of the Collaborative Intelligence revolution. Responding effectively requires full-spectrum integration across technology, talent, and service models—operationalized as *Adaptive Orchestration*.

- **Operating Environment Forces** reshape the competitive terrain where all workforce decisions must unfold. Market dynamics shift as digital-first competitors rewrite industry rules overnight. Regulatory requirements diverge across regions, demanding adaptable workforce models. And cultural transformation becomes essential as traditional management structures break down in networked, platform-based organizations. Together, these forces determine whether your workforce strategy enables or constrains competitive response.

- **Macro Pressure Forces** create the broader societal context no workforce strategy can ignore. Economic and geopolitical volatility make prediction obsolete. Demographic shifts trigger knowledge retention crises. Social movements elevate equity and inclusion from values to strategic imperatives. And resource constraints blur the lines between workforce efficiency and environmental responsibility. These external forces set the long-term conditions under which short-term workforce strategies must operate.

- **Strategic Transformation Forces** emerge when external pressures force internal reinvention. Business model innovation—platform coordination, ecosystem orchestration,
  service-based value creation—demands entirely new workforce structures and capabilities. When your business model evolves, your workforce architecture must evolve with
  it—or risk becoming the constraint that kills transformation.

As you work through these ten drivers, you'll find practical self-assessment tools designed
to help you identify which forces most powerfully impact your organization. Some will
immediately resonate as pressure points. Others may reveal untapped opportunities for
strategic differentiation. The goal isn't to tackle all ten equally—but to understand which
combination defines your current operating reality and future trajectory.

This systematic assessment serves a crucial purpose: building leadership alignment around
the *why* of workforce transformation. Too often, workforce initiatives fail not because of
poor execution, but because stakeholders lack a shared understanding of the forces making
change necessary. By identifying and prioritizing the drivers affecting your organization,
you create the foundation for meaningful, sustained transformation.

Each driver section follows a consistent structure: a focused explanation of the force at work,
real-world examples, and a practical evaluation tool. Each assessment takes only minutes
to complete, and together they provide a comprehensive map of your transformation
landscape.

Let's begin by examining how these forces are reshaping workforce models across industries—starting with the Digital Acceleration Forces at the core of the shift to adaptive
operating models.

3.1 Technological Evolution and Integration

Technological evolution is the most visible and rapidly accelerating driver of workforce transformation in the Collaborative Intelligence Era. AI, robotics, and digital infrastructure are redefining how work gets done, who does it, and which skills matter most; *Adaptive Orchestration* aligns these shifts with outcomes.

Evolution alone is insufficient. Integration—the thoughtful embedding of technology into human workflows—determines whether organizations capture value or create chaos. The most successful companies are not those with the most advanced tools, but those that master human–machine collaboration.

For example, Target uses AI for demand forecasting and personalization to help merchandisers spot trends and respond to local conditions[32]. In 2024, Target also rolled out a GenAI "Store Companion" across nearly 2,000 stores and introduced GenAI-enhanced product pages and guided search[33]. By contrast, IBM Watson for Oncology—despite analyzing more than 600,000 medical documents and achieving 81.52% concordance with physicians[34]—did not adapt autonomously to new knowledge and required ongoing human input[35]. Together, these examples show that effective AI implementations enhance, rather than replace, human judgment.

The pace is exponential. Since November 2022, GPT-3.5 and successors have reshaped customer service operations. The imperative is clear: build continuous adaptation into the workforce.

Three technological shifts demand immediate workforce attention:

AI and Machine Learning have moved from specialized tools to general-purpose technologies. Modern language models draft documents, analyze data, and generate code. Every role must reimagine how human expertise combines with AI capabilities.

Collaborative Robotics extends beyond manufacturing. "Cobots" now work in warehouses, hospitals, and restaurants, handling repetitive tasks while humans focus on problem solving and quality control.

Digital Infrastructure—cloud computing, APIs, real-time data—enables new work models. Systems that connect previously siloed functions create flexibility unimaginable five years ago.

The most valuable employees are not those who program AI, but those who partner with it effectively. This requires knowing what machines do well (processing data, identifying patterns) and what humans do best (contextual judgment, creative problem solving, ethical reasoning).

Organizations that thrive invest in continuous learning infrastructure, not one-time training. They measure success by human–machine collaboration effectiveness. Most importantly, they recognize that technological evolution is not about replacing human intelligence—it is about building adaptive ecosystems that amplify both.

Technological Evolution Assessment

Key Questions: How are AI and automation creating competitive advantages? Which workflows could benefit most from human-AI collaboration? Where could technology free your workforce for uniquely human contributions?

Technological Evolution Indicators	Yes / No
Competitors use AI to deliver superior customer experiences	[ ] Yes / [ ] No
Manual processes limit your ability to scale operations	[ ] Yes / [ ] No
Your workforce lacks training on AI collaboration	[ ] Yes / [ ] No
Data silos prevent leveraging predictive analytics	[ ] Yes / [ ] No
Technology adoption has stalled due to workforce resistance	[ ] Yes / [ ] No
You lack metrics for human-AI collaboration effectiveness	[ ] Yes / [ ] No
Critical decisions rely on intuition rather than data insights	[ ] Yes / [ ] No
AI initiatives focus on automation, not collaboration with human expertise	[ ] Yes / [ ] No
Digital infrastructure limits real-time coordination across teams	[ ] Yes / [ ] No
Your organization lacks a strategy for continuous adaptation to emerging technologies	[ ] Yes / [ ] No

Scoring:
0-3 "Yes" = Technology is likely not a critical constraint
4-6 "Yes" = Significant opportunities for improved integration exist
7-10 "Yes" = Technological gaps are actively undermining competitiveness

What your score reveals:

High scores signal you're still operating with yesterday's tools in tomorrow's market. The gap compounds daily as AI capabilities advance exponentially. Your first priority: shift from episodic technology adoption to continuous capability evolution. Start by identifying one high-impact workflow where human-AI collaboration could transform outcomes within 90 days.

3.2 Customer Behavior and Expectation Shifts

Customer expectations have fundamentally transformed workforce management requirements. Only 3% of companies achieve true customer obsession, but those that do report 41% faster revenue growth[36]. This transformation demands workforce strategies that can deliver personalized, omnichannel, proactive experiences—capabilities that require human-AI collaboration at scale.

The data reveals a persistent perception gap: many companies believe they deliver personalized experiences, yet customers often report otherwise. McKinsey's State of the Consumer 2025 identifies personalization and targeted marketing as strategic imperatives that allow consumer companies to unlock growth[37]. Companies that close this gap can outperform their peers.

Three shifts define the new reality:

Channel Complexity Explosion: Customers commonly use multiple touchpoints before purchasing, often engaging across several channels. Companies with robust omnichannel strategies tend to outperform those with weaker approaches[38].

Proactive Service Imperative: Customers increasingly want companies to contact them proactively. Evidence from large-scale implementations shows that AI-enabled customer service with predictive capabilities can reduce service interactions by 40–50% and cut costs by over 20%[39].

Workforce Transformation Requirements: The World Economic Forum reports that 59% of the global workforce will require training by 2030, with service orientation and customer service among the top 10 core skills, and AI and big data showing the largest net increase in importance (+87 percentage points)[40].

Success examples prove the payoff. Leading institutions report major gains in client growth and digital engagement. Hyperscale cloud and enterprise CX platforms report strong revenue momentum alongside broad adoption of AI-assisted service.

The path forward requires acknowledging that BCG's research on AI transformation emphasizes proper resource allocation: 10% to algorithms, 20% to technology and data, and 70% to people and processes[41]. Organizations must enable *Adaptive Orchestration*—combining human judgment with machine scale to deliver results neither could achieve alone.

Customer Expectation Readiness Assessment

Key Questions: Where are customer expectations outpacing your current delivery? What barriers prevent your workforce from delivering personalized, omnichannel, proactive service?

Customer Expectation Indicators	Yes / No
Customer satisfaction scores decline despite personalization investments	[ ] Yes / [ ] No
Service escalations increase due to unmet personalization expectations	[ ] Yes / [ ] No
Employees lack real-time access to comprehensive customer data	[ ] Yes / [ ] No
Customers experience friction when moving between touchpoints	[ ] Yes / [ ] No
Channel silos prevent seamless journey management	[ ] Yes / [ ] No
High volume of preventable contacts and escalations	[ ] Yes / [ ] No
Limited predictive analytics for proactive intervention	[ ] Yes / [ ] No
Teams organized by function rather than customer journey	[ ] Yes / [ ] No
Limited autonomy to resolve customer issues creatively	[ ] Yes / [ ] No
Technology limits rather than enables employee effectiveness	[ ] Yes / [ ] No

Scoring:
0-3 "Yes" = Isolated challenges that may benefit from targeted improvements
4-6 "Yes" = Multiple interconnected gaps requiring systematic transformation
7-10 "Yes" = Comprehensive organizational rewiring required

What your score reveals:

High scores expose the 25-point perception gap that separates customer-obsessed organizations from the rest. Unlike technology gaps that require investment, expectation gaps demand organizational rewiring focused on 70% people and processes, 20% data infrastructure, and only 10% algorithms. Organizations succeeding here don't add more channels—they eliminate the boundaries between them while empowering employees with both advanced technology and creative autonomy.

3.3 Workforce Expectations Revolution

The pandemic didn't just change where we work—it fundamentally rewired what workers expect from work itself. McKinsey's research reveals that COVID-19 caused two-thirds of employees to reflect on their life purpose, with nearly half reconsidering the type of work they do[42]. Meanwhile, their Global Institute found that 20-25% of workforces in advanced economies could work remotely 3-5 days weekly without productivity loss[43].

The business impact is undeniable. McKinsey Health Institute's 2025 analysis estimates $3.7–$11.7 trillion in global economic value from investing in holistic employee health[44]. Independent analyses indicate that investments in well-being generate a strong, positive return.

Four seismic shifts define the new workforce reality:

Flexibility as foundation: Today's workforce expects real control over when, where, and how they work. In PwC's 2024 survey of 56,600 workers, 28% say they are extremely or very likely to change employers in the next 12 months; those planning to switch are nearly twice as likely to prioritize learning and development opportunities (67% vs. 36%)[45]. Large cross-country samples also link flexibility shortfalls to turnover intent: in Future Forum's Winter 2022–2023 snapshot, flexibility ranks second only to compensation for job satisfaction, and among workers dissatisfied with their level of flexibility, 75% plan to look for a new opportunity within a year[46].

Purpose over paycheck: Purpose is now a core job attribute. It shapes employer choice, engagement, and retention across career stages and industries. Roughly nine in ten Gen Zs (89%) and millennials (92%) say a sense of purpose is important to job satisfaction and well-being[47], and workers increasingly choose employers that prioritize DE&I (63% overall; 73% of Gen Z)[48].

Well-being as business strategy: Poor mental health carries large, measurable costs, while targeted investments deliver returns. The WHO estimates depression and anxiety cost the global economy about $1 trillion annually and account for roughly 12 billion lost workdays[49]. A WHO-led analysis finds that every $1 invested in treatment yields about $4 in improved health and productivity[50]. Company studies find positive ROI from sustained workplace mental health programs[51].

Continuous growth imperative: Learning is a primary lever for retention and performance. Organizations with strong learning cultures see higher retention, and many companies cite learning as a top retention strategy[52]. Skills-based organizations are more likely to achieve business outcomes[53], and industry benchmarks show continued investment in employee development.

Yet the gap between recognition and action remains. Many leaders acknowledge these shifts, but few have redesigned work, management, and systems accordingly. The advantage goes to organizations that make flexibility the default, embed purpose in daily work, treat well-being as a strategic investment, and build continuous growth into the operating model for adaptive workforce systems.

Workforce Expectations Revolution Assessment

Key Questions: Is your workforce strategy aligned with what employees actually want? Where do outdated policies create retention risks? How can meeting evolving expectations become your competitive advantage?

Workforce Expectations Indicators	Yes / No
High performers leave despite competitive compensation	[ ] Yes / [ ] No
Rigid policies prevent flexible work arrangements	[ ] Yes / [ ] No
Exit interviews cite lack of growth opportunities	[ ] Yes / [ ] No
Employee engagement scores trend downward	[ ] Yes / [ ] No
Mental health issues impact productivity	[ ] Yes / [ ] No
Top talent rejects offers citing culture concerns	[ ] Yes / [ ] No
Learning programs focus on compliance, not growth	[ ] Yes / [ ] No
Purpose and values feel disconnected from daily work	[ ] Yes / [ ] No
Manager behavior contradicts stated culture	[ ] Yes / [ ] No
Younger employees express highest dissatisfaction	[ ] Yes / [ ] No

Scoring:

0-3 "Yes" = Workforce expectations largely met

4-6 "Yes" = Significant gaps requiring attention

7-10 "Yes" = Fundamental transformation needed

What your score reveals:

High scores indicate you're fighting a talent war with outdated weapons. While competitors offer flexibility, purpose, and growth as core operating principles, you're still treating them as retention programs. The fix isn't adding perks—it's fundamentally rethinking how work gets done. Start where it matters most: give your highest performers the autonomy they crave and watch what happens.

3.4 Market Dynamics and Competition

The competitive landscape isn't just changing—it's shape-shifting. Platform businesses decimated traditional competitors in record time: within a decade of its 2008 founding, Airbnb amassed more *listings* than any single hotel chain's *rooms*[54, 55]; and TikTok reached one billion monthly active users in roughly five years—far faster than earlier social platforms[56, 57]. These aren't anomalies. They're the new normal.

The drivers are clear: digital platforms enabling instant scale, AI lowering barriers to entry, and talent accessible globally rather than locally. Traditional competitive moats—capital, distribution, even brand—erode while new ones emerge: data network effects, ecosystem orchestration, and workforce agility.

Four market forces demand immediate workforce strategy response:

Platform competition: Platform businesses command valuation premiums. In a study of 959 unicorns, platform models averaged $4.3 billion versus $2.5 billion for non-platforms (a 72% premium)[58]. Public markets show a similar pattern, with platforms trading at about $2.1 \times$ the EV/revenue multiple of traditional SaaS peers[59]. The workforce implication: shift from producing value to orchestrating it across networks[60].

Talent arbitrage: GitLab operates as a remote-only company with approximately 2,375 team members across 60 countries and no headquarters[61]. Geography no longer determines capability.

Industry convergence: Software capability now cuts across sectors. As boundaries blur, industry-anchored playbooks date quickly, elevating skills portability and role mobility. Leaders report the need to keep human capabilities in step with technology, yet few report progress; skills-based organizations are more likely to achieve outcomes, and workers spent about 50% more time learning in 2024 than in 2023[53].

Speed premium: AI startups are reaching $1B valuations faster and with smaller teams than non-AI peers[62]. AI also accounts for a growing share of new unicorns—nearly half in 2024 and a majority in early 2025[63]. This pace favors workforce models that scale through automation, partnerships, and flexible talent networks.

Static org charts give way to dynamic team assembly. Five-year workforce plans compress to quarterly sprints. Skills inventory management becomes as critical as financial management. Advantage shifts from owning resources to orchestrating capabilities.

Market Dynamics Assessment

Key Questions: How are new competitors disrupting your talent model? Where do rigid structures limit your market responsiveness? What workforce capabilities create genuine competitive advantage?

Market Competition Indicators	Yes / No
New entrants attract your best talent with innovative work models	[ ] Yes / [ ] No
Geographic hiring constraints limit access to critical skills	[ ] Yes / [ ] No
Platform competitors achieve more with smaller workforces	[ ] Yes / [ ] No
Industry convergence creates unfamiliar talent requirements	[ ] Yes / [ ] No
Speed to market suffers due to lengthy hiring processes	[ ] Yes / [ ] No
Functional silos prevent rapid response to market shifts	[ ] Yes / [ ] No
Workforce planning cycles can't match market volatility	[ ] Yes / [ ] No
Critical capabilities exist outside your traditional talent pools	[ ] Yes / [ ] No
Competitive threats emerge from unexpected industries	[ ] Yes / [ ] No
Your workforce model assumes stable, predictable competition	[ ] Yes / [ ] No

Scoring:
0-3 "Yes" = Competitive position secure
4-6 "Yes" = Market vulnerabilities emerging
7-10 "Yes" = Urgent competitive transformation needed

What your score reveals:

High scores suggest you're organized for stability in a world that rewards speed. Platform competitors aren't just moving faster—they're playing a different game entirely. Traditional workforce planning assumes predictable competition, but today's threats emerge from blind spots. Your next step: identify which workforce constraints would cripple you if a platform player entered your market tomorrow.

3.5 Regulatory and Compliance Evolution

The regulatory landscape has become a geopolitical battlefield where workforce strategies must navigate opposing philosophies. The EU's AI Act prohibits workplace emotion recognition systems as of February 2025[64]. Meanwhile, U.S. policy signals have emphasized innovation alongside emerging safeguards. This divergence creates an unprecedented challenge: building workforce models flexible enough to operate across radically different compliance regimes.

The whiplash is real. California's AB5 reshaped gig worker classification, yet enforcement has varied. GDPR fines reached €1.97 billion in 2023[65], while U.S. regulators have, in some cases, scaled back worker protections. Companies operating globally must now maintain multiple workforce playbooks—one for privacy-first Europe, another for a more deregulatory U.S. context.

Three compliance fractures demand immediate workforce attention:

The Privacy Paradox: AI development requires massive data collection, yet privacy regulations restrict it. European companies increasingly rely on synthetic data to navigate privacy constraints. Meanwhile, U.S. competitors leverage real user data—though recent European enforcement actions highlight the risks. Your workforce must master both approaches.

Labor Classification Chaos: Recent "rider" rulings in Europe have pushed platforms toward employment models. The UK Supreme Court's Uber ruling established five key factors for worker classification[66]. California's Prop 22 created contractor exemptions following significant platform spending. Organizations need workforce strategies that can shift between models as regulations change.

Compliance as Competitive Weapon: McKinsey research shows 87% of consumers refuse business with companies having poor security practices[67]. Industry surveys indicate the benefits of privacy investment often exceed the costs. Workforce readiness for compliance becomes a differentiator.

The workforce implications extend beyond legal teams. Every employee becomes a compliance officer when regulations touch daily work. Data scientists must understand privacy engineering. HR teams need real-time classification systems. Traditional compliance training—annual sessions on static rules—becomes obsolete when regulations shift quarterly.

Most organizations treat compliance as a cost center rather than capability. They react instead of anticipating. They centralize expertise instead of distributing it. They assume today's regulatory environment will persist, despite evidence of accelerating change.

Winners build compliance agility into workforce DNA. They track regulatory trends like market opportunities. They create modular workforce models that reconfigure for new requirements. In a world of competing regulatory philosophies, the ability to operate effectively across all of them becomes the ultimate competitive advantage.

Regulatory Compliance Assessment

Key Questions: Which regulatory shifts threaten your current workforce model? Where does compliance friction slow innovation? How can regulatory readiness become a competitive edge?

Regulatory Compliance Indicators	Yes / No
Different regulations across markets require multiple workforce models	[ ] Yes / [ ] No
Privacy laws conflict with your AI/data strategy needs	[ ] Yes / [ ] No
Labor classification uncertainty affects staffing decisions	[ ] Yes / [ ] No
Compliance requirements slow product development cycles	[ ] Yes / [ ] No
Regulatory changes catch your organization unprepared	[ ] Yes / [ ] No
Compliance expertise remains siloed in legal/HR departments	[ ] Yes / [ ] No
Training programs can't keep pace with regulatory shifts	[ ] Yes / [ ] No
Competitors use regulatory arbitrage against you	[ ] Yes / [ ] No
Cross-border operations face conflicting requirements	[ ] Yes / [ ] No
Your workforce model assumes stable regulations	[ ] Yes / [ ] No

Scoring:
0-3 "Yes" = Compliance under control
4-6 "Yes" = Regulatory risks emerging
7-10 "Yes" = Compliance strategy overhaul needed

What your score reveals:

High scores signal you're fighting tomorrow's battles with yesterday's compliance playbook. While competitors build regulatory agility, you're still perfecting adherence to rules that may vanish with the next election. The fix isn't more lawyers—it's embedding compliance thinking throughout your workforce. Start by identifying which regulations create real risk versus mere friction, then build the organizational muscle to adapt faster than requirements change.

3.6 Organizational Culture Transformation

Culture has become the new battlefield for talent—and most organizations are losing.
A large perception gap persists: 82% of executives rate their culture as good or excellent,
but only 47% of individual contributors agree[68]. This disconnect helps explain why
roughly 70% of transformations fail[69]: you can't transform a workforce that doesn't
believe in where you're heading.

The pandemic exposed cultural fault lines that had been papered over for decades. Remote
work revealed which companies actually trusted their employees versus those merely
claiming to. Social justice movements forced organizations to confront the gap between
DEI statements and lived experiences. Mental health crises showed whether "people first"
was policy or platitude.

Three cultural shifts now separate thriving organizations from the struggling majority:

From Control to Context: Netflix's culture deck popularized "context, not control"—giving
employees the information to make smart decisions rather than rules to follow. Companies
embracing this shift report meaningful productivity gains. Managers must evolve from
supervisors to context-providers, sharing the why behind decisions, not just the what.

From Perks to Purpose: Free lunch and foosball tables don't create culture—shared
mission does. Purpose-driven companies tend to see higher retention and stronger innovation. Organizations that commit to rigorous, values-aligned standards often report strong
retention.

From Diversity Theater to Inclusion Reality: Publishing diversity statistics means nothing
if underrepresented employees leave within two years. For every 100 men promoted to
manager, only 81 women were promoted in 2024—down from 87 in 2022–2023[70].
Psychological safety—the belief you can speak up without punishment—supports learning
behaviors and better performance outcomes, with leadership as a key antecedent[71].

The workforce implications cascade through every interaction. Hiring shifts from skills-
matching to values-alignment. Performance reviews evolve from individual metrics to
team outcomes. Most critically, culture becomes everyone's job, not HR's project.

Yet most culture transformations fail because they treat symptoms, not systems. They
launch initiatives without changing incentives. They preach collaboration while rewarding
competition. This theatrical approach to culture change exhausts employees who've seen
too many "transformations" that transform nothing.

Winners in cultural evolution share observable behaviors: they make hard choices that
prove values aren't just words—pausing high-velocity initiatives that conflict with service
standards and removing incentives that drive corner-cutting. They measure culture with
behavioral analytics rather than relying on engagement surveys, using these signals to
identify cultural indicators with greater precision than traditional approaches. In the
Collaborative Intelligence Era, culture determines whether humans and AI enhance or
undermine each other, and adaptive operating routines make that culture measurable and
repeatable.

Culture Transformation Assessment

Key Questions: Does your stated culture match employees' lived experience? Where do systems contradict values? How can authentic culture become your talent magnet?

Culture Transformation Indicators	Yes / No
High performers leave citing cultural misalignment	[ ] Yes / [ ] No
Stated values contradict daily management behaviors	[ ] Yes / [ ] No
DEI initiatives feel performative rather than substantive	[ ] Yes / [ ] No
Employees fear speaking up about problems or ideas	[ ] Yes / [ ] No
Remote workers feel excluded from advancement opportunities	[ ] Yes / [ ] No
Innovation attempts meet bureaucratic resistance	[ ] Yes / [ ] No
Culture initiatives launch without measurable goals	[ ] Yes / [ ] No
Individual rewards undermine collaborative values	[ ] Yes / [ ] No
Leadership talks change but models status quo	[ ] Yes / [ ] No
Culture strategy remains separate from business strategy	[ ] Yes / [ ] No

Scoring:
0-3 "Yes" = Culture aligned with aspirations
4-6 "Yes" = Cultural gaps undermining performance
7-10 "Yes" = Culture actively impeding success

What your score reveals:

High scores indicate your culture is theater, not reality. Employees see through the performance and vote with their feet. The fix starts with brutal honesty: identify where your systems reward behaviors opposite to your stated values. Then change the systems, not the slogans. Remember: culture is what gets rewarded, not what gets posted on walls.

3.7 Economic and Geopolitical Uncertainty

The old playbook for managing economic uncertainty assumed predictable cycles. That playbook no longer fits the facts. We've entered an era where black swan events arrive in flocks: a pandemic shutters global commerce, supply chains snap without warning, inflation spikes unexpectedly, and wars reshape energy markets. The question isn't whether the next disruption will hit—it's whether your workforce can pivot when it does.

Traditional workforce planning built on five-year forecasts has become organizational malpractice. Consider the whiplash: early-pandemic employment shocks were followed by acute talent shortages within a year. Those who maintained flexible capacity adapted faster; those who cut to the bone often struggled to rebound.

Three uncertainty patterns demand new workforce approaches:

Volatility as the Baseline: Economic disruption now arrives in waves: pandemic employment shocks in 2020, supply chain breakdowns through 2022, regional banking failures in 2023, persistent inflation volatility. Organizations clinging to annual planning cycles find themselves perpetually behind. Build systems that reconfigure monthly, not annually.

Geopolitical Fragmentation: The global market is fracturing as firms re-route supply chains toward allies ("friend-shoring"). IMF scenarios estimate that such fragmentation could trim long-run global GDP by around 1.8%[72]. Mexico has also emerged as the United States' top goods trading partner, reflecting nearshoring and supply-chain reconfiguration[73].

Skills Half-Life Compression: Economic disruption accelerates capability obsolescence. Software development skills can become outdated quickly, compressing the time workers have to stay current. Banking's traders became data scientists. Manufacturing's line workers became robot supervisors. Tomorrow's disruption will demand capabilities we can't yet name.

The workforce implications upend every assumption. Permanent headcount gives way to capability networks. The contingent workforce market has expanded rapidly in recent years and continues to grow. Location strategies shift from cost arbitrage to risk mitigation. Learning systems evolve from training programs to continuous adaptation where a very large share of the global workforce will require reskilling within just a few years.

Yet most organizations still operate like uncertainty is temporary. They treat each crisis as exceptional rather than expected. They maintain rigid structures while preaching agility. This cognitive dissonance between recognition and action creates competitive vulnerability.

Winners in uncertainty share distinct characteristics: They scenario-plan constantly, not annually. They measure workforce adaptability, not just productivity. They build redundancy into critical capabilities. Most importantly, they recognize that in an uncertain world, the ability to change direction quickly matters more than the efficiency of moving straight ahead.

Economic Uncertainty Assessment

Key Questions: Which economic shifts would break your current workforce model? Where does geographic concentration create vulnerability? How fast can you reconfigure when assumptions shatter?

Economic Uncertainty Indicators	Yes / No
Recent disruptions caught your workforce planning unprepared	[ ] Yes / [ ] No
Fixed cost structures limit ability to adapt to revenue swings	[ ] Yes / [ ] No
Critical capabilities concentrated in single geographic regions	[ ] Yes / [ ] No
Annual planning cycles can't match market volatility	[ ] Yes / [ ] No
Talent strategies assume continued global mobility	[ ] Yes / [ ] No
Skills development lags behind capability requirements	[ ] Yes / [ ] No
Workforce costs rise faster than productivity gains	[ ] Yes / [ ] No
Contingency plans exist on paper but not in practice	[ ] Yes / [ ] No
Leadership treats each crisis as unique versus systemic	[ ] Yes / [ ] No
Your workforce model optimizes for efficiency over resilience	[ ] Yes / [ ] No

Scoring:
0-3 "Yes" = Reasonable uncertainty preparedness
4-6 "Yes" = Vulnerability to disruption growing
7-10 "Yes" = Workforce model brittle in volatile world

What your score reveals:

High scores indicate you're optimized for a world that no longer exists—one where disruptions were rare and recovery predictable. Your efficiency has become fragility. The path forward requires accepting uncertainty as permanent and building workforce systems that thrive on change rather than resist it. Start by identifying which assumptions about stability create your greatest vulnerabilities.

3.8 Demographic and Social Changes

The workforce is reshaping across age, gender, geography, and preferences—faster than traditional models anticipate. The risk is not fracture but mismatch: a workforce mix evolving faster than roles, policies, and pipelines, creating capability gaps if organizations do not adapt.

The numbers tell a stark story: in some large enterprises, sizable cohorts are already retirement-eligible, and waves of departures can occur within a single month. Yet academic research consistently debunks generational stereotypes, showing more similarities than differences between age groups [74]. The real challenge isn't managing generations—it's managing the intersection of demographic shifts with accelerating social expectations.

Three demographic realities demand immediate workforce attention:

The Knowledge Exodus: As the Federal workforce continues to age and employees look to retire, much of the institutional knowledge once available to agencies through long-term and tenured employees has been lost [75]. Meanwhile, labor force participation rates will fall from 62.6% in 2023 to 61.2% by 2033 [76]. Organizations clinging to informal knowledge transfer risk losing decades of institutional wisdom overnight.

Progression and Participation Imbalance: For every 100 men promoted to manager, only 54 Black women are promoted—the lowest rate since 2020 [70]. When underrepresented groups stall at entry and feeder levels, the future leadership slate shrinks regardless of hiring volume.

Cohort Preferences and Constraints: Work flexibility preferences vary systematically by race and ethnicity, with 88% of Asian/Asian American workers and 79% of White workers preferring location flexibility [77]. Caregiving, commuting radius, visa status, and hybrid expectations now shape supply as much as pay.

Most organizations treat demographic change as separate programs for different groups instead of integrated strategies. They measure diversity statistics rather than retention outcomes. They assume goodwill generates results rather than building systems that reward inclusive behaviors.

Winners in demographic transformation implement structured knowledge transfer before retirements accelerate. They measure and address pay equity proactively. They create reverse mentoring so experience flows both directions. Most importantly, they recognize that in the Collaborative Intelligence Era, diverse perspectives are a competitive advantage no AI can replicate, and *Adaptive Orchestration* routes those perspectives into decisions at pace.

Demographic and Social Changes Assessment

Key Questions: Where will retirement eligibility and attrition create capability gaps? Which critical roles rely on single geographies or visa pipelines? Where are feeder roles underrepresented by cohort? How many roles can flex hours/location without performance loss?

Demographic and Social Changes Indicators	Yes / No
>15% of critical roles reach retirement eligibility within 3 years	[ ] Yes / [ ] No
Promotion rates in feeder roles differ materially by cohort	[ ] Yes / [ ] No
Key capabilities concentrated in a single geography or time zone	[ ] Yes / [ ] No
Visa/permit dependency creates single-point-of-failure exposure	[ ] Yes / [ ] No
Hybrid/remote preferences are known but not reflected in role design	[ ] Yes / [ ] No
Caregiver constraints materially limit shift coverage or availability	[ ] Yes / [ ] No
Part-time or flexible paths are unavailable for critical roles	[ ] Yes / [ ] No
Feeder-role representation does not match intended leadership mix	[ ] Yes / [ ] No
Knowledge capture/transfer is ad hoc or episodic	[ ] Yes / [ ] No
Talent mapping ignores cross-border or cross-business mobility options	[ ] Yes / [ ] No

Scoring:
0-3 "Yes" = Demographic shifts under management
4-6 "Yes" = Demographic risks building pressure
7-10 "Yes" = Demographic crisis requiring immediate action

What your score reveals:

High scores indicate a structural mismatch: the workforce you have and the one you need are drifting apart by age mix, geography, and progression rates. The priority is to rebalance supply and pathways—capture knowledge before it exits, widen feeder pipelines, de-risk location and visa concentration, and align roles to real preferences and constraints.

3.9 Resource Scarcity and Sustainability

Resource constraints are reshaping workforce strategies as organizations navigate talent shortages, environmental pressures, and sustainability mandates. The World Economic Forum projects 170 million new jobs by 2030, yet 92 million will be displaced, creating a net gain of only 78 million positions[40]. Climate change adaptation is expected to contribute meaningfully to employment growth.

This tension between scarcity and opportunity demands workforce models that optimize human capital while advancing sustainability goals. Organizations can no longer separate workforce efficiency from environmental responsibility—the two have become inseparable drivers of long-term competitiveness.

Three critical patterns define the resource scarcity challenge:

Skills Scarcity Accelerating Green Transformation: Traditional energy sectors struggle to attract skilled workers as talent chooses renewables and emerging technologies[78]. The U.S. Bureau of Labor Statistics projects wind turbine service technicians and solar photovoltaic installers among the fastest-growing occupations over the coming decade, though the absolute number of new jobs remains relatively small[79–81]. Organizations investing in green skills development report higher engagement in sustainability initiatives.

Remote Work as Resource Optimization: Studies indicate that remote and hybrid work can materially reduce environmental impact while maintaining productivity. Distributed teams have also demonstrated high rates of operational waste diversion. This creates workforce models where environmental sustainability directly enhances operational efficiency.

Circular Economy Workforce Models: Meta-analysis of 137 studies across 43 countries confirms that Green Human Resource Management practices directly improve economic, environmental, and social performance[82]. Companies are operationalizing this by tying elements of compensation to sustainability outcomes and allocating paid time for community or environmental initiatives.

The workforce implications cascade through every organizational level. Hiring shifts from skills-matching to sustainability alignment. Training evolves from compliance-driven to purpose-driven. Most critically, workforce planning must balance immediate operational needs with long-term resource constraints and environmental commitments.

Organizations succeeding in this transformation share common approaches: They measure workforce impact on sustainability goals, not just productivity metrics. They create career pathways connecting individual growth with organizational environmental objectives. They recognize that in an era of resource scarcity, the most sustainable resource is a workforce aligned with both operational excellence and planetary stewardship.

Resource Scarcity and Sustainability Assessment

Key Questions: Where do talent shortages constrain your sustainability goals? How can workforce optimization reduce environmental impact? Which green skills gaps limit competitive advantage?

Resource Scarcity and Sustainability Indicators	Yes / No
Talent shortages limit sustainability initiatives	[ ] Yes / [ ] No
Workforce models fail to optimize energy and waste	[ ] Yes / [ ] No
Employees lack circular economy and sustainability training	[ ] Yes / [ ] No
Remote work policies ignore environmental benefits	[ ] Yes / [ ] No
Recruitment ignores green skills and sustainability alignment	[ ] Yes / [ ] No
Supply disruptions reveal workforce capacity gaps	[ ] Yes / [ ] No
Sustainability goals disconnect from workforce metrics	[ ] Yes / [ ] No
Skills programs exclude environmental competencies	[ ] Yes / [ ] No
Performance systems don't reward sustainable behaviors	[ ] Yes / [ ] No
Workforce strategy assumes unlimited resources	[ ] Yes / [ ] No

Scoring:
0-3 "Yes" = Sustainability workforce alignment
4-6 "Yes" = Resource optimization opportunities emerging
7-10 "Yes" = Critical need for sustainable workforce transformation

What your score reveals:

High scores indicate your workforce model treats sustainability as separate from operational efficiency. While competitors build resource-conscious capabilities, you're optimizing for an abundant world that no longer exists. The solution isn't adding sustainability training—it's embedding resource optimization into every workforce decision. Start by identifying where talent scarcity and environmental constraints intersect, then build workforce systems that turn these constraints into competitive advantages.

3.10 Business Model Innovation

Business model innovation has become the ultimate workforce stress test, revealing which organizations can adapt and which will be disrupted to irrelevance. Platform economies reshape workforce management through algorithmic coordination rather than traditional employment structures [83]. Subscription models demand customer success capabilities that extend well beyond traditional sales and support. Ecosystem partnerships require orchestration skills spanning organizational boundaries, as platforms function less like traditional hierarchies and more like coordinated networks of independent participants [84].

The transformation cuts deeper than operational adjustments. Adobe's Creative Cloud transition moved from 18-24 month release cycles to continuous delivery requiring DevOps expertise, cloud infrastructure capabilities, and organizational restructuring including 12% workforce growth [85, 86]. Apple's App Store ecosystem illustrates how developer relations functions can scale to support a vast developer community. Automattic exemplifies globally distributed operations coordinated primarily through asynchronous practices.

Five business model shifts create workforce requirements that legacy structures cannot support:

Platform Coordination: Uber coordinates a large, technology-enabled marketplace at global scale[87]. Traditional hiring processes become irrelevant when your workforce operates through APIs.

Customer Success Management: Subscription businesses need specialized workforce models where managers handle ongoing client relationships rather than one-time sales. Product sales training becomes obsolete when revenue depends on retention.

Ecosystem Orchestration: Organizations with a significant share of external contributors require boundary-spanning capabilities and hybrid governance competencies. Managing employees is simple compared to orchestrating networks.

Outcome-Based Services (products $\rightarrow$ outcomes): Siemens complements products with data-driven services built on IoT platforms[88]. Roles shift from manufacturing excellence to lifecycle value delivery and customer success.

Remote-First Distribution: Microsoft research revealed firm-wide remote work causes collaboration networks to become more static, demanding shifts from synchronous to asynchronous communication [89].

Most organizations treat business model innovation as strategy while ignoring workforce implications. They announce transformations without building capabilities. They adopt new models using old management approaches.

Winners recognize that business model innovation is workforce innovation. They develop hybrid governance capabilities balancing hierarchical management with network coordination. They build asynchronous coordination systems before going remote-first.

Business Model Innovation Assessment

Key Questions: Which business model shifts demand new workforce capabilities? Where do traditional management approaches fail in network-based models? How can workforce transformation enable rather than constrain innovation?

Business Model Innovation Indicators	Yes / No
Platform or ecosystem models expose traditional management gaps	[ ] Yes / [ ] No
Subscription services require customer success capabilities you lack	[ ] Yes / [ ] No
External contributors represent 20%+ of your workforce	[ ] Yes / [ ] No
Service-based models need outcome management skills	[ ] Yes / [ ] No
Remote-first operations demand asynchronous coordination	[ ] Yes / [ ] No
Traditional hiring processes fail for gig-based talent	[ ] Yes / [ ] No
Boundary-spanning roles lack clear management structures	[ ] Yes / [ ] No
Continuous development cycles overwhelm project-based teams	[ ] Yes / [ ] No
Network business models operate despite hierarchical organization	[ ] Yes / [ ] No
Innovation initiatives fail due to workforce capability gaps	[ ] Yes / [ ] No

Scoring:
0-3 "Yes" = Workforce aligned with business model
4-6 "Yes" = Growing capability-strategy gaps
7-10 "Yes" = Business model innovation constrained by workforce

What your score reveals:

High scores signal your business model is writing checks your workforce can't cash. You're trying to operate platform businesses with hierarchical management, run subscription models without customer success capabilities, and manage ecosystems through traditional employment structures. The fix isn't better training—it's fundamental workforce architecture redesign. Start by identifying which business model requirements most conflict with current workforce structures.

3.11 Strategic Focus for Workforce Transformation

You've now examined ten critical forces reshaping workforce management in the Collaborative Intelligence Era. The patterns you've identified through these assessments aren't academic exercises—they guide the *Adaptive* roadmap by revealing the specific pressures and opportunities that will determine your transformation priorities.

As you worked through each driver, certain ones likely resonated as immediate challenges in your organization. Others may have revealed blind spots you hadn't fully recognized. Some might have highlighted untapped opportunities where workforce innovation could create competitive advantage.

This awareness becomes crucial as you move forward. When the time comes to make the case for workforce investments—whether for new technology capabilities, cultural transformation initiatives, or fundamental operating model changes—the insights from these assessments will ground your arguments in business reality rather than theoretical possibility.

The change drivers where you identified the most significant gaps or opportunities will become your strongest leverage points. They provide the compelling "why" that transforms workforce initiatives from siloed projects into business imperatives across operations. They also help you sequence investments, focusing resources on the areas where external forces create the greatest urgency for change.

Part II shifts from understanding these forces to acting on them. You'll explore practical frameworks to advance to *Adaptive Orchestration*, and develop tools to translate your change-driver insights into strategic workforce initiatives that deliver measurable results.

The forces reshaping workforce management won't wait for perfect planning or complete consensus. But armed with a clear understanding of which drivers most powerfully affect your organization, you're prepared to lead rather than react to the transformation ahead.

4 Frameworks for Operational Transformation

Introduction: The Power of Frameworks in Workforce Management

Workforce Management is more than just scheduling employees or tracking performance—it is the strategic alignment of people, processes, and technology to drive operational success. As businesses enter the Collaborative Intelligence Era, leaders need *Adaptive* frameworks to navigate complexity, optimize workforce efficiency, and orchestrate systems that can thrive amid constant change. This is where frameworks play a crucial role.

Why Frameworks Matter

Frameworks provide structured approaches to tackling challenges, ensuring that leaders move beyond intuition-based decision-making toward repeatable, scalable methodologies. They bridge the critical gap between high-level strategy and day-to-day execution, ensuring that workforce initiatives align with broader business objectives while adapting to organizational realities.

Well-designed frameworks enable organizations to:

- **Scale workforce strategies** consistently across different environments and business units
- **Measure progress** systematically using proven methodologies rather than ad hoc approaches
- **Implement best practices** that have been validated across multiple organizational contexts
- **Make data-driven improvements** in real-time while maintaining strategic coherence

Balancing Efficiency, Flexibility, and Employee Well-being

The fundamental challenge in workforce transformation lies in harmonizing three often competing forces:

Operational Efficiency: Ensuring the right number of employees are in the right place at the right time to meet demand while optimizing resource utilization and cost management.

Organizational Flexibility: Adapting quickly to changing business needs, market conditions, technological advancements, and unexpected disruptions while maintaining operational stability.

Employee Well-being: Creating work environments that support engagement, retention, and productivity while fostering personal growth and career satisfaction.

An effective workforce management strategy must harmonize rather than optimize these forces in isolation. Frameworks provide the structured tools to achieve this balance, enabling organizations to pursue multiple objectives simultaneously while making informed trade-offs when conflicts arise.

Three Essential Frameworks for Strategic Transformation

This chapter introduces three powerful frameworks that serve as the backbone of strategic workforce transformation. Each addresses different dimensions of the workforce management challenge while working synergistically to create comprehensive transformation capabilities:

The STaRS Framework: Understanding organizational context and choosing the right workforce strategy based on whether a company is in Startup, Turnaround, Realignment, or Sustaining Success mode [90]. This framework ensures that workforce strategies align with organizational lifecycle realities.

The Service-Profit Chain: Linking employee satisfaction to customer experience and business profitability, demonstrating how investing in workforce engagement drives measurable business outcomes [91]. This framework quantifies the return on workforce investment.

The GRPIT Framework: A comprehensive approach to aligning Goals, Roles, Processes, Interpersonal Relationships, and Technology to optimize workforce management. This synthesis extends Beckhard's four-element diagnostic framework [92] by integrating technology as a fifth strategic dimension drawn from Leavitt's Diamond Model [93], ensuring systematic implementation across all organizational dimensions.

These frameworks complement the variance management principles explored in Chapter 5 and the maturity progression detailed in Chapter 6, creating a comprehensive toolkit for workforce transformation.

Framework Selection and Integration

Not all frameworks apply universally or simultaneously. The key to effective workforce transformation lies in selecting and combining frameworks based on your organization's unique challenges, objectives, and stage of development.

Organizations undergoing significant change benefit from starting with the **STaRS framework** to understand their current context and align workforce strategies accordingly. Those prioritizing the connection between employee engagement and business performance find the **Service-Profit Chain** provides compelling evidence for workforce investment decisions. Organizations seeking systematic implementation across multiple dimensions rely on the **GRPIT framework** to ensure comprehensive transformation.

The most successful transformations leverage multiple frameworks in concert, adapting and combining elements to address specific organizational needs while maintaining flexibility to evolve as circumstances change.

Bridge to Adaptive Workforce Management

These frameworks prepare organizations to embrace the *Adaptive* workforce management principles that follow in Part II of this book. They provide the conceptual foundation for understanding how to build workforce capabilities that thrive on variance rather than fight it, how to progress systematically through maturity levels, and how to implement Collaborative Intelligence approaches that enhance rather than replace human capabilities.

In the following sections, we explore each framework in detail, providing practical guidance for selection, implementation, and integration. By developing mastery of these methodologies, workforce leaders can shift from reactive decision-making to proactive, strategically aligned approaches that drive sustainable competitive advantage.

The frameworks serve as your navigation tools for the workforce transformation journey ahead. Let's begin.

4.1 The STaRS Framework

Introduction to STaRS

The STaRS framework, developed by Michael D. Watkins in his influential work *The First 90 Days* (2003), provides a powerful lens for understanding organizational contexts and adapting workforce strategies accordingly [90]. Originally designed for leadership transitions, STaRS has proven equally valuable for strategic workforce management, helping leaders recognize that different organizational situations demand fundamentally different approaches to managing people, processes, and performance.

Watkins' original framework identifies five organizational stages, though workforce management practitioners often find four stages most applicable to operational contexts. Understanding where an organization sits on the STaRS spectrum enables workforce leaders to align their strategies with broader business objectives, ensuring that Workforce Management decisions support rather than hinder organizational success.

The four stages most relevant to workforce management are:

- **Startup**: Building foundational workforce structures and capabilities
- **Turnaround**: Stabilizing operations and restructuring for improvement
- **Realignment**: Adapting established operations to shifting conditions
- **Sustaining Success**: Optimizing performance while fostering innovation

Watkins' complete framework also includes **accelerated growth** (the lowercase 'a' in STaRS)—organizations experiencing rapid expansion after initial success. While this stage presents unique workforce challenges around scaling culture, hiring velocity, and system capacity, our experience in contact center environments suggests the four stages above capture the most common strategic contexts. Organizations experiencing true accelerated growth may benefit from exploring Watkins' complete framework, particularly for challenges around maintaining quality during rapid scaling.

The framework's power lies not in providing universal solutions, but in helping leaders ask the right questions: What workforce challenges are we actually facing? What strategies align with our current organizational reality? How can we build workforce capabilities that support our specific stage of development?

The Four Stages of STaRS and Workforce Applications

1. Startup: Building the Workforce Foundation

Characteristics: Organizations in startup mode are establishing new business models, launching operations, or building capabilities from the ground up. These environments are characterized by resource constraints, high uncertainty, and the need for rapid adaptation as market feedback shapes strategic direction.

Workforce Strategy:

- Focus on **speed and cultural alignment** in hiring, prioritizing adaptability and learning potential over perfect skill matches
- Design **cross-functional roles** where employees contribute across multiple areas, fostering collaboration and organizational agility
- Implement **flexible workforce models** that can scale quickly in response to evolving business needs and market opportunities
- Invest early in **culture-building and leadership development** to establish strong foundations for future growth

Common Challenges:

- High employee turnover due to unclear role expectations and organizational uncertainty
- Limited historical data for workforce forecasting, requiring intuitive and adaptive planning approaches
- Balancing lean operations with employee workload sustainability as teams stretch across multiple priorities

Example: A technology startup launching a SaaS platform builds an initial customer support team of generalists who handle technical support, customer onboarding, and account management. The Workforce Management strategy emphasizes flexibility and rapid skill development over specialized efficiency, with scheduling models that adapt quickly to customer acquisition patterns and product evolution.

2. Turnaround: Stabilizing and Restructuring the Workforce

Characteristics: Organizations in turnaround mode face performance crises requiring rapid diagnosis and decisive action. These situations demand immediate stabilization while building foundations for sustainable improvement.

Workforce Strategy:

- Conduct **comprehensive workforce audits** to identify performance gaps, inefficiencies, and improvement opportunities
- Implement **data-driven performance management** systems that enable informed staffing decisions and talent retention
- Pursue **automation and process optimization** to reduce operational costs while maintaining or improving service quality
- Prioritize **employee engagement and communication** to retain top talent during organizational uncertainty

Common Challenges:

- Declining morale and increased attrition due to restructuring efforts and organizational instability
- Resistance to change from employees invested in existing processes and familiar ways of working

- Balancing immediate cost pressures with long-term workforce sustainability requirements

Example: A financial services contact center experiencing deteriorating service levels and rising customer complaints implements rapid workforce stabilization through enhanced real-time management, performance coaching programs, and technology upgrades. The approach emphasizes quick wins to restore confidence while building systematic improvements for sustained performance.

3. Realignment: Adapting to Changing Conditions

Characteristics: Realignment organizations have established operations that function adequately but require adjustment to address external shifts, evolving customer expectations, or strategic redirection. The challenge lies in strategic evolution rather than crisis management.

Workforce Strategy:

- Conduct **skills gap analyses** to identify capabilities needed for future success versus current workforce strengths
- Develop **flexible workforce models** including hybrid arrangements, gig workers, and cross-functional teams
- Implement **continuous learning and reskilling programs** to evolve employee capabilities with business requirements
- Deploy **predictive workforce analytics** to anticipate and prepare for changing demand patterns

Common Challenges:

- Organizational inertia and comfort with existing approaches that may no longer optimize performance
- Securing leadership buy-in for changes that may not seem urgent given adequate current performance
- Managing employee resistance to new ways of working that disrupt established routines and expectations

Example: A retail company's customer service operation adapts to increasing digital channel preferences by retraining voice agents for chat and email support, implementing omnichannel workforce management, and developing new performance metrics that reflect customer journey complexity rather than single-channel efficiency.

4. Sustaining Success: Optimizing While Innovating

Characteristics: Organizations in sustaining success mode have achieved operational stability and must focus on continuous improvement without becoming complacent. These organizations face the challenge of maintaining excellence while fostering innovation and preparing for future disruption.

Workforce Strategy:

- Implement **sophisticated workforce engagement programs** that retain top talent and foster continuous improvement culture
- Optimize **workforce automation** to increase efficiency while enabling employees to focus on higher-value activities
- Invest in **leadership pipeline development** to ensure long-term stability and prepare for succession challenges
- Create **innovation frameworks** that encourage experimentation while maintaining operational excellence

Common Challenges:

- Preventing complacency that can lead to gradual performance decline as success breeds overconfidence
- Retaining high-performing employees who may seek new challenges when operations become routine
- Preparing for external disruptions while maintaining current operational excellence and market position

Example: A global e-commerce company with mature Workforce Management capabilities leverages AI-driven forecasting and dynamic scheduling to maintain peak performance while piloting new workforce models like flexible gig integration and predictive employee experience management. The focus balances operational excellence with continuous innovation to sustain competitive advantage.

Understanding these four stages is essential because workforce strategies that excel in one context can fail spectacularly in another. The following table distills the core workforce priorities for each STaRS stage:

STaRS Stage	Workforce Focus	Key Initiatives
Startup	Rapid hiring, culture-building	Agile workforce models, cross-functional roles, speed in on-boarding
Turnaround	Workforce stabilization	Performance audits, automation, cost optimization, engagement retention
Realignment	Workforce adaptation	Reskilling programs, flexible staffing, predictive workforce analytics
Sustaining Success	Continuous optimization	AI-driven forecasting, employee retention strategies, workforce innovation

Table 4.1: STaRS Framework Applied to Workforce Management

Applying STaRS to Workforce Management

The STaRS framework transforms workforce management from a one-size-fits-all approach to a contextually intelligent discipline. By identifying where an organization sits on the STaRS spectrum, leaders can make targeted workforce decisions that align with broader business objectives and organizational realities.

As Watkins emphasizes, organizations may simultaneously experience different STaRS stages across various departments or business units, requiring segmented workforce approaches rather than uniform strategies [90]. A technology company might have startup-mode product teams, sustaining success customer service operations, and realignment-phase sales organizations—each requiring different workforce management strategies despite operating within the same corporate structure.

Integration via Adaptive Orchestration

In the era of Collaborative Intelligence, the STaRS framework is a situational strategy model that helps leaders choose the right path for the organization's stage. It does not prescribe orchestration mechanics; instead, it sets priorities, sequencing, risk posture, and decision rights, and indicates which *Adaptive Orchestration* patterns, investments, and guardrails fit the context. Each STaRS stage presents distinct opportunities and constraints for AI-enhanced workforce strategies:

- **Startup** organizations can build AI collaboration into their workforce DNA from inception
- **Turnaround** situations may leverage AI for rapid performance improvement and cost optimization
- **Realignment** contexts often require AI to bridge skill gaps and enable new capabilities
- **Sustaining Success** environments can pursue sophisticated AI applications for competitive advantage

Contextual Workforce Strategy

The STaRS framework transforms workforce decision-making from generic best practices to contextually intelligent strategies. Success depends not on having the single best approach, but on aligning workforce initiatives with organizational realities to create sustainable competitive advantage through situational awareness.

4.2 The Service-Profit Chain

Introduction to the Service-Profit Chain

The Service-Profit Chain represents one of the most influential frameworks for under-standing how operational decisions cascade through employee experience to customer satisfaction and financial outcomes. Introduced by Heskett, Jones, Loveman, Sasser, and Schlesinger in their landmark 1994 Harvard Business Review article and expanded in their 1997 book, this framework established a data-driven perspective on business performance [91].

At its core, the Service-Profit Chain demonstrates that business success is fundamentally rooted in employee experience. A well-supported, engaged workforce delivers superior customer service, leading to higher satisfaction, stronger loyalty, and sustained profitability. This framework holds particular significance for Workforce Management, where employee well-being directly influences customer interaction quality and service delivery outcomes.

The chain illustrates that organizations cannot separate employee experience from customer experience—they are inextricably linked in a causal relationship that determines business success. By aligning workforce strategies with Service-Profit Chain principles, organizations create virtuous cycles where investments in employee well-being generate measurable returns through enhanced customer loyalty and financial performance.

The Seven Links of the Service-Profit Chain

The Service-Profit Chain consists of seven interconnected relationships that collectively drive business success, forming a causal sequence from internal operations to financial outcomes:

Internal Service Quality
↓
Employee Satisfaction
↓
Employee Loyalty
↓
Employee Productivity
↓
External Service Value
↓
Customer Satisfaction
↓
Customer Loyalty
↓
Revenue Growth and Profitability

Link 1: Internal Service Quality

Internal service quality encompasses the policies, tools, training, and work environment that enable employees to deliver excellent service. This foundational element determines whether employees have the resources and support needed to succeed in their roles.

In Workforce Management applications, internal service quality manifests through:

- Automating manual scheduling processes to reduce administrative burden and scheduling conflicts
- Providing real-time performance dashboards that help employees understand their impact
- Ensuring equitable workload distribution to prevent burnout and maintain fairness
- Implementing AI-powered coaching tools that enhance training effectiveness and career development

Organizations that invest in robust internal service quality create the fundamental conditions for employee success, establishing the foundation for all subsequent chain links.

Link 2: Employee Satisfaction

Employee satisfaction reflects how valued, motivated, and empowered employees feel in their roles. Satisfied employees demonstrate greater engagement and productivity while contributing to lower turnover and reduced recruitment costs.

Workforce Management strategies that enhance satisfaction include:

- Implementing flexible scheduling options that balance operational needs with personal preferences
- Creating transparent performance metrics that employees understand and can influence
- Providing clear career growth pathways with skill development opportunities
- Establishing fair and consistent recognition programs that reward excellence

Research consistently shows that satisfied employees are more likely to stay with organizations, develop deeper expertise, and deliver superior customer experiences.

Link 3: Employee Loyalty

Employee loyalty extends beyond satisfaction to establish long-term organizational commitment. Loyal employees not only remain with the company longer but also develop institutional knowledge and stronger customer relationships that become competitive advantages.

Workforce Management approaches that build loyalty include:

- Providing predictable schedules that enable work-life balance planning
- Using data-driven insights to recognize and reward top performers consistently
- Creating employee voice mechanisms that involve staff in operational decision-making

- Investing in long-term skill development rather than focusing solely on immediate needs

The reduction in turnover from increased loyalty creates substantial cost savings while preserving valuable organizational knowledge and customer relationships.

Link 4: Employee Productivity

Employee productivity represents the ability to deliver high-quality service efficiently. Productive employees simultaneously improve customer experience and operational cost management, creating sustainable competitive advantages.

Workforce Management enhances productivity through:

- Real-time analytics that dynamically adjust staffing to match demand patterns
- Automation of repetitive tasks, allowing employees to focus on value-added activities
- Performance management systems that provide actionable feedback and coaching
- Cross-training programs that increase workforce flexibility and capability

Importantly, productivity improvements driven by employee engagement create reinforcing cycles rather than the burnout often associated with efficiency-focused approaches.

Link 5: External Service Value

External service value encompasses the quality and efficiency of customer-facing service delivery. This represents the direct output of engaged, productive employees and serves as the critical bridge between internal operations and customer outcomes.

In Workforce Management contexts, external service value is enhanced through:

- Optimizing service level adherence while maintaining employee sustainability
- Using predictive staffing models to ensure adequate coverage during demand peaks
- Implementing continuous feedback loops to measure and improve service quality
- Personalizing customer-agent interactions through better workforce planning and training

Customers consistently recognize and value interactions with knowledgeable, engaged employees who demonstrate genuine commitment to problem resolution.

Link 6: Customer Satisfaction and Loyalty

Customer satisfaction and loyalty represent the market validation of effective service delivery. Heskett and colleagues demonstrated that satisfied customers become loyal advocates who remain with brands, increase spending, and generate referrals.

Research in this stream indicates that even small improvements in customer loyalty can yield substantial profitability gains, though the magnitude varies by industry and context [91]. For Workforce Management, this emphasizes the importance of:

- Maintaining appropriate staffing levels to prevent excessive wait times
- Providing ongoing employee development to refine customer interaction skills
- Leveraging technology to enable more personalized and effective service delivery
- Creating seamless omnichannel experiences through coordinated workforce planning

Link 7: Revenue Growth and Profitability

Revenue growth and profitability represent the financial validation of Service-Profit Chain investments. Organizations with engaged employees and loyal customers consistently outperform competitors across key financial metrics, demonstrating measurable returns on workforce investment.

This final link provides compelling business justification for workforce strategies that prioritize employee experience alongside operational efficiency.

Transforming Workforce Management Through the Service-Profit Chain

Traditional workforce planning often focuses narrowly on cost control, leading to understaffing, burnout, and higher turnover—creating hidden costs that exceed apparent savings. The Service-Profit Chain challenges this perspective by demonstrating that employee investments generate substantial long-term financial returns.

Organizations that embed Service-Profit Chain principles into Workforce Management can:

- Transform from cost-minimization to value-creation approaches
- Reduce turnover while improving service quality simultaneously
- Build compelling business cases for workforce technology investments
- Create cross-functional alignment around shared employee and customer outcomes
- Develop sustainable competitive advantages through workforce excellence

The framework also enables powerful cross-functional collaboration by providing a common reference point for workforce management, customer service, and financial planning functions to align efforts around shared outcomes.

Strategic Implementation

Successful Service-Profit Chain implementation requires systematic measurement across all seven links, combining quantitative metrics with qualitative insights from employee surveys, customer feedback, and operational analytics. Organizations must establish clear indicators for internal service quality, employee engagement, productivity, and customer outcomes to understand how workforce decisions impact the entire value chain.

The framework transforms Workforce Management from cost-minimization to value-creation, enabling organizations to reduce turnover while improving service quality, build compelling business cases for workforce investments, and develop sustainable competitive advantages through workforce excellence.

4.3 The GRPIT Framework

Introduction to GRPIT: Synthesizing Organizational Frameworks

The GRPIT framework represents the synthesis of two foundational organizational models that have proven their value across decades of application. By combining Richard Beckhard's diagnostic framework (1972) [92] with Harold Leavitt's Diamond Model (1965) [93], GRPIT provides a comprehensive methodology specifically designed for modern Workforce Management challenges.

Beckhard's framework focuses on four essential elements: Goals, Roles, Processes, and Interpersonal relationships. Leavitt's Diamond Model emphasizes the interdependence of Tasks, People, Structure, and Technology, recognizing that changing any element necessitates adjustments in others. GRPIT integrates these insights into a unified framework, extending Beckhard's diagnostic approach with Leavitt's technology dimension to address the complexity of contemporary workforce transformation.

The integrated GRPIT framework (Goals, Roles, Processes, Interpersonal relationships, and Technology) provides a structured methodology for designing workforce strategies that simultaneously optimize operational efficiency, enhance employee engagement, and leverage emerging technologies. This balanced approach is essential for building adaptive systems that sustain performance as conditions change.

Source Framework	Contribution to GRPIT
GRPI (Beckhard)	Goals, Roles, Processes, Interpersonal relationships
Leavitt's Diamond	Tasks (Goals), People (Roles), Structure (Processes), Technology

Table 4.2: Theoretical Foundations of the GRPIT Framework

Each GRPIT component addresses a critical dimension of workforce transformation. These elements function as an integrated system where changes in one area inevitably affect others, requiring coordinated rather than isolated optimization approaches.

Goals (G): Aligning Workforce Strategies with Business Objectives

Goals define desired outcomes for Workforce Management initiatives, ensuring that staffing strategies support service level expectations, financial targets, and employee experience objectives. Without this alignment, sophisticated workforce planning can deliver impressive operational metrics while missing broader business value.

Effective workforce goals typically span multiple domains:

- **Service level targets** establish customer-facing performance expectations (e.g., 80/30 service level standards)
- **Cost efficiency objectives** optimize labor expenses while maintaining service quality through automation and scheduling optimization
- **Employee well-being metrics** recognize sustainability requirements including work-life balance, job satisfaction, and career development

These goals often create productive tensions that workforce management must navigate. Maximizing service levels may require higher staffing costs, while optimizing employee preferences can add scheduling complexity. Effective goal-setting finds the intersection where business performance and employee experience reinforce each other.

Roles (R): Structuring Responsibilities for Maximum Impact

Clear role definition ensures accountability across all aspects of workforce planning, from long-term forecasting to real-time adjustments. Role clarity prevents duplication while encouraging specialization and expertise development within scalable organizational structures.

Essential Workforce Management roles include:

- **Forecasters** apply statistical methods and business intelligence to predict workload patterns and staffing requirements
- **Schedulers** develop shift patterns balancing coverage requirements with employee preferences and regulatory constraints
- **Real-time analysts** monitor operations and make dynamic staffing adjustments as conditions change
- **Strategic workforce planners** align workforce capabilities with long-term business growth trajectories

As organizations advance through the maturity levels detailed in Chapter 6, roles evolve from generalized to specialized and from tactical to increasingly strategic, reflecting workforce management's growing business impact.

Processes (P): Standardizing Workforce Planning Excellence

Processes provide the operational backbone ensuring consistency, scalability, and continuous improvement in workforce planning. Well-designed processes enable data-driven decision-making rather than reactive management, creating foundations for systematic optimization.

Core workforce processes include:

- **Capacity planning** sets medium to long-term staffing and budget envelopes, translating demand outlooks, service targets, and productivity assumptions into hiring plans, vendor mix, and overtime/part-time guardrails
- **Forecasting** translates historical data into predictions across multiple time horizons, decomposing patterns into baseline, seasonality, trends, and event impacts
- **Scheduling** transforms forecasts into work assignments, balancing coverage requirements with employee preferences and operational constraints
- **Intraday management** provides real-time adjustments responding to forecast deviations while protecting employee development activities

These processes interconnect systematically: capacity planning establishes forecasting boundaries, forecasting enables scheduling, and intraday management creates feedback loops for continuous improvement. This integration transforms workforce management from reactive administration into strategic capability.

Interpersonal relationships (I): Creating Workforce-Centric Culture

Interpersonal relationships address the human dynamics underlying effective workforce management, encompassing how workforce teams interact internally, engage with employees, and collaborate across organizational functions to balance operational excellence with employee well-being.

Strong interpersonal relationships produce measurable benefits including improved employee engagement, enhanced cross-functional collaboration, and shifted organizational perceptions of workforce management from rule enforcement to strategic enablement. These outcomes directly support the Service-Profit Chain principles explored earlier in this chapter.

Practical applications include:

- **Bidirectional feedback loops** ensuring workforce decisions incorporate frontline realities through focus groups and employee representation
- **Transparent communication** about scheduling rationale and workload expectations to build trust and acceptance
- **Thoughtful technology implementation** that improves employee experience through AI-powered coaching and self-service scheduling tools
- **Flexible work arrangements** aligning employee preferences with business needs in increasingly competitive talent markets

Technology (T): Leveraging AI and Automation for Workforce Optimization

Technology encompasses the digital tools, artificial intelligence, and automation that increasingly reshape workforce management possibilities. Rather than merely enabling existing processes, technology expands workforce management capabilities and organizational influence.

Transformative technology domains include:

- **AI-powered forecasting** using machine learning to identify complex patterns and incorporate diverse data sources for unprecedented prediction accuracy
- **Automated scheduling** through optimization engines balancing multiple constraints and preferences simultaneously
- **AI assistants** augmenting human decision-making with recommendations, risk identification, and insight surfacing
- **Employee experience platforms** using predictive analytics to identify engagement risks and personalize work assignments

Successful technology implementation requires balanced approaches considering implications for all GRPIT elements rather than focusing solely on technical capabilities. This reinforces the framework's integrated nature and the importance of coordinated transformation efforts.

GRPIT Integration and Implementation

The GRPIT framework's power lies in recognizing these components as an integrated system rather than independent elements. Changes in one area require coordinated adjustments across others, demanding systematic rather than piecemeal approaches to workforce transformation.

Organizations implement GRPIT differently based on their position in the maturity progression detailed in Chapter 6:

- **Lower maturity levels** focus on establishing basic GRPIT elements: clear goal alignment, defined roles, standardized processes, improved communication, and foundational technology
- **Higher maturity levels** optimize GRPIT integration: dynamic goal adjustment, role specialization, process automation, engagement personalization, and predictive technology applications

The framework provides both diagnostic capability for identifying gaps and roadmap guidance for building workforce management capabilities that support organizational success across the STaRS lifecycle stages.

Strategic Workforce Transformation

GRPIT enables organizations to evolve from compliance-driven workforce management focused on meeting basic service levels and minimizing costs toward strategic workforce optimization that balances operational efficiency with employee well-being while leveraging technology for competitive advantage.

This transformation becomes increasingly essential as organizations navigate talent scarcity, technological disruption, and evolving employee expectations. The framework ensures that workforce management advances contribute to rather than conflict with broader organizational objectives, creating sustainable competitive advantages through integrated workforce excellence.

4.4 Framework Integration and Selection

The frameworks explored in this chapter—STaRS, the Service-Profit Chain, and GR-PIT—provide structured approaches to workforce transformation that balance operational efficiency, employee well-being, and organizational adaptability. Each methodology offers distinct insights while collectively forming a comprehensive toolkit for aligning workforce strategy with business success.

The power of these frameworks lies in their complementary nature. The STaRS framework provides contextual awareness for adapting strategies to organizational lifecycle stages. The Service-Profit Chain demonstrates quantifiable linkages between employee investment and business performance. The GRPIT framework offers systematic implementation methodology across goals, roles, processes, interpersonal dynamics, and technology.

Selecting the Right Framework

Different situations call for different frameworks. Use this matrix to choose, combine, and sequence STaRS, the Service-Profit Chain, and GRPIT:

Framework	Best For	Key Question	Deliverables
STaRS	Contextual diagnosis	What stage defines our current reality?	Strategic focus areas, stage aligned goals
Service-Profit Chain	Business case development	How will workforce investments drive measurable ROI?	ROI models, performance cascades
GRPIT	Implementation execution	Which elements must align to ensure sustainable change?	Process redesigns, role definitions

Table 4.3: Framework Selection Matrix

How to combine: Diagnose organizational context with STaRS, justify investments with the Service-Profit Chain, and operationalize change with GRPIT. When phases shift, re-run STaRS; when outcomes drift, revisit the Service-Profit Chain; when execution stalls, adjust GRPIT.

Additional Strategic Methodologies

Beyond these core frameworks, workforce leaders may draw upon additional methodologies to address specific challenges:

Strategic Planning Frameworks

- **Balanced Scorecard** [94] – Links workforce initiatives to financial, customer, internal process, and learning perspectives
- **Porter's Five Forces** [95] – Analyzes industry pressures affecting talent requirements and organizational structure
- **Intel-style MBOs** [96] – Creates alignment between individual performance and organizational priorities

Change and Leadership Frameworks

- **Situational Leadership** [97] – Adapts leadership approaches based on employee competence and commitment levels
- **Kotter's 8-Step Change Model** [98] – Provides structured approach for implementing workforce transformation initiatives
- **Job Characteristics Model** [99] – Guides job design decisions through skill variety, task identity, autonomy, and feedback dimensions

Operational Excellence Frameworks

- **Lean Management** – Reduces waste in workforce processes while improving service delivery efficiency
- **Theory of Constraints** [100] – Identifies and addresses bottlenecks limiting overall workforce system performance
- **Agile Methodology** – Enables iterative, responsive approaches to workforce planning and implementation

These supplementary frameworks integrate with the core methodologies to address specific organizational contexts and challenges.

Implementation Foundation

Successful framework application requires systematic rather than piecemeal approaches. Organizations must consider their STaRS context when selecting methodologies, build compelling Service-Profit Chain business cases for workforce investments, and use GRPIT to ensure coordinated implementation across all organizational dimensions.

These frameworks provide conceptual structure for the practical capabilities explored in subsequent chapters: variance management techniques that build resilience into workforce planning, maturity progression models that guide systematic capability development, and *Adaptive Orchestration* operating routines that embed human–AI collaboration in workforce decisions.

By mastering these foundational frameworks, workforce leaders can transform their function from reactive administration to strategic enablement that creates sustainable competitive advantage through integrated workforce excellence.

5 Variance and Volatility - Why Planning Matters More than the Plan

Introduction: Beyond the Illusion of Perfect Planning

Traditional workforce management operates on a seductive but dangerous assumption: that superior planning can eliminate uncertainty. Organizations invest millions in sophisticated forecasting systems, detailed capacity models, and elaborate scheduling processes, believing that if they can just plan precisely enough, they can control operational outcomes.

But this assumption is fundamentally flawed—and it's costing organizations dearly.

Why Perfect Planning Fails

The reality confronting every workforce manager is that business environments are inherently unpredictable. Customer demand fluctuates unexpectedly. Employees call in sick without warning. Market conditions shift overnight. External events—from weather to economic disruptions—create operational challenges that no amount of historical analysis could have anticipated.

Most organizations respond to these inevitable uncertainties by seeking even more precise forecasting and tighter control mechanisms. They treat variance as a planning failure rather than a mathematical certainty. This approach creates brittle organizations that excel under normal conditions but fracture when reality deviates from expectations.

The Strategic Imperative for Adaptive Planning

The frameworks introduced in Chapter 4—STaRS, Service-Profit Chain, and GR-PIT—provide the structural foundation for workforce transformation. But implementing these frameworks effectively requires a fundamental shift in how we approach uncertainty itself.

This chapter establishes the strategic foundation for this shift by exploring two critical distinctions:

Variance vs. Volatility: Understanding why small, predictable fluctuations require different responses than fundamental disruptions, and why confusing the two leads to either overreaction or dangerous complacency.

Planning vs. Plans: Recognizing why the process of continuous planning matters far more than the accuracy of any individual plan, and how this insight transforms workforce management from reactive firefighting to proactive adaptation.

Learning from Military Strategy

The principles we explore draw heavily from military strategy—not because business is warfare, but because military leaders have confronted the challenge of planning under uncertainty longer than any other profession. From Helmuth von Moltke's insights about adaptive strategy to Dwight Eisenhower's D-Day preparations, military thinking offers proven frameworks for thriving amid unpredictability.

The Foundation for Strategic Transformation

This chapter serves as the conceptual bridge between the transformation frameworks of Part I and the systematic implementation approach that follows in Chapter 6. The principles we establish here provide the strategic rationale for why workforce management must evolve from static planning to adaptive capabilities.

Organizations that master the distinction between variance and volatility—and build appropriate responses for each—position themselves to thrive in uncertain environments rather than merely survive them. We continue pursuing forecast accuracy, but we build organizational capabilities that excel when forecasts inevitably prove imperfect.

The frameworks from Chapter 4 showed you how to structure transformation. This chapter shows you why that transformation must embrace uncertainty as a strategic asset rather than an operational liability.

5.1 The Fallacy of the Perfect Plan

Businesses love certainty. Whether it's a meticulously crafted annual budget, a strategic five-year roadmap, or an intricately detailed workforce schedule, organizations invest enormous time and energy into creating the perfect plan. The assumption is simple: if we can plan well enough, we can control the future.

But that assumption is fundamentally flawed.

The Illusion of Control

Most business environments, particularly those in high-variability fields like customer service, logistics, healthcare, and finance, are filled with natural variance—the small but persistent fluctuations that impact operations daily. Unexpected sick calls, higher-than-forecasted customer demand, delayed marketing campaigns, or sudden supplier disruptions can immediately render a carefully crafted plan obsolete.

This is where most businesses fail—not because they lack a plan, but because they put too much faith in it. They operate under the illusion that precision in planning translates to precision in execution, despite overwhelming evidence to the contrary. Even sophisticated mathematical models like Erlang-C, which have served workforce management for decades, assume static conditions that rarely exist in dynamic business environments [15].

Moltke's Wisdom: No Plan Survives First Contact with Reality

One of the most widely quoted military maxims in both warfare and business comes from Helmuth von Moltke the Elder, the 19th-century Prussian military strategist. The commonly cited version states:

> "No plan survives first contact with the enemy."

However, this modern paraphrase simplifies Moltke's more nuanced original statement, written in 1871:

> "Kein Operationsplan reicht mit einiger Sicherheit über das erste Zusammentreffen mit der feindlichen Hauptmacht hinaus."
>
> [No plan of operations extends with any certainty beyond the first encounter with the main enemy forces.]
>
> —Helmuth von Moltke the Elder, 1871 [101]

Moltke's full principle conveys a more sophisticated idea: strategy must be fluid, evolving with circumstances rather than being rigidly fixed. His complete philosophy emphasized that *"strategy is a system of expedients; it is more than knowledge, it is the application of knowledge to practical life, the development of an original guiding idea under constantly changing circumstances"* [101].

Historical Context: How Moltke Transformed Military Strategy

To understand the full impact of Moltke's philosophy, we must examine his historical role in reshaping modern warfare. As Chief of the Prussian General Staff from 1857 to 1888, Moltke revolutionized military campaign planning and execution through his doctrine of **Auftragstaktik** (mission-type tactics) [102].

Before Moltke, European armies followed centralized, rigid command structures where generals devised meticulous plans that field officers were expected to execute precisely. This approach was effective when battles unfolded as predicted but disastrous when unexpected events arose.

Moltke's revolutionary approach emphasized:

- **Decentralized Decision-Making:** Field commanders received broad objectives but had autonomy to adjust tactics based on real-time battlefield conditions
- **Continuous Reassessment:** Commanders evaluated unfolding events and modified strategies dynamically
- **Flexibility over Fixed Plans:** Warfare was viewed as a constantly evolving problem requiring rapid, informed adaptation

This philosophy proved decisive in the Franco-Prussian War (1870–1871), where Prussian forces using adaptive command structures outmaneuvered French armies that relied on rigid, hierarchical planning [103].

Eisenhower's Planning Paradox

Dwight D. Eisenhower drew a sharp distinction between static plans and the discipline of planning. In his 1957 remarks, he put it plainly:

> "Plans are worthless, but planning is everything."
>
> —Dwight D. Eisenhower, 1957 [104]

His point was pragmatic: emergencies are, by definition, unexpected, so leaders must be ready to discard plans and adapt, yet the act of planning equips teams with shared context, decision rights, and rehearsed responses. For modern operations, treat planning as a continuous practice—scenario work, clear integration contracts, and pre-agreed triggers—so adaptation is fast, coordinated, and repeatable.

Churchill's Insight: The Art of Adaptive Execution

Winston Churchill, though often misquoted on planning matters, provided his own wisdom about the relationship between preparation and execution in his 1941 autobiography:

> "...the best generals are those who arrive at the results of planning without being tied to plans."
>
> —Winston S. Churchill, *A Roving Commission: My Early Life*, 1941 [105, p. 213]

Churchill's observation captures a fundamental truth: success comes not from perfect prediction, but from maintaining strategic intent while adapting tactical execution to emerging realities.

The Mathematical Reality of Variance

Military strategists understood intuitively what mathematics confirms: perfect prediction is impossible in complex systems. A.K. Erlang's pioneering work in queuing theory, originally developed for telephone traffic in 1917, demonstrated that even in highly controlled environments, arrival patterns follow probabilistic distributions with inherent variance [15].

This mathematical reality explains why static workforce plans consistently fail. Call volume, handle times, and agent availability all exhibit natural variance that cannot be eliminated through more precise forecasting. The illusion of control comes from confusing statistical averages with operational certainties.

Applying Military Wisdom to Workforce Management

The lessons of Moltke, Eisenhower, and Churchill apply directly to modern workforce management, particularly in environments where variance and volatility are the norm. Instead of asking, "How do we create the perfect plan?" organizations should be asking:

- How do we build adaptability into our operations at every level?
- What systems enable dynamic adjustment when conditions shift?
- How can we leverage real-time data for informed decision-making?
- What tools and technologies support intelligent responses to uncertainty?
- How do we balance efficiency with the flexibility required for resilience?

These questions form the foundation for the adaptive planning principles we will explore throughout this chapter—principles that acknowledge uncertainty as inevitable and transform it from a threat into a strategic advantage.

The Difference Between Planning and Plans

The military strategists we've examined understood a critical distinction that most businesses miss: the difference between *planning* as an ongoing, adaptive process and *plans* as static documents. Successful organizations master the art of continuous planning—remaining strategically focused while tactically flexible.

This distinction becomes the foundation for understanding why some organizations thrive amid uncertainty while others struggle. As we will see in the following sections, the key lies not in eliminating variance and volatility but in building organizational capabilities that can harness them as competitive advantages.

5.2 The Nature of Variance and Volatility in Business

In business operations, variance and volatility are often confused or used interchangeably, yet understanding their fundamental differences is critical to designing effective workforce strategies. While both introduce uncertainty into planning and execution, they operate on different scales, have different causes, and require entirely different approaches to management.

This distinction provides the strategic foundation for building adaptive workforce capabilities: organizations that treat both variance and volatility identically—as planning failures to be eliminated through better forecasting—create brittle systems. Those that understand the differences can build appropriate responses for each type of uncertainty.

Understanding Variance: The Predictable Unpredictability

Variance represents the small, inevitable fluctuations that occur within expected ranges—the day-to-day deviations that are statistically predictable in aggregate yet individually unpredictable. A contact center forecasting 200 calls per hour will rarely receive exactly 200 calls in any given hour, even when demand patterns are stable. Statistical models based on queuing theory show this variation is mathematically inevitable [15].

Variance exists because:

- **Customers behave unpredictably** at the individual level—purchase decisions, service requests, and interaction patterns naturally fluctuate
- **Employees are human**—productivity, adherence, and availability vary from person to person and day to day
- **Small inefficiencies accumulate**—minor delays, slightly longer interactions, and micro-disruptions create cumulative effects
- **External factors introduce variability**—weather, traffic, competing events affect customer and employee behavior in ways difficult to quantify precisely

The critical insight about variance is that it represents normal system behavior, not planning failure. Organizations that build variance management into their operational design—rather than fighting it through ever-more-precise forecasting—gain significant competitive advantages.

Volatility: When Fundamental Assumptions Break

Volatility represents disruptions that break expected ranges entirely, forcing organizations to rethink their fundamental approach to operations. Unlike variance, which fluctuates around stable patterns, volatility creates new patterns that render historical data temporarily or permanently irrelevant.

Volatility occurs when external or internal forces cause demand, supply, or operational rules to change suddenly and significantly:

- **Market Shocks:** Economic downturns, regulatory changes, competitive disruptions that reshape entire industries

- **Technological Disruptions:** Breakthrough innovations or critical system failures that render established processes obsolete
- **Black Swan Events:** Pandemics, natural disasters, geopolitical conflicts that fundamentally alter business environments
- **Social and Cultural Shifts:** Rapid changes in consumer preferences or behaviors that transform market dynamics

Volatility represents disruptions that break expected ranges entirely—*at any horizon*—forcing organizations to rethink their fundamental approach to operations. Unlike variance, which fluctuates around stable patterns, volatility creates new patterns that can render historical data temporarily or permanently irrelevant.

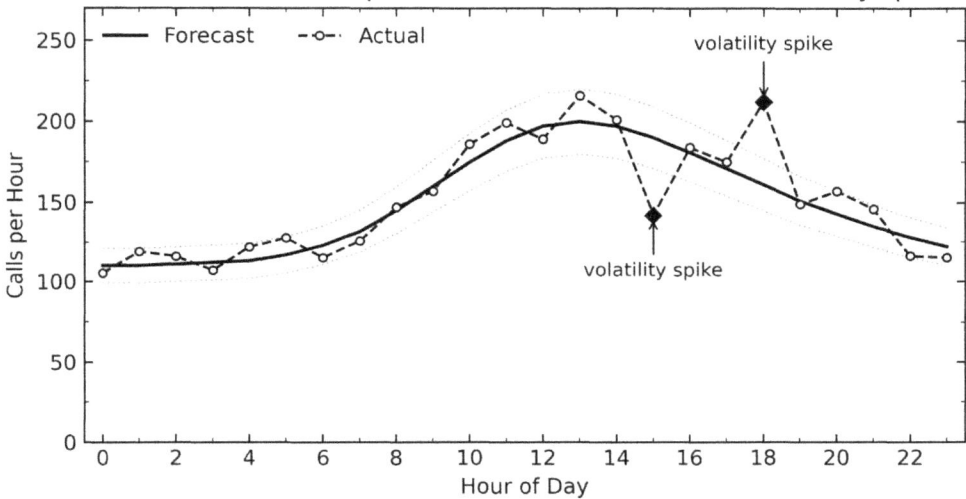

Figure 5.1: Intraday example: variance band with two out-of-band volatility spikes.

Case Study: COVID-19 as Volatility vs. Variance

The COVID-19 pandemic provides a stark illustration of volatility versus variance in action. Before March 2020, most companies' workforce plans assumed normal office attendance, predictable consumer behavior, and stable supply chains. Call volume fluctuations of ±10-15% represented normal variance that could be managed through traditional workforce management approaches.

Within days, however, offices shut down globally, call volumes in some industries surged sharply while collapsing in others, and entire sectors shifted to remote work virtually overnight. This wasn't variance—it was pure volatility that broke every planning assumption.

Organizations with rigid workforce models struggled or collapsed entirely. Their detailed forecasting models and capacity plans proved useless when fundamental assumptions became invalid. Conversely, companies that had built adaptability into their operational DNA pivoted quickly:

- Retailers with omnichannel capabilities rapidly scaled digital operations

- Contact centers with cloud-based technologies transitioned to remote work within days
- Organizations with cross-trained workforces redeployed resources to meet shifting demands

Why Organizations Fail to Distinguish Variance and Volatility

Most businesses treat variance and volatility identically, leading to ineffective decision-making and resource misallocation. This failure manifests in two dangerous patterns:

Treating Variance Like Volatility (Overreaction): When organizations mistake normal statistical fluctuations for fundamental shifts, they overreact with unnecessary disruption. A company sees a small dip in performance and immediately launches a complete process overhaul, when the issue was simply normal variance that required minor tactical adjustments.

Treating Volatility Like Variance (Underreaction): Equally dangerous is interpreting fundamental shifts as mere fluctuations, leading to complacency. Early signs of major market shifts get dismissed as temporary variations rather than indicators of permanent change requiring strategic response.

The COVID-19 pandemic revealed both patterns: some organizations panicked at normal business fluctuations while others dismissed clear signals of permanent change as temporary disruptions.

Building Capabilities for Both Challenges

Organizations that excel in dynamic environments design strategies addressing both variance and volatility, recognizing that each requires fundamentally different approaches:

Factor	Managing Variance	Managing Volatility
Approach	Tactical flexibility	Strategic resilience
Tools	Real-time automation, dynamic scheduling	Scenario planning, probabilistic modeling
Decision Speed	Immediate adjustment	Deliberate strategic shifts
Investment	Operational efficiency	Adaptive capacity
Mindset	Variance as asset	Volatility as opportunity

Table 5.1: Distinct Approaches to Managing Variance vs. Volatility

This dual approach enables organizations to optimize day-to-day operations through variance management while building strategic resilience against volatility. Rather than viewing uncertainty as a problem to be solved, they treat it as a competitive advantage to be leveraged.

Understanding the distinction between variance and volatility becomes the foundation for building adaptive workforce capabilities. Organizations that master this difference can design appropriate responses for each type of uncertainty, positioning themselves to thrive in dynamic business environments.

5.3 When Variance Becomes Asset: Evidence from the Field

Organizations that recognize variance as a predictable operational pattern—rather than a planning failure—transform it from cost burden to competitive advantage. The evidence is consistent: companies that manage variance through tactical flexibility deliver superior financial performance, higher customer satisfaction, and better employee experience versus those that try to eliminate it through rigid plans. The following field examples show why variance demands different capabilities than volatility.

Tax Season at Scale: Intuit's Cloud Transformation

Intuit's contact center operations provide an archetypal case of effective variance management. Every year, with calendar precision, the company scales from 6,000 agents to 11,000 agents during U.S. tax season—an 83% increase that recurs predictably from January through April [106]. This is not volatility; it is variance at massive scale.

Before migrating to cloud infrastructure, Intuit required six months of preparation to handle this predictable surge. The company maintained multiple contact center servers year-round, carrying licenses and hardware that sat idle for most of the year. Scaling meant ordering equipment, provisioning circuits, and hoping demand projections proved accurate.

The shift to Amazon Connect changed the economics entirely. As Jerry Lekhter, Director of Contact Center Engineering at Intuit, explains: "Scaling our solution for tax season only takes a few minutes now, and it doesn't require us to manage and maintain contact centers for 11,000 agents all year." The system has been load-tested to support up to 20,000 agents—nearly double current peak needs—providing buffer for unexpected variance within the expected pattern [106].

The financial impact is direct: fixed capacity became elastic capacity. Pay-per-use cost models align spend with demand realization. This isn't about forecasting more precisely; it's about building infrastructure that treats variance as normal.

Insurance's Annual Tsunami: Engineering for Extremes

Health insurers face even more dramatic, yet calendar-anchored, variance patterns. During Open Enrollment Periods (OEPs)—October through December for Medicare, November through January for ACA marketplace plans—contact centers often experience multi-fold increases over steady state. Public CMS snapshots illustrate the pattern: Marketplace call-center volume rose from *293,511* calls in Week 1 of the 2022 OEP (Nov. 1–6, 2021) to *1,299,313* around the Dec. 15 deadline, roughly a 4.4× surge within the same season [107, 108]. Top-tier analyses of government-benefits contact centers report similar "surging call volumes" and operational strain during eligibility events, compounding staffing challenges [109].

The complexity extends beyond volume. Licensed insurance agents typically command materially higher bill rates than non-licensed staff and must often hold licenses across multiple states, constraining resource pools. Training requirements commonly run 4–6 weeks before an agent can handle enrollment calls independently. Treating this as an annual crisis leads to chronic inefficiency; treating it as engineered variance changes the playbook:

- Business Process Outsourcing (BPO) partnerships that activate dormant capacity on demand
- Cloud contact center platforms enabling instant geographic distribution
- Automated deflection that absorbs a significant share of routine enrollment questions
- Year-round retention of a core seasonal workforce that returns annually

The strategic shift is clear: Open Enrollment is not a disruption. It is the high end of normal variance, designed into operating DNA.

Retail and Travel Rhythms: Seasonal Patterns as Edge

Airlines and retailers show how mastering seasonality becomes competitive advantage. European low-cost carriers see pronounced summer and winter peaks that are printed on calendars years in advance; the winners build systems around those rhythms. One successful carrier reported maintaining high utilization across the year while materially reducing Average Handle Time (AHT) through cross-training, flexible scheduling, and automated callbacks—capabilities tuned to predictable peaks rather than heroic recoveries after the fact.

Retail contact centers show similar cadence: the Thanksgiving–Cyber Monday window produces the year's most concentrated surge in traffic, orders, and service contacts. Leaders no longer treat Black Friday as an emergency; they pre-build capabilities that activate specifically for those moments—seasonal hiring that begins in September, auto-scaling cloud infrastructure tied to web telemetry, and automation that satisfies order-status inquiries without agent intervention.

The Variance Playbook: Common Success Patterns

Across industries, organizations that excel at variance share four traits:

Temporal Predictability. Variance follows patterns. Tax season, enrollment deadlines, holiday shopping, summer travel—these are scheduled. The exact volume may vary by ±20%, but timing is certain. Preparation replaces scrambling.

Bounded Magnitude. Variance has limits. Intuit's seasonal spike may reach 83%, but not 800%. OEP demand can drive multi-fold increases (e.g., 3–8×), but not 50×. Capacity is planned to ranges, not point estimates, enabling investment for the 95th percentile without gold-plating for impossibilities.

Elastic Infrastructure. Fixed capacity gives way to elastic capability. Cloud, flexible labor models, and automation create capacity that expands and contracts with demand. Economics shift to pay-for-what-you-use when you use it.

Operational Integration. Variance management is not a side project; it is embedded. Scheduling assumes seasonality, hiring anticipates peaks, and technology prioritizes flexibility.

Why Variance Differs from Volatility

The evidence above shows variance as *structured uncertainty*: timing is knowable, magnitude is bounded, and responses can be designed in advance. Volatility is different: it breaks those bounds. Because peaks and shocks occur across *multiple time horizons* (intraday, daily, weekly, seasonal), the tell is not the clock but the behavior of systems when limits are exceeded.

Warning signs you have crossed into volatility

- *Out-of-band scale or timing* across any horizon (intraday spikes or off-season surges that ignore calendars and exceed planned bands).

- *Non-linear failure modes:* critical systems do not slow—they hard-stop (queuing/crew/IVR/scheduling subsystems flip from degraded to unavailable).

- *Cascades and cross-domain spillover:* one failure begets many (operations → customer service → workforce → compliance), and recovery spans multiple horizons (minutes to stabilize, days to clear backlogs, weeks to repair trust).

- *Priors lose power:* historical patterns, control limits, and trained models stop helping because the event has no close precedent.

- *Broken proportionality:* costs and outcomes decouple from volume (SLA collapse, write-offs, penalties) rather than scaling linearly.

So variance stretches systems; volatility breaks them. The organizations above win at variance by treating calendar-anchored surges as normal and engineering elasticity accordingly. Next, we turn the lens to *volatility*: pattern-breaking shocks—visible even intraday, as in the spiky departures from a smooth forecast—where assumptions fail, cascades form, and the playbook, math, and governance must change to operate beyond planning ranges.

5.4 When Planning Breaks: Volatility's Operational Cascade

While variance represents predictable patterns within expected ranges, volatility shatters those ranges entirely. It does not merely stress-test systems—it breaks them. The distinction is critical: organizations that confuse routine variance with true volatility either overreact to normal fluctuations or, more dangerously, underreact to fundamental disruptions. The following cases demonstrate why volatility requires fundamentally different organizational capabilities than variance.

Southwest's $140 Million Warning: When Systems Cascade into Chaos

Southwest Airlines' December 2022 operational collapse provides a textbook study in volatility's compounding effects. Between December 21 and December 31, the airline canceled roughly 16,900 flights, stranding more than two million passengers during peak holiday travel [110]. On peak disruption days, Southwest accounted for the vast majority of cancellations[111].

The apparent trigger—a winter storm—was manageable across the industry. The difference was system fragility under stress. As reporting and subsequent investigations noted, outdated crew-scheduling technology and manual fallbacks could not handle the volume of reassignments required, turning localized disruption into a network-wide cascade [111]. Contact channels were overwhelmed, and recovery required a systemwide "reset." Regulators later imposed a $140 million penalty—the largest consumer-protection penalty in DOT history—and documented failures to provide adequate customer service assistance and prompt flight-status notifications. DOT also ensured more than $600 million in refunds and reimbursements were delivered to passengers [110]. In short: variance-era fixes (trim schedules, reoptimize) could not arrest a volatility event that broke underlying assumptions.

Banking's COVID Crucible: Demand Without Precedent

Financial-services contact centers in early 2020 faced a volatility shock, not a seasonal spike. McKinsey's global retail-banking review found that from December 2019 to April 2020, *call volumes rose about 29% and waiting times quadrupled*, with the severity varying by market maturity [112]. Simultaneously, physical networks seized up: roughly a quarter of branches closed in March 2020 and about 15% remained closed in May, abruptly shifting traffic into remote channels and contact centers [112].

Consumer distress surfaced in government data as well: the CFPB logged approximately *542,300* complaints in 2020—about a 54% year-over-year increase—concentrated in core banking categories [113]. Criminal exploitation rose in parallel: the FBI's IC3 recorded *791,790* internet-crime complaints in 2020, a *69%* increase from 2019, with pandemic-related scams prominent [114].

This was not variance scaling up; it was new demand with different topics, customer intents, and handling effort—arriving faster than static plans could adapt.

The Volatility Signature: Why Traditional Planning Fails

Volatility exhibits distinct characteristics that render variance-based planning insufficient:

Magnitude shock. Volatility does not nudge demand 10–20%; it can push systems multiple times beyond typical operating ranges. Linear scaling assumptions fail at these levels.

Technology failure under stress. Stacks optimized for efficiency degrade gracefully within bands of variance—but at volatility levels they can fail discontinuously (e.g., scheduling and notification systems that stop functioning rather than merely slowing).

Cascading secondary failures. One system's failure (crew scheduling, branch access, identity verification) drives overload elsewhere (operations, contact centers, fraud controls), amplifying losses.

Planning assumptions destroyed. Historical patterns lose relevance. Stimulus-check questions, hardship programs, or system-wide network resets have no historical twins to train on.

Extended recovery windows. Variance spikes decay quickly; volatility leaves operational and reputational damage that persists well beyond the initial trigger.

The False Promise of Better Forecasting

Leaders often answer volatility with "better prediction." That misses the point. Volatility is unpredictable not because data are scarce, but because the event breaks the model: new policies, new intents, and new interdependencies invalidate learned relationships. Southwest had decades of operational data; the problem was the interaction between weather, process bottlenecks, and brittle tools at scale [110, 111]. Banks had sophisticated journey analytics; they did not have historical data for pandemic relief and policy-driven surges [112]. Survival depends less on anticipating the exact shock than on absorbing and adapting to *any* shock.

Volatility's Strategic Message

Variance-optimized systems are volatility-fragile. Lean staffing, just-in-time schedules, and tightly coupled technology produce enviable efficiency in normal times—and brittleness when assumptions fail. The remedy is not prophecy; it is capability: redundant pathways that maintain partial function during failure, surge capacity that scales nonlinearly, decision frameworks that work when precedent does not, and recovery mechanisms that restore operations after fundamental disruption [112]. These can appear inefficient through a variance lens. They are essential through a volatility lens.

In the next section, we outline the operating capabilities and governance patterns that allow organizations to function *beyond planning ranges*—a playbook designed for environments where the game itself can change.

5.5 Operating Doctrine for Variance and Volatility

The core lesson of this chapter is not to "forecast harder," but to build adaptive operating systems that run at two tempos of uncertainty. Some surges are patterned and bounded; others break patterns and bounds. Both can appear intraday or seasonally, and both matter. In the Collaborative Intelligence Era—and in the context of the change dynamics outlined in Chapter 3—the organizations that outperform are those that design for these dual realities on purpose.

What we now know

- *Uncertainty is plural.* Variance is structured and recurrent; volatility is structure-breaking. Treating them as one problem guarantees the wrong trade-offs.
- *Different physics, different tools.* Variance yields to elasticity and banded plans; volatility requires resilience, decoupling, and rapid reconfiguration.
- *Edge speed matters.* Time-to-decision and time-to-action improve when intent and guardrails are clear and authority sits close to the work.
- *Horizon awareness prevents over/under-reaction.* Recovery must be gated by horizon—minutes for intraday stabilization, days for backlog clearance, weeks for reputational repair—not by a single SLA.
- *Learning compounds performance.* Spikes and shocks are inputs, not anomalies; they should tighten bands, update runbooks, and harden failovers.

Doctrine for operating beyond planning ranges

- *Plan to bands, not points.* Express demand and supply as ranges with triggers; make fan-charts first-class artifacts.
- *Pre-wire elasticity for variance.* Cross-train, schedule flexibly, and use pay-per-use capacity so costs stay proportional as demand moves.
- *Design graceful degradation for volatility.* Decouple critical paths, define fallback modes, and rehearse system "resets" under load.
- *Push decisions to the edge with intent.* Replace permission with principles; give front lines clear objectives and bounded authority.
- *Instrument and remember.* Capture intraday signals, run after-action reviews, and convert lessons into updated bands, playbooks, and contracts.

Variance and volatility are not side topics—they are why Workforce Management must advance. The Collaborative Intelligence Era raises the pace and degree of change; Chapter 3 explains why it will keep accelerating. *Adaptive Orchestration* absorbs that volatility. Entry-level practices saturate quickly. The upgrade is two engines in parallel: *elasticity* for patterned demand and *resilience* when patterns break—together turning uncertainty into advantage.

This doctrine now becomes an operating model: capabilities, artifacts, and governance that make banded plans real and recoveries reliable. The imperative is simple: mature Workforce Management so your operation performs within bands—and beyond them—whatever tempo arrives.

6 The WFM Labs Maturity Model: A Framework for Transformation

Introduction: Your Roadmap from Theory to Practice

The workforce management landscape is undergoing a radical transformation. Traditional scheduling and forecasting methods—rooted in historical data and rigid capacity planning—are no longer sufficient in an era defined by real-time adaptability, automation, and employee-centric (EX-first) workforce strategies. Organizations that continue to rely on static workforce planning models face growing inefficiencies, increased attrition, and an inability to respond dynamically to the variance and volatility we explored in Chapter 5.

The frameworks in Chapter 4—STaRS, Service-Profit Chain, GRPIT, and understanding variance management—provide the strategic foundation for transformation. But how do you actually implement them?

The WFM Labs Maturity Model™ is your roadmap from where you are to where you need to be.

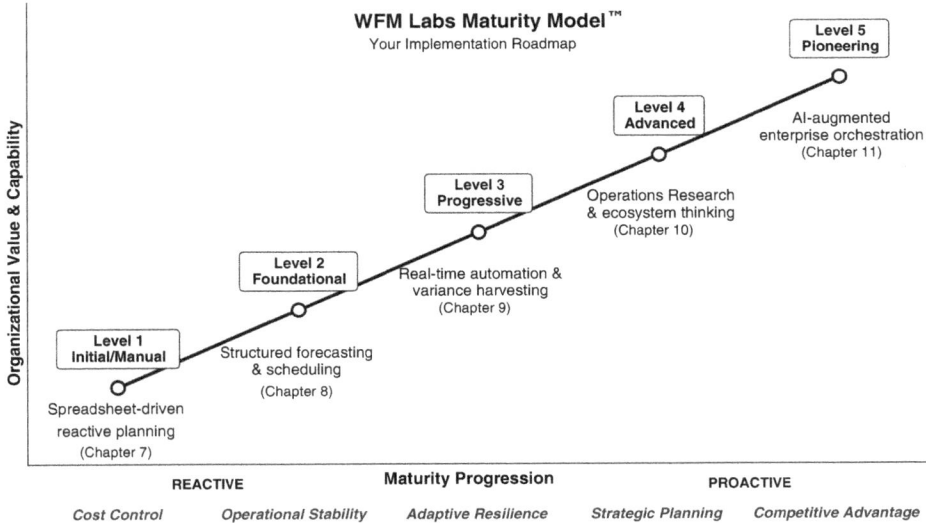

Figure 6.1: WFM Labs Maturity Model™

Five Levels, Five Chapters, One Clear Path

This model distills decades of workforce management evolution into five progressive levels. Each level represents a fundamental shift in capability and is summarized in Table 6.1. Unlike academic maturity models that describe ideal states, this framework is built from real implementations. Every level reflects what actually works in practice, not what sounds good in theory. The progression isn't just about technology—it's about fundamentally changing how organizations think about their workforce as a strategic asset.

From Cost Center to Competitive Advantage

Most organizations still treat workforce management as a cost-control function: minimize labor expense while hitting service targets. This mentality guarantees mediocrity. The Collaborative Intelligence Era demands a different approach—*Adaptive Orchestration*—where workforce optimization becomes a source of competitive advantage through employee engagement, operational resilience, and customer value creation.

The maturity model shows this evolution clearly. At Level 1, you're fighting fires with spreadsheets. By Level 5, you're orchestrating enterprise-wide intelligence—*integration without ownership* of data—making workforce management a strategic differentiator. The journey between these points is systematic, measurable, and achievable.

Table 6.1: WFM Labs Maturity Model™ — Your Implementation Roadmap

Level	Core Capability	Deep-Dive
Level 1: Initial/Manual	Spreadsheet-driven reactive planning	Chapter 7
Level 2: Foundational	Structured forecasting & scheduling	Chapter 8
Level 3: Progressive	Real-time automation & variance harvesting	Chapter 9
Level 4: Advanced	Operations Research & ecosystem thinking	Chapter 10
Level 5: Pioneering	AI-augmented enterprise orchestration	Chapter 11

How to Use This Model

First, assess where you are today. Unlike other maturity models that describe organizations scattered across multiple levels, workforce management maturity tends to cluster around specific stages. At the time of this publication, approximately 85% of contact centers operate at either Level 1 or Level 2, with the distinction often determined by scale and investment capacity.

Many smaller contact centers remain at Level 1—managing operations through spreadsheets and manual processes—either because they haven't reached the scale requiring formal WFM software investment or are just beginning to grow into that requirement. The majority sit at Level 2, having invested in traditional WFM software and established the legacy processes that define this level: building detailed plans, pre-scheduling training and coaching, and reacting to variance as it unfolds.

A smaller but growing portion of the industry has advanced to Level 3, where they've fundamentally rethought these legacy processes, invested in automation software, and transformed variance from enemy to asset through dynamic delivery of training and development. Level 4 represents organizations that have broken free from deterministic capacity planning and migrated to ecosystem thinking—an even smaller group. Level 5 encompasses those pioneering enterprise-wide orchestration capabilities.

Second, understand that progression isn't strictly linear. You might implement Level 3 real-time capabilities before perfecting Level 2 processes. The model provides guardrails, not rigid sequencing. What matters is building capability that supports your specific business context—the STaRS framework from Chapter 4 helps determine where to focus first.

Third, recognize that each level unlocks different value. Level 2 brings operational stability. Level 3 enables automation and adaptive resilience. Level 4 provides strategic planning capability. Level 5 creates competitive differentiation. Your organization's urgency and resources should guide how fast you advance.

The Implementation Reality

Transformation is hard. Every level requires not just new technology but new ways of thinking, working, and measuring success. You'll face resistance from people comfortable with current processes. You'll encounter vendors selling solutions that promise to skip levels. You'll discover gaps between what you thought you needed and what actually drives results.

This is why Part II exists. Rather than theoretical descriptions, you'll follow Sarah Chen's real-world journey through each level. You'll see the specific challenges she faces, the decisions she makes, and the results she achieves. Her story becomes your implementation guide, showing not just *what* to do but *how* to do it effectively.

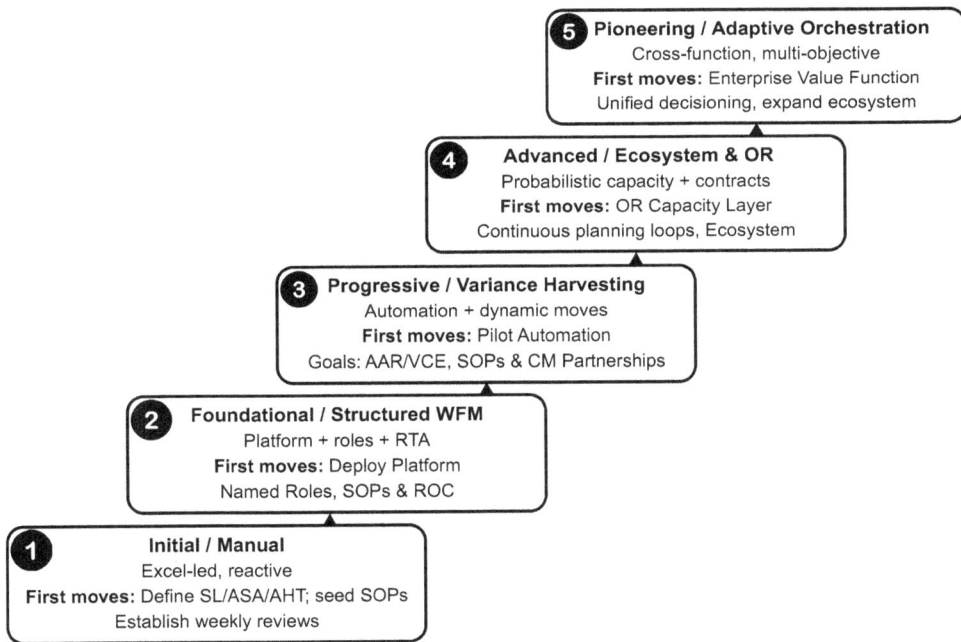

5 Pioneering / Adaptive Orchestration
Cross-function, multi-objective
First moves: Enterprise Value Function
Unified decisioning, expand ecosystem

4 Advanced / Ecosystem & OR
Probabilistic capacity + contracts
First moves: OR Capacity Layer
Continuous planning loops, Ecosystem

3 Progressive / Variance Harvesting
Automation + dynamic moves
First moves: Pilot Automation
Goals: AAR/VCE, SOPs & CM Partnerships

2 Foundational / Structured WFM
Platform + roles + RTA
First moves: Deploy Platform
Named Roles, SOPs & ROC

1 Initial / Manual
Excel-led, reactive
First moves: Define SL/ASA/AHT; seed SOPs
Establish weekly reviews

Figure 6.2: Implementation Path

Your Preview of the Journey Ahead

This chapter now sketches each level—what defines it, why organizations get stuck, and which capabilities unlock the next step—while showing how GRPIT and variance/volatility practices mature across the spectrum. Use this overview as the map for Part II's implementation stories.

6.1 Level 1: Initial/Manual — The Excel Foundation

Level 1 organizations run workforce operations through spreadsheets, manual processes, and reactive adjustments. This is the *Excel stage*: scheduling happens in workbooks, forecasting leans on recent history, and real-time management means supervisors phoning and messaging when problems emerge. It often fits smaller contact centers—frequently under 100 agents—before a dedicated WFM function exists.

This approach works at small scale but has predictable limits. Without an interval forecast (15–30 minutes) and a clear translation from the service promise (e.g., 80/30) to staffing, teams cannot tell normal pattern drift from a real disruption. Routine changes—volume up a few points, AHT creeping—may go unnoticed until backlog and ASA jump, prompting *basic, reactive* moves (calls, texts, sliding lunches) rather than planned levers. Because queue dynamics are non-linear, small staffing changes can produce outsized service swings (the "Power of One").

Operational profile (GRPIT)

- **Goals (G):** Daily promise stated but not enforced at the interval level; no posted occupancy band (e.g., 78–88%); shrinkage treated as a fuzzy buffer rather than a policy.
- **Roles (R):** No dedicated WFM owner; forecasting, scheduling, and real-time split across supervisors and an "Excel power user."
- **Processes (P):** Weekly roster from historical averages; ad hoc intraday changes; no Rule→Trigger→Action playbook or variance log.
- **Interpersonal (I):** Goodwill bridges gaps, but unpredictability taxes agents (overtime asks, sliding lunches, canceled coaching).
- **Technology (T):** Excel/email/whiteboards as the system; no ACD↔WFM link; limited interval visibility.

Why instability appears. Customer arrivals are random, handle times vary, and agents have real constraints. An Erlang-C baseline translates interval workload (arrivals × AHT) into staffing for a timeliness promise—but Level 1 typically discovers this relationship through service failures rather than proactive planning. Pairing SL with ASA and an occupancy band exposes the depth and cost of misses. A clear short-abandon policy (e.g., exclude abandons under 5–10 seconds) keeps definitions honest.

Growth and integration pressure. Manual scheduling that works for 50 agents becomes unmanageable at 150. Spreadsheet coordination fails when multiple supervisors need simultaneous edits. Acquisitions magnify the pain: different Excel formats, scheduling philosophies, and coordination methods collide; what functioned separately becomes chaos when merged without common definitions and cadence. Employee experience erodes as unpredictability drives turnover, which steals more capacity from the plan.

The minimum path forward. Advancing from Level 1 requires four concrete steps that stabilize today and enable Level 2:

1. **Name ownership.** Assign a WFM owner (even part-time) who curates definitions and handoffs across forecasting, scheduling, and real-time.

2. **Post the instruments.** Publish interval SL, an occupancy band (e.g., 78–88%), a shrinkage policy, and a short-abandon rule; use an Erlang-C sheet to translate promises into required staff.

3. **Run a simple rhythm.** Weekly interval forecast → shrinkage-aware roster → intraday micro-moves via a small Rule→Trigger→Action log → two-line variance log at day's end.

4. **Tool the basics.** Keep Excel systematic (one source-of-truth workbook); prepare for a starter WFM platform by standardizing inputs and guardrails rather than chasing features.

Why Level 1 matters. Level 1 is the common starting point. Naming its limits makes the business case for structure without blaming people. Teams typically see quick gains in service stability, efficiency, and morale once interval goals, occupancy bands, shrinkage, and a few repeatable intraday moves are in place. The move to Level 2 is then an upgrade of habits already working, not a reboot.

6.2 Level 2: Foundational — Structured Workforce Management

Level 2 is where most contact centers operate today. Organizations establish dedicated workforce management functions, implement a WFM platform, and document processes that turn manual chaos into professional operations. Service levels stabilize, interval goals are tracked, and schedules arrive predictably. This structure delivers clear improvements over Level 1's reactive firefighting.

Built-in constraint (made explicit). The same strengths become limits. Planning remains largely *deterministic* (often in external spreadsheets), and *no real-time automation* executes micro-moves. When reality deviates—a mathematical certainty in queues—the system reacts through manual edits rather than adapting in minutes. Multi-channel mixes (voice/chat/email) expose rigidity as cross-channel shifts are slow and policy-bound. Staffing baselines are often *abandonment-blind* (Erlang-C), optimistic when queues are tight unless short-abandon treatment or abandonment-aware thinking is applied.

Operational profile (GRPIT)

- **Goals (G):** SL is formal (e.g., 80/30) and visible with ASA; *publish* short-abandon policy, an *occupancy band* (e.g., 78–88%), and a *shrinkage policy* to balance service, people, and cost.
- **Roles (R):** Dedicated forecasters, schedulers, and real-time analysts exist; handoffs work, but learning loops are weak across silos.
- **Processes (P):** Capacity planning deterministic; schedules post on cadence; intraday adjustments are manual; coaching often yields under pressure.
- **Interpersonal (I):** Professional structure improves predictability, yet rigid adherence and repeated training cancellations erode flexibility and growth.
- **Technology (T):** The WFM platform is the single source of truth for rosters and targets. You can see issues, but fixes still require people to push buttons—changes roll out at human speed without automation.

The Professional Structure

Level 2 builds impressive capabilities within traditional frames. Forecasters maintain seasonality and event calendars and project demand months ahead, assuming patterns repeat with modest variation. Schedulers optimize staffing with precision, balancing breaks and lunches down to minutes. Real-time analysts monitor SL, ASA, abandon, and adherence, processing exceptions when agents deviate from the plan. These are real advances over Level 1.

The limits are predictable. Functions operate as strong *silos*: forecasters measure accuracy against history but rarely integrate fast floor signals; schedulers assume perfect adherence and static forecasts; real-time reacts to variance rather than feeding design changes upstream. Traditional platforms excel at making detailed plans visible; they struggle to *execute small, timely corrections* across skills and channels. Dashboards show variance with precision; responses still arrive at human speed.

The Human Reality

Professionalization brings wins—schedules are posted further in advance with fewer last-minute changes, processes are clearer, and operational visibility improves. Yet rigid templates and policy-heavy adherence trap employees in patterns that ignore life's unpredictability. Training cancellations protect short-term SL at the expense of long-term capability. Over time, the metric trio that signals Level 2 "success"—forecast accuracy, schedule adherence, service level attainment—can incentivize defending a static plan instead of building adaptive capacity. Turnover follows, often misattributed to "the industry" rather than design choices.

The ROC Evolution

Progressive Level 2 organizations stand up a *Resource Optimization Center (ROC)* that reframes real-time from exception processing to operational coordination. The ROC treats variance as expected and manages it with *Rule→Trigger→Action* ladders. Its value is visibility that *quantifies* Level 2's limits and the opportunity cost of manual speed: every manual intervention becomes a candidate for automation; every delay has a measured impact (e.g., *time-to-stabilize* and *protected-time retention*). This evidence builds the business case for Level 3 automation grounded in your own intervals.

The Industry Reality

Most centers remain at Level 2 because structure "works well enough" and looks professionally sophisticated. A mature vendor ecosystem has optimized for *static planning plus reactive management*. External pressure is changing the math: customers expect immediacy and personalization; employees expect flexibility; market cycles compress. Level 2, once revolutionary, becomes increasingly inadequate in dynamic environments.

The Path Forward

Advancing beyond Level 2 does not discard investments; it *transcends* their limits. Forecasting engines become inputs to *automated* decision systems; scheduling platforms generate *flexible frames* with guardrails; real-time moves from exception handling to *variance harvesting*. Concretely: publish SL/ASA/short-abandon, an occupancy band, and shrinkage policy; close role handoffs with a daily variance loop; codify micro-moves so the ROC can act consistently now and automation can safely press the same buttons at Level 3. Level 2 is a foundation, not a destination—the platform from which dynamic workforce management becomes possible.

6.3 Level 3: Progressive — Real-Time Variance Harvesting

Level 3 upgrades the operation from *defending a plan* to *continuously planning*. An automation layer sits between ACD, WFM, and LMS/Comms, reads live signals, and executes small, safe actions in seconds. Variance stops being the enemy; it becomes fuel for stability, development, and cost control—simultaneously.

Design principle (made explicit). Variance is expected and instrumented. Published guardrails (SL/ASA/short-abandon, occupancy band, shrinkage policy) remain the rules of the game; automation enforces them at machine speed. Agents keep control (accept/defer where appropriate); every action is auditable and written back to systems of record.

Operational profile (GRPIT)

- **Goals (G):** Classic KPIs persist, now joined by *service-level stability (SLS)*, *Automation Acceptance Rate (AAR)*, and *Variance Capture Efficiency (VCE)*. Supervisor time shifts from admin to coaching (track a *focus* metric).

- **Roles (R):** Real-time analysts become *rule orchestrators*; forecasters publish risk bands; schedulers design flexible frames; many shops add an *automation strategist*. The ROC stewards rules and learning.

- **Processes (P):** Dynamic training/coaching, break/lunch protection, end-of-shift and VTO/VOT automation; exceptions disappear by design; rule registry and weekly tune-ups replace manual workarounds.

- **Interpersonal (I):** Trust grows as prompts explain *why*, options replace mandates, and supervisors return to coaching. Transparency and co-design matter more than slogans.

- **Technology (T):** Real-time automation ingests ACD signals live, with bi-directional reads/writes to WFM and LMS on their native cadences (often every few minutes). Analysts author rules; sub-minute actuation happens where the ACD is the source, and all updates are auditable—the value is orchestration, not another dashboard.

The Operating Model

Where Level 2 had strong silos and precise dashboards, Level 3 adds *actuation*. Rules convert signals to the smallest effective move: deliver micro-learning in safe lulls, protect breaks when calls overrun, surface long-call assists with context, nudge early/late meals within the occupancy band, offer VTO ahead of surplus. The WFM platform remains the schedule source of truth; automation updates it in-line so audits and trust hold.

The Human Reality

The day becomes more humane: fewer adherence tickets, preserved development, less firefighting. Agents gain real flexibility (accept/defer with no penalty); supervisors stop policing minutes and coach; RTAs design and tune rules instead of chasing the board. Adoption hinges on simple, honest copy (*"Your call ran long; your break moved +6 to protect adherence."*) and visible wins.

The ROC, Evolving

The *Resource Optimization Center* is a natural extension of Level 2—not a new bureaucracy. It keeps the same real-time visibility and coordination role, but now also *owns the rulebook*:

what the system may do, when, and with what agent choices. When guardrails wobble, automation takes the first safe step; the ROC confirms or overrides and handles the few cases that require human judgment. Recurring patterns are codified into rules; effective rules become part of the standard frame. Over time, more fixes happen in seconds, and the ROC concentrates on tuning rules, managing judgment-heavy exceptions, and introducing or retiring rules as the operation learns.

The Industry Reality

The legacy ecosystem optimized for static planning + reactive management. Level 3 changes the cost curve: steadier SL with lower planned shrinkage and higher delivered development. As peers adopt, standing still raises your relative unit cost and erodes talent appeal.

The Path Forward

Keep the Level 2 guardrails; let automation press the buttons. Institutionalize a rule registry, a weekly tune-up, and shared dashboards for AAR, VCE, and SLS. Treat the ROC as rule mission control. The data you generate (signals → actions → outcomes) becomes the runway for Level 4 prediction and Level 5 orchestration.

6.4 Level 4: Advanced — The Ecosystem Revolution

Level 4 is the pivot from spreadsheet arithmetic to *Operations Research* at ecosystem scale. Organizations replace point estimates with *probability ranges*, and monolith thinking with *composable* planning: a best-in-breed WFM core, a real-time automation layer, an OR-driven capacity engine, and an analytics workspace wired by APIs and data contracts. The result is a *living* capacity plan that updates as drivers change and expresses staffing as P50/P80/P95 bands rather than single numbers.

Scientific premise (made explicit). We plan for distributions, not points. Inputs (arrivals, AHT, shrinkage, attrition, deflection) are modeled as uncertain; outputs are *envelopes with confidence* and *playbooks for tails*. Leadership chooses risk posture (e.g., staff to P80), and automation executes within those bands day-to-day. Assumptions, constraints, and model limits are published as *model cards* with a versioned *constraint register*.

Operational profile (GRPIT)

- **Goals (G):** Optimize across *service stability, cost, agent experience, resilience*—measured as hit-rates to targets (e.g., P_{85} of meeting 80/30), total cost (incl. OT/BPO risk), schedule quality, and robustness under stress tests. Report ranges (P50/P80/P95) and sensitivities, not single asks.
- **Roles (R):** Add a *Capacity Planning Data Scientist* (probabilistic models, simulation), an *OR–WFM Translator* (turns policies into constraints and trade-offs into decisions), and an *Automation Orchestrator* (links bands to real-time rules). Core WFM upskills to probabilistic literacy.
- **Processes (P):** Move from annual snapshot to *continuous refresh*: daily/weekly range updates, monthly calibration, quarterly stress scenarios. Standard artifacts: *staffing envelope, constraint register, model cards*, and *decision packs*.
- **Interpersonal (I):** Shift from handoffs to *joint ownership of uncertainty*: one model, many role-based views (Ops/Finance/Marketing), explicit triggers, and blameless post-mortems that update models—no "precision theater."
- **Technology (T):** Ecosystem architecture: API-first WFM single source of truth (SSoT); intraday automation for variance harvesting; OR planning layer (Monte Carlo, simulation, optimization); analytics workbench; event streaming + governed data contracts for ranges/constraints/outcomes.

Mathematical sophistication (right-sized). Monte Carlo replaces single-point staffing with confidence bands; discrete-event simulation handles multi-skill routing, abandonment, and policy tests; linear/mixed-integer programming optimizes across constraints (labor, skills, preferences) and objectives. Leaders pick from *Pareto-efficient* options rather than defend "exactly 287 agents."

Ecosystem architecture (how it fits together). Keep your WFM core for scheduling/adherence; add an *OR capacity layer* for ranges and scenarios; use *real-time automation* to enforce the selected service posture; and operate an *analytics workspace* to back-test, explain, and learn. Integrations are bi-directional: planning publishes bands/guardrails; automation returns telemetry (acceptance, micro-availability, drift) that tightens distributions.

Strategic business intelligence (why it matters). With ranges tied to business drivers, WFM becomes a strategy partner: Finance prices cost/risk, Marketing schedules campaigns within capacity envelopes, HR times classes to band thresholds, and Ops selects posture by line of business. Decisions come with *confidence, triggers, and residual risk*—not wishful precision.

Implementation and evolution. Phase in: (1) establish probabilistic literacy and data contracts; (2) run side-by-side pilots that publish P50/P80/P95 and sensitivities; (3) formalize governance (model cards, calibration cadence, rollback); (4) scale across units and feed bands to automation. Level 4 lays the foundation for Level 5's autonomous optimization by making plans living, transparent, and machine-consumable.

6.5 Level 5: Pioneering — Adaptive Orchestration

Level 5 is workforce management's next frontier—from contact center optimization to enterprise-wide *Adaptive Orchestration*. Organizations transcend WFM's boundaries to coordinate human capability, artificial intelligence, and business purpose across functions, turning the operation into a *living* intelligence system that senses, decides, and adapts.

The defining shift reframes the question from "Will AI replace workers?" to "How do we *optimize* human–AI collaboration for multi-stakeholder value (customers, employees, business, and risk)?" Level 5 ecosystems amplify human potential rather than replace it, using portfolio decisioning to route each interaction to the highest-value handler—human, AI, or hybrid.

This isn't "better WFM tools." It is WFM becoming the enterprise *decisioning platform*: a federated *orchestration layer* that connects to truths where they live (CRM, HR, Finance, Marketing) and a *decision layer* that balances objectives and constraints in real time. The result is a self-evolving system that learns continuously.

Enterprise Integration and Predictive Operations

Level 5 dissolves the artificial boundary that confined WFM to service. Intelligence is *federated*: the platform queries authoritative systems at decision time (integration without ownership), reconciles by policy, and publishes insights back.

Workforce choices ripple across the enterprise: marketing spend shifts demand; product launches alter intent; competitor moves change sentiment. Level 5 systems ingest these signals *before* impacts arrive—digital exhaust, journey patterns, and social sentiment—and pre-position resources accordingly. Questions become: "What's the enterprise value and workforce impact of +30% marketing spend?" or "How should we posture resources for the competitor outage we just detected?" Predictive operations prevent problems and accelerate opportunities.

Adaptive Human–AI Collaboration

Level 5 mathematically optimizes *how* people and AI work together: AI as *tool* (intelligence amplification), AI as *teammate* (task specialization), and AI as *orchestrator* (dynamic allocation). Each request routes based on expected value across complexity, emotion, risk, and capability—choosing human, AI, or hybrid.

Crucially, human value is *quantified*: empathy lift to lifetime value, creative problem-solving to saves/referrals, and judgment in novel or ethical contexts. Boundaries shift with evidence, not belief, within fairness and compliance guardrails.

Autonomous Operations with Human Governance

Autonomy increases human value. Self-optimizing systems make thousands of micro-decisions per second—routing, scheduling, interventions—while escalating novelty, ambiguity, or high-stakes situations. Reinforcement loops improve decisions where safe; optimization handles constrained trade-offs elsewhere.

Humans set goals and constraints; the platform acts within them. Every action is explainable and auditable (model cards, decision traces, overrides). Autonomy serves human flourishing: AI handles routine optimization; people focus on relationships, creativity, ethics, and the moments that create durable value.

Continuous Innovation and Future Readiness

Level 5 advantages compound. Competitors can buy tools; they cannot copy federated relationships, learning loops, or culture. The platform runs *always-on* experiments (champion–challenger), scales winners automatically, and retires losers with learning credits. Architecture remains modular and vendor-agnostic, preserving option value and scenario robustness across uncertain AI and regulatory futures.

The Ultimate Transformation

Level 5 prepares for unknowable futures by building adaptive capacity: orchestration that accepts new AI services as they emerge, learning algorithms that improve regardless of vendor, and human development that increases the value of distinctly human skills as automation scales. WFM completes its shift from cost center to strategic differentiator and becomes the enterprise's orchestration function.

Level 5 is not an end state but a beginning—continuous evolution where the ability to blend human and artificial intelligence becomes the ultimate, sustainable advantage.

From Framework to Implementation

Part II applies the model through a running case. You'll work alongside Sarah as she inherits an operation and moves it forward. Each chapter opens with her context and constraints, then walks the same pattern: diagnose what she has, choose the minimum viable moves, set guardrails, and define checkpoints. The artifacts and checklists are designed to be lifted and adapted.

Read with your own numbers in hand. Locate your current level, map Sarah's steps to your environment, and take the next bounded move.

Part II

The Five-Level Playbook to Enterprise Orchestration

7 Level 1: Initial/Manual – The Excel Foundation

7.1 Introduction: Sarah's Proving Ground

Sarah Chen set down her coffee and surveyed Midwest Mutual's specialty lines floor for the first time as WFM Manager. Forty-five agents handled niche insurance products—collectibles, marine, aviation—the profitable oddities that larger divisions wouldn't touch. Two supervisors walked the aisles between cubicles. The ACD hummed. Excel spreadsheets covered three monitors at what passed for the command center.

"Congratulations on the promotion," said Marcus Webb, the senior supervisor who'd been running scheduling in his spare time. His tone suggested condolences might be more appropriate. "Fair warning—we're absorbing two acquisitions next quarter. Vintage Auto Specialists and Classic Marine Insurance. Twenty more agents, different systems, and nobody's modeled the impact."

Sarah had earned this chance after three years as a senior analyst in the main contact center, watching opportunities disappear into politics and inertia. Corporate gave her specialty lines as a test: stabilize this operation, prove her ideas worked, and maybe—maybe—they'd let her touch the 3,000-agent main floor.

"Show me how you forecast," she said.

Marcus pulled up Excel. The roster was neat—names, shifts, time blocks—but static. No 15-minute intervals. No connection to the ACD. No automated reconciliation between plan and reality.

"We look at last month's call counts and add bodies when it seems busy," he admitted. "Monday mornings are rough. Lunch hurts. Fridays are light except month-end." No interval service-level target translated into staffing. No shrinkage segmentation for breaks, training, or PTO. Occupancy wasn't even measured, let alone used as a guardrail.

Sarah watched the floor through the morning. By 10 AM, three agents were out sick. A product update had pushed aviation quotes from five to eight minutes. The queue for marine claims stretched to twelve calls.

"Pull Jenkins from training," Marcus called to the other supervisor. "Cancel the coaching session for Smith—third time this month. Tell everyone breaks are sliding fifteen minutes."

This was **Level 1: Manual Operations**—competent people compensating for missing instruments. Excel and email carried the load. Decisions happened in real-time crisis. Variance was treated as betrayal rather than input.

Discovering the Reality

Sarah spent her first week documenting what actually happened versus what was planned. The patterns were predictable:

- No annual or monthly capacity plan guiding hiring or backfill—just reactive requisitions when pain became unbearable.
- No 15–30 minute targets or guardrails to steer the day—only end-of-day autopsies.
- Intraday adjustments through overtime heroics, emergency call-ins, and perpetually canceled development.

Wednesday brought the proof point. A marine underwriter released new documentation requirements without warning. Handle times jumped 40%. The queue backed up. Service levels crashed from 82% to 31% in two hours.

"All hands!" Marcus shouted. Break schedules collapsed. The training coordinator became a temporary agent. Sarah watched $8,000 in overtime authorize itself while three agents' certification training—required for next month—got pushed again.

"This happens every time," said Patricia, the other supervisor, exhaustion clear in her voice. "Marketing launches something. Product changes something. Weather hits somewhere. We scramble, people burn out, someone quits, and we're deeper in the hole."

The death spiral was obvious: crisis drives canceled development, which degrades quality, which extends handle times, which creates more crises. No one was negligent. There simply wasn't a system.

Finding the Leverage

That evening, Sarah mapped the operation against what she'd learned in the main center. The tools existed—the ACD could export interval data, Excel could run Erlang calculations, patterns were visible if anyone looked. The gap wasn't technology; it was instrumentation and discipline.

She pulled three years of historical data, working until midnight. Patterns emerged:

- Mondays ran 18% above weekly average, concentrated 9–11 AM
- Marine insurance spiked with weather systems (trackable via NOAA)
- Aviation quotes clustered around air show season and tax deadlines
- Collection appraisals surged after estate tax announcements

The business was more predictable than anyone realized. It just required looking.

The Proposition

Thursday morning, Sarah presented Marcus and Patricia with a simple framework:

"We're going to install basic instrumentation. Not a platform—we don't have budget. Not transformation—we don't have time. Just enough structure to stop drowning."

She outlined three foundations:

1. Interval Visibility: Export ACD data every 15 minutes. Track service level, calls offered, calls handled, and ASA. Build a simple Excel heat map showing where reality diverged from plan. "We can't fix what we don't measure at the right granularity."

2. Erlang-Based Staffing: One formula, consistently applied. Input: calls, handle time, service goal. Output: bodies needed. "It's imperfect but infinitely better than guessing. We'll adjust for reality, but we start with math."

3. Protected Minimums: Define non-negotiable shrinkage for breaks, training, and development. Calculate the true bodies needed including shrinkage. "When we cancel training, we're borrowing from next month's capacity. That debt compounds."

Marcus looked skeptical. "Corporate won't approve overtime for proper staffing."

"They will when I show them the math," Sarah replied. "We're already paying overtime—just reactively, at premium rates, after service fails. I'm proposing we staff correctly upfront."

Week Two: Installing the Foundation

Sarah started with small, visible wins:

Monday: Created the first interval staffing requirement chart. The 9–11 AM gap was stark—six bodies short every Monday. "We've been failing before lunch for three years," Patricia said, seeing it clearly for the first time.

Tuesday: Built a simple shrinkage tracker. Actual shrinkage: 28%. Planned shrinkage: "What's shrinkage?" The gap explained everything.

Wednesday: Implemented the first "rule trigger": If service level drops below 60% for two consecutive intervals, authorize overtime immediately rather than waiting for end-of-day approval. Simple, clear, executable.

Thursday: Created a one-page "State of the Floor" report—interval performance, shrinkage actuals, top variance drivers. Replaced seventeen ad-hoc reports nobody read.

Friday: Held the first proper planning session. Reviewed the week's patterns, identified three specific improvements for next week, assigned owners. Thirty minutes, focused, actionable.

The Acquisition Test

Week three brought the integration kickoff. Twenty agents from two acquired companies would join in six weeks. The old approach would have been: "We'll figure it out when they get here."

Sarah's approach:

- Pulled historical volume from both acquisitions
- Modeled the combined operation using Erlang calculations
- Identified the critical gaps: Monday coverage, marine expertise, aviation certification timing
- Built a ramp plan with specific weekly checkpoints

"We need four more bodies for Mondays, two marine specialists, and aviation certification for six agents," she told corporate. "Here's the math, the cost of not doing it, and the ROI."

For the first time, specialty lines presented a capacity plan backed by data. Corporate approved—not because they loved spending, but because the alternative was obviously worse.

Six Weeks Later: The Quiet Victory

The acquisitions integrated on a Tuesday. By Thursday, operations were stable. No heroics. No crisis. Just the plan working as designed.

"I kept waiting for the explosion," Marcus admitted. "It just... didn't happen."

Service levels held at 83%. Overtime dropped 30%. Smith finally completed his certification. Patricia ran her first full coaching session without interruption.

More importantly, patterns emerged that pointed toward Level 2:

- Erlang worked, but multi-skill complexity needed better tools
- Excel reached its limits at 65 agents and three distinct products
- Manual intraday adjustments consumed two hours of supervisor time
- The business case for a proper WFM platform was now obvious

The Recognition

The quarterly business review brought unexpected visitors. David Kim, COO of Midwest Mutual, had noticed something unusual in the metrics: specialty lines' service improved while cost per contact dropped.

"Walk me through what changed," he said.

Sarah presented the journey from chaos to control. Simple disciplines. Basic math. Protected development. Clear rules. Nothing revolutionary—just fundamentals properly applied.

"Could this scale?" David asked.

"With the right tools and team, absolutely," Sarah replied. "But we'd need to move beyond Excel. The foundation is proven; now we need infrastructure."

David exchanged glances with the head of the main contact center operation. "We're restructuring workforce management for our primary operation—3,000 agents, multiple sites, seven-figure SLA penalties. Interested?"

Sarah thought of Smith finally getting trained, Patricia coaching again, Marcus no longer firefighting every day. Level 1 had stabilized. The foundation was solid.

"When do I start?"

Operational Profile: Level 1 Essentials

As Sarah prepared to hand specialty lines to her successor, she documented what made Level 1 sustainable:

- **Scale & Tools:** Works up to 100 agents; Excel-based but systematic; one source of truth for roster, PTO, and changes
- **Roles:** Blended responsibilities acknowledged and protected; scheduling gets dedicated time; reporting automated where possible
- **Planning:** Basic interval forecasting (15–30 min); Erlang-based staffing; explicit shrinkage calculation
- **Scheduling:** Still manual but rules-based; protected development minimums; clear escalation triggers
- **Metrics:** Interval visibility standard; variance tracked and discussed; simple root-cause hygiene
- **Behavior Under Variance:** Rules trump panic; overtime authorized proactively; development protected by policy

The specialty lines team gathered for Sarah's farewell. Marcus spoke for the group: "You didn't just fix our operations. You showed us we weren't broken—we just needed a system."

Patricia added, "Three months ago, I was ready to quit. Now I'm actually teaching other supervisors how to forecast."

Sarah looked at the heat map on the wall—mostly green now, with variance contained rather than cascading. Level 1 wasn't sophisticated, but it was stable. The Excel foundation could hold.

As she packed her desk, an email arrived from David Kim: "Main operations Monday, 8 AM. Bring the specialty lines playbook. We're going to need it."

The foundation was built. The journey to Level 2 was about to begin.

7.2 What Defines Level 1?

Level 1 is the manual baseline. Competent people hold the day together with spreadsheets, hallway asks, and overtime when variance spikes. Plans exist as artifacts (tabs, emails), not as a loop that connects forecast, schedule, and intraday action. When the day stays average, the operation looks fine; when demand bends, outcomes depend on individual heroics rather than a designed system. This section names the operating reality of Level 1 so we can improve it deliberately in Section 7.3 and beyond.

Scope and scale. Teams typically range from a few dozen to low hundreds of agents, often in a single site or two, with one primary channel and light spillover into email/chat. Interval forecasts (if any) live apart from the roster, and there is no consistent link between "what we thought would happen" and "what hit the queues." Hiring and overtime tend to be reactive; scenario work is episodic rather than planned.

Roles that exist—without clear boundaries. Forecasting, scheduling, and real-time monitoring are *activities* shared across supervisors and an "Excel owner," not distinct *roles* with explicit accountabilities. When service slips, fixes arrive through one-off messages and ad hoc favors. Wins and misses rarely roll into a repeatable learning loop because no one is tasked to keep it. (Later, Section 7.7 will name minimal role ownership without changing headcount.)

Metrics and limits. SL/ASA/AHT may appear on wallboards, but definitions vary, data sources shift, and interval red/green is inconsistently captured. Daily rollups can mask volatile 15–30 minute windows customers actually experience. Occupancy is described as "busy" or "light," not governed against a band. Shrinkage is a remembered percentage, not a managed component. In Section 7.4 we lock definitions and point them to a single source of truth; here we simply acknowledge the current ambiguity.

Technology reality. The ACD routes and reports; nearly everything else is manual. Exports are copy/paste, time zones drift, and interval alignment is inconsistent. There is no reliable way to convert a signal (unexpected arrival rate, sudden handle-time change) into a small, timely move. Level 1 does not require a platform upgrade to improve; it requires naming the few signals that matter and agreeing how they will be seen. (Mechanics follow in Section 7.4)

Culture and agent experience. Adherence is a feeling, not a contract. Breaks and lunches are honored when the queue allows; development time is scheduled optimistically and often sacrificed to defend SL. Rules can feel rigid but are enforced unevenly, leading to fairness questions and fatigue. Level 1's cultural signature is good intent plus inconsistent follow-through—it works until the day deviates.

Sarah's read.   On the floor, Sarah sees a neat roster and engaged supervisors—and the gaps that make days brittle: no common interval view behind the schedule, no shared definitions of "good," and no pre-agreed small moves that anyone can trigger without a meeting. The operation survives variance but does not *harvest* it into learning.

Operational profile (summary)

- **Tech:** ACD + spreadsheets; no single interval source of truth; manual exports and reconciliation; no real-time automation.

- **Roles:** Activities spread across supervisors and a spreadsheet owner; no dedicated forecaster/scheduler/RTA; learning loop informal.

- **Process:** Weekly roster publication; intraday changes via overtime and ad hoc asks; development time frequently canceled to defend SL.

- **Metrics:** SL/ASA/AHT present but inconsistently defined; interval visibility patchy; occupancy unmanaged as a band; shrinkage approximated.

- **Risk:** Narrow daily wins that hide interval misses, fairness concerns, fatigue from constant trade-downs, and fragile performance under variance.

This is Level 1—*manual*, not broken. By naming the work and aligning on shared definitions and visibility, we create the footing for Chapter 7's goals and guardrails (Section 7.4) and the role clarity that follows (Section 7.7). The "how" begins there; this section's job is simply to define the baseline with precision.

7.3 Key Challenges at Level 1

Level 1 struggles not from negligence but from missing intraday mechanisms that turn variance into action. Spikes, callouts, and AHT drift recur; SL swings; manual workarounds multiply; engagement erodes. These are the problems we must name and fix.

Service-level instability.   Because interval targets were never defined and no forecast was translated into staffing, the morning spike becomes a bottleneck. Without shrinkage segmented and protected, breaks cluster and development is the first thing to go. Waits lengthen; the afternoon overcorrects into idle time. The day averages out on paper, but customers lived peaks and troughs.

Operational inefficiency.   Manual rosters are slowest to change precisely when speed matters. Back-of-envelope staffing (volume × AHT) correctly totals workload, but when occupancy bands and shrinkage are omitted there's no headroom for natural variability—so preventable overtime becomes routine. By late day, you've paid twice: first in delays, then in labor.

Engagement and retention.   Agents feel the instability first. Shifts slide, lunches move, PTO feels arbitrary, and coaching evaporates. Supervisors multi-hat all day and coach at night—or not at all. Burnout accelerates turnover; turnover increases nesting load; nesting steals more capacity; the loop tightens.

Cultural barriers.   From the conference room, the spreadsheet looks "good enough." Tools read as overhead, not instrumentation. Without shared vocabulary—occupancy bands, shrinkage components, interval targets—improvement arguments sound like opinion, not math. Investment waits until the pain is undeniable.

None of these problems require a moonshot to fix. The path out depends on context:

If you are a Startup, you need speed with just enough structure: a weekly interval forecast, a declared SL target, a simple shrinkage policy, and a roster that respects both. Keep the process light, the data visible, and iterate.

If you are in Turnaround, stabilize hard and fast: publish interval targets, protect breaks and training, run a daily interval review, and implement a lightweight WFM tool to replace ad hoc edits. You are buying back trust as much as minutes.

If you are in Realignment, reconnect operations to strategy: make the service promise explicit, align quality and SL, and use shared enterprise tools to accelerate capability without new spend.

If you are Sustaining, invest from strength: formalize forecasting, scheduling, and intraday guardrails before growth multiplies today's rough edges.

What this means in practice (summary)

- **Instability → math gap:** No interval forecast, no SL translation, no occupancy band, no segmented shrinkage.

- **Inefficiency → speed gap:** Manual exceptions and no intraday rules create slow, expensive recoveries.

- **Engagement → design gap:** Schedules lack preference inputs and guardrails that protect development time.

- **Culture → language gap:** Decisions lack a common vocabulary and a shared source of truth.

Lay the groundwork with GRPIT (minimum viable foundation). You do not need a full program to leave Level 1—you need a baseline you can run tomorrow:

- **Goals (G):** Declare SL (e.g., 80/20) and a planning occupancy band (e.g., 78–88%); publish shrinkage components (breaks, meetings, training, PTO).

- **Roles (R):** Name a WFM owner (even part-time); separate scheduling from QA/training where possible.

- **Processes (P):** Produce a weekly 15–30 minute forecast; translate SL to interval staffing; build a shrinkage-aware roster; run a short daily interval review.

- **Interpersonal (I):** Make adherence a support mechanism; use transparent PTO/shift-bid rules; protect coaching/training with simple guardrails.

- **Technology (T):** Stand up a shared source-of-truth workbook or entry-level WFM tool; link ACD data; enable same-day roster adjustments.

With the problem stated and the minimum viable foundation defined, we turn next to the metrics and misconceptions that commonly derail early progress (Section 7.5) and introduce a simple, shrinkage-aware baseline the team can adopt immediately.

7.4 Goals (G) — Building Core Metrics

A plan is only a picture until the team agrees on a handful of goals that turn intent into behavior. *Clarity beats complexity*: choose a few metrics, define them precisely, and let those definitions drive staffing, scheduling, and intraday decisions. As the organization matures, the set can evolve—but the muscle you need now is agreeing on goals, using them daily, and refining them together.

Why goals matter first

Without clear goals, debates collapse into anecdotes. With clear goals, the conversation becomes math. If the service promise is 80/30 and we see 76% at 10:00, we don't argue about feelings; we ask what changed in volume, handling time, or staffing. If occupancy runs at 93% for hours, we don't celebrate "efficiency"; we recognize risk to quality and burnout. Goals translate intent into interventions.

The AQEE lens (story before numbers)

A practical Level-1 foundation fits on one page and in one meeting. Use four lenses—**Availability**, **Quality**, **Efficiency**, and **Expense** (AQEE)—to keep the conversation complete without being complicated.

Availability: can customers reach us when they try? A **service level (SL)** such as *80% answered within 30 seconds* anchors responsiveness, with **average speed of answer (ASA)** and **abandon rate** providing context. The goal is not a pretty daily average—it is *stable intervals*. Interval targets (15–30 minutes) give supervisors something to steer toward in real time.

Quality: did we solve the right problem well? At Level 1, Quality is often measured by **CSAT** and a simple **first-contact resolution (FCR)** read. WFM influences Quality more than it seems: a smoother day (stable SL) increases the chance of patient, thorough conversations. Over time, **forecast accuracy** becomes part of the quality story—better forecasts reduce avoidable stress on customers and agents.

Efficiency: are we using capacity wisely without burning people out? Two numbers matter most early: **occupancy** (share of time agents are engaged on work) and **average handle time (AHT)**. Set an *occupancy band* (e.g., 78–88%) and treat excursions outside it as signals, not sins. High, sustained occupancy predicts quality drift and attrition; very low occupancy flags waste or misaligned staffing.

Expense: what does it cost to deliver today and keep delivering tomorrow? Track a basic **cost per contact** and watch **turnover rate**. At Level 1, turnover is often the hidden tax on the other metrics; every replacement cycle increases nesting load and steals capacity from the plan.

Make definitions explicit (and write them down)

Numbers without definitions create arguments. Decide *now* how you will calculate service level, how often you'll measure it, and how you will treat abandons. Three common choices exist:

Exclude abandons entirely. Simple and agent-centric, but can mask long waits.

Include all calls. Customer-centric, but can punish the operation for "micro-abandons" (e.g., 1–5 seconds).

Exclude short abandons. A practical middle ground: ignore abandons under a small threshold (e.g., 5–10 seconds), include the rest. *Document the threshold.*

Apply the same discipline to occupancy (what counts as "engaged" time), AHT (components included), and cost per contact (labor-only vs. fully loaded).

Intervals beat averages

Two days can both end "green" and feel completely different. On Day 1 the operation holds near the target most of the day; on Day 2 it swings—overstaffed in the morning, underwater after lunch. Customers remember swings, not averages. Measure and manage SL at 15–30 minute intervals; use the daily roll-up for storytelling, not steering. This is variance management made practical.

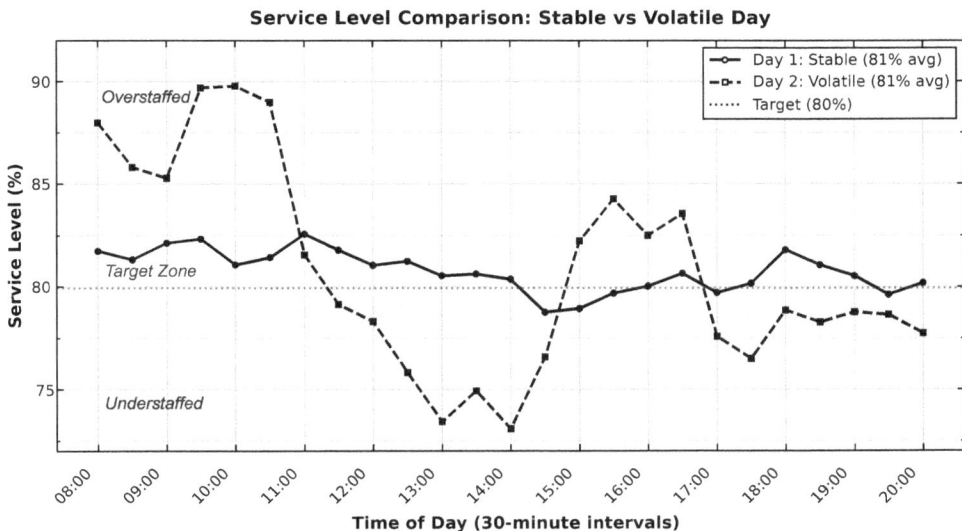

Figure 7.1: Two "green" days: one stable, one volatile. Stability wins for customers, agents, and cost.

From goals to behavior (tomorrow morning at 9:00)

Here is how goals change the day:

- **Before the day:** Review a simple interval forecast, the SL goal (e.g., 80/30), and the occupancy band (e.g., 78–88%). Place breaks and training with shrinkage assumptions, not "where they fit."
- **During the day:** Watch interval SL and occupancy. If SL dips and occupancy rises, trigger a predefined move (pull one non-phone task, nudge breaks). Training is protected unless a defined threshold is crossed.
- **After the day:** Spend ten minutes on two or three outlier intervals. Ask "volume, AHT, or staffing?" and log the answer. Tomorrow's roster improves by one inch.

A minimal starter set (so you can start now)

Keep it small and real:

- **Availability:** SL target (e.g., 80/30) measured in 15–30 minute intervals; ASA and abandon rate as context.
- **Efficiency:** Occupancy planning band (e.g., 78–88%); AHT tracked daily by queue/skill.
- **Quality:** CSAT (or a proxy) and a simple FCR signal.
- **Expense:** Cost per contact (labor view) and turnover rate.

These goals do not require a new platform; they require agreement and consistency. In Section 7.5 we clarify what *service level is not*—the common misconceptions that derail good intent—and show how clean definitions prevent later rework.

7.5 Service Level: Common Misconceptions

Service level (SL) is essential as a promise of speed, but misleading when treated as a proxy for quality, utilization, or satisfaction. Use SL for staffing; pair it with ASA and abandon rate to understand experience and behavior, and read it alongside an occupancy band to avoid burnout disguised as efficiency.

What SL is not (so we use it wisely)

SL is not average wait time, not customer satisfaction, not a productivity target, and not a guarantee that *every* customer experienced the promised wait. It is the share of interactions answered within a chosen threshold. Powerful for staffing; dangerous when stretched beyond its job.

Not average wait (that's ASA). Two intervals can both report 80% at 30 seconds while producing very different experiences. In one, most callers are answered near the threshold; in the other, many are answered instantly *and* a minority wait minutes. SL hides the tail by design. **Average speed of answer (ASA)** exposes the magnitude of waits and belongs next to SL whenever you narrate the day.

Not quality or resolution. Good SL creates the *opportunity* for a good conversation; it does not guarantee correctness or empathy. First-contact resolution (FCR) and CSAT live here. Treating SL as a quality proxy produces brittle behaviors (rush the answer, defer the fix) that degrade outcomes.

Not a utilization goal. Overstaffing can lift SL while occupancy sinks and cost per contact rises. Squeezing staff until occupancy runs at 93% may hold SL briefly and then collapse under variance. Read SL alongside an *occupancy band* to balance service, people, and cost (Section 7.4).

Not channel-agnostic or universal. An 80/30 voice target says little about asynchronous channels. Chat, email, and messaging require channel-specific timeliness promises and instruments. For voice, the 30-second threshold is a policy choice, not a law of nature; revisit it as your market and mix change.

How ASA and abandon rate complete the picture

In Section 7.4 we argued for intervals over averages. Here is how to *read* those intervals.

ASA: the depth of the red. When SL dips, ASA tells you whether callers waited 45 seconds or four minutes. That difference drives sentiment, second-order volume (repeats, escalations), and agent stress. Use ASA to prioritize which intervals need structural change (break placement, training blocks, micro-moves), not just heroics.

111

Abandon rate: patience under pressure. Abandonment is behavior—shaped by urgency, alternatives, and expectations. A high abandon rate in a sales or retention queue often equals lost revenue; in an info line it can signal that customers are finding answers elsewhere *or* giving up unsatisfied. Build a simple "patience curve" periodically: plot individual waits vs. whether callers stayed. Expect it to shift with seasonality, policy, and brand promises.

Why small staffing errors hit SL so hard (Power of One)

Queues are non-linear. Arrivals are random and handle times vary, so performance falls off a cliff once the system is tight. In one case, with 200 forecasted calls and 415 seconds AHT aiming at 80/30, *52 agents* met the target, *51* dropped to ~73%, and *50* to ~65%. One agent sounds trivial; in the math, it is decisive. As Penny Reynolds describes in *The Power of One* [115], small staffing changes produce outsized SL swings because the queue amplifies variance.

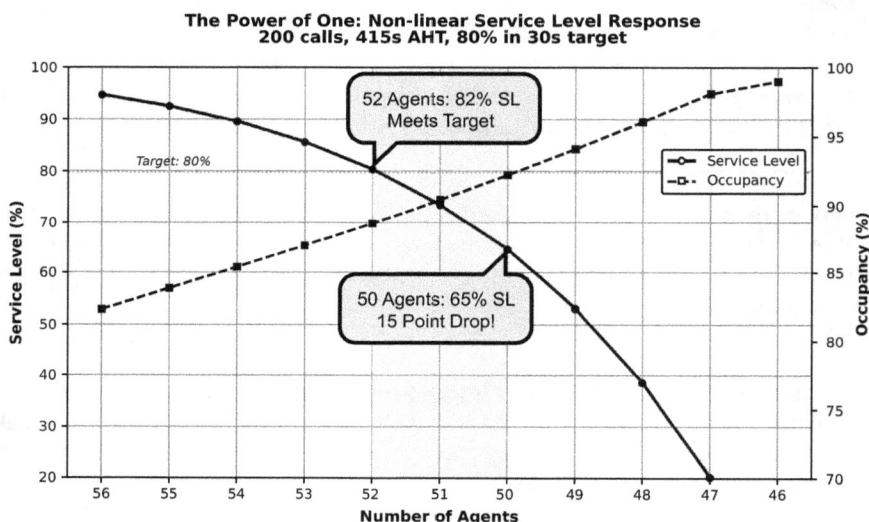

Figure 7.2: Power of One: non-linear SL response to small staffing changes (voice, 80/30 target).

Bottom line. Don't autopsy the miss—diagnose the lever. Read SL as a staffing instrument alongside ASA and abandon to see depth and behavior, then check occupancy to choose the next move. If occupancy is high, free capacity (pull non-phone work, nudge breaks, protect training); if it's low with poor SL, suspect routing or interval-mix issues. The goal isn't to rescue a daily average—it's to steer the *next* interval.

7.6 Erlang: The Mathematical Foundation

Every day, someone asks the most expensive question in the building: *How many is enough?* Erlang is the math behind that answer. It translates *workload* (arrivals and handle time) into *staffing* under explicit queueing assumptions. At Level 1, you do not need to perfect the formula—you need to use it consistently as a baseline and then correct it in the day.

What Erlang-C gives you (and what it assumes)

Erlang-C estimates the probability of waiting and, from that, the staffing needed to meet a timeliness promise (e.g., 80/30). It works when the interval is reasonably stable and when its assumptions are close enough to reality:

- Poisson arrivals (random), exponential service (memoryless), FIFO queue.
- No abandonment within the interval, single skill, stationary conditions.

These are strong assumptions. They are why we pair the baseline with interval rules and intraday moves (Section 7.8), and why we treat SL as a *guardrail*, not a proxy for quality.

From workload to staffing (the minimal recipe)

Let λ be the arrival rate (calls per second) and s the average handle time (seconds). Offered load in erlangs is

$$R = \lambda \cdot s.$$

Given R and a trial number of agents N, the Erlang-C waiting probability $P(\text{wait})$ is

$$P(\text{wait}) = \frac{\dfrac{R^N}{N!}\dfrac{N}{N-R}}{\displaystyle\sum_{k=0}^{N-1}\dfrac{R^k}{k!} + \dfrac{R^N}{N!}\dfrac{N}{N-R}},$$

and the probability of answering within a target T seconds is

$$P(\text{answer} \leq T) = 1 - P(\text{wait})\, e^{-(N-R)T/s}.$$

Increase or decrease N until the interval target (e.g., 80/30) is achieved, then adjust for shrinkage to convert to scheduled heads.

A concrete example (matches our "Power of One" case)

- Interval: 30 minutes; volume: 200 calls; AHT: 415 seconds.
- Workload: $R = \dfrac{200 \times 415}{30 \times 60} \approx 46.1$ erlangs.

Solving for an 80/30 goal:

- $N = 52$ agents $\Rightarrow$ meets target,
- $N = 51$ agents $\Rightarrow$ ~73%,
- $N = 50$ agents $\Rightarrow$ ~65%   (illustrating the "Power of One").

After you find N, divide by $(1 - \text{shrinkage})$ to get *scheduled* heads. With 30% shrinkage, $52/(1 - 0.30) \approx 74.3 \Rightarrow 75$ scheduled.

How to use Erlang well at Level 1

- **Keep intervals consistent:** use the same interval length in the forecast, ACD data, and staffing math.
- **Publish the assumptions:** what counts as AHT, the abandon treatment, the SL threshold, and shrinkage segments.
- **Pair with guardrails:** set an occupancy band (e.g., 78–88%) so "hitting SL" does not mask burnout (Section 7.4).
- **Correct in real time:** use a small Rule→Trigger→Action log to adjust breaks, pull non-phone work, and protect training (Section 7.8).

When Erlang-C misleads (and what to do)

- **Abandonments present:** Erlang-C overstates staffing. Either treat short abandons explicitly (definition in Section 7.4) or use an abandonment-aware model (Erlang-A/Erlang-X) as you mature.
- **Multi-skill routing:** Interactions and skills interact non-linearly. Start with single-skill baselines per queue and validate with splits or simple simulation before adding complexity.
- **Choppy intervals:** If marketing spikes or outages make the interval non-stationary, shorten the interval or apply intraday rules; do not chase exactness in the formula.

Bottom line. Erlang-C is a useful baseline to translate service goals into initial staffing; it is not a full description of the day. Keep the plan honest with interval visibility and intraday rules: steer by explicit guardrails and pre-agreed micro-moves—hold occupancy within band, defend protected coaching, and trigger the smallest action ladder when intervals drift (Section 7.8, Section 8.4). As you progress toward Level 2, standardizing inputs and shrinkage strengthens the baseline; higher levels introduce richer models where warranted.

7.7 Roles (R) — Defining Essential Functions

Most Level 1 operations run on people wearing multiple hats. Supervisors and operations managers keep the day together: the numbers-savvy lead pulls reports, sketches a quick forecast, and tweaks the roster; the long-tenured supervisor shepherds onboarding and training; another watches queues between one-on-ones. A dedicated "WFM role" may not exist—and that's okay. *Roles exist as work, not titles.* The work is forecasting, scheduling, and real-time management; the question is who owns each part today, and whether the handoffs are intentional or improvised.

How the work actually flows (a morning in three moves)

1) Forecasting — the silent first move. Someone, often unofficially, decides what "busy" means today. They glance at last Tuesday, note the email campaign landing at noon, and adjust by feel. That quick call becomes the plan's center of gravity. Even at Level 1, naming this responsibility matters. A lightweight interval view (15–30 minutes) and two posted notes—"campaign at 12:00," "AHT up 0:30 since policy change"—turn a hunch into a shared starting point.

2) Scheduling — turning intent into seats and time. The roster looks tidy until the first absence hits. Breaks cluster by habit rather than design; coaching finds leftover spaces. When scheduling is just "who works when," the day is one surprise away from a scramble. When scheduling is "who works when *to serve this forecast, with shrinkage protected*," the same spreadsheet becomes an operating instrument. The difference is not software; it is ownership of rules: where breaks land, what protects training, and how swaps happen without unraveling the interval plan.

3) Real-time — steering the next interval, not judging the last. Reality edits the plan. Without a named real-time role, the floor reacts via group chat: "Anyone extend lunch?" "Can you jump on phones?" With a named role—even if it is the same person wearing a second hat—the conversation shifts to *pre-agreed levers*: pull one back-office task, nudge two breaks by five minutes, keep training unless SL drops below the threshold for two intervals. These micro-moves are small by design; their power is consistency.

Why naming the roles matters (even when one person does all three)

Level 1 rarely affords three specialists. That's fine. What matters is clarity of *which hat is on* and *how the handoff works*. When the same person forecasts and schedules, they still document the assumptions that real-time will inherit (expected volume, AHT, protected coaching). When a supervisor owns real-time for the morning, they need a one-page playbook that converts "SL dipping" into an agreed sequence of actions before canceling development. Clarity reduces firefighting and gives coaching time back to leaders otherwise stuck moving blocks.

A Level-1 role charter (lightweight, real-world)

Two pages are enough to turn tacit habits into shared practice:

Forecasting (owner: *Name/Role*). Weekly 15–30 minute view; note known events; publish AHT assumption and service promise; record two uncertainties for the day. Hand off by 3:00 p.m. the prior day.

Scheduling (owner: *Name/Role*). Build to the forecast and shrinkage policy; place breaks to protect peaks; lock coaching windows with a save/skip rule. Hand off roster and "what changed" note by 5:00 p.m.

Real-time (owner: *Name/Role*). Monitor SL and occupancy bands; apply micro-moves before canceling development; log two intervals where reality diverged and why. Hand back the log at day's end to improve tomorrow's forecast.

Skills that matter now (and scale later)

You do not need unicorns; you need three muscles that compound: *pattern sense* (seeing interval shapes), *math humility* (pairing every number with its assumption), and *clean communication* (explaining a staffing constraint in one sentence to a busy supervisor). Prior WFM software experience helps, but the habit of documenting assumptions and protecting shrinkage will pay off more than any tool at Level 1—and makes the Level 2 transition faster when the tool arrives.

What changes tomorrow

Give the hats names. Publish a one-page role charter. Start a tiny "interval variance" log. Those three steps reclaim supervisor time for coaching, make scheduling more than calendar art, and give forecasting a feedback loop. The team will still improvise—only now, they'll improvise on purpose.

Bottom line. Roles at Level 1 are not about headcount; they are about *ownership of decisions* that already exist. Name the work, agree the handoffs, and your operation stops reliving the same bad morning. In Section 7.8 we turn these roles into repeatable processes so the play looks the same on Thursday as it did on Tuesday.

7.8 Processes (P) — Creating Manual Rhythms

Level 1 runs on people, not platforms—but people need a rhythm. Processes give the day a beat: *what we do before the day, during the day, and after the day*, and how those moments roll up into the week and month. The goal is simple: make recurring work happen the same way twice so decisions arrive sooner and with less drama.

The minimum viable rhythm (week → day → interval)

Weekly. Publish a one-page *Week Brief*: a 15–30 minute forecast for core hours, the key assumptions (AHT, drivers), the shrinkage policy, a calendar of known events, and two risks with planned responses. This is the working reference for the week.

Daily. Build the roster to the Week Brief: place breaks against peaks, lock coaching on purpose, and mark which shrinkage is protected versus flexible. Ship a short "what changed" note (absences, AHT, event timing).

Intraday. Every interval, read SL/ASA/occupancy against bands, then apply small, pre-agreed moves (pull one back-office task, nudge two breaks) before canceling development. Log the variance and action so tomorrow's forecast learns.

This rhythm isn't software; it's sequence and handoff. Forecasting hands *assumptions* to scheduling; scheduling hands *constraints and protections* to real-time; real-time hands *variance notes* back to forecasting. When those handoffs are written, the same three people stop re-having the same Monday.

The backbone artifacts (four pages you can run tomorrow)

1) Source-of-truth workbook. One shared file, one tab per week, interval rows, and columns for forecast arrivals, AHT, required staff (Erlang-C), shrinkage, and scheduled staff. Lock definitions; change inputs, not formulas.

2) Shrinkage policy (one page). Name components (breaks, meetings, training, PTO, unplanned) and target rates; say how you apply them (to *required* staff to get *scheduled* staff) and when you protect training (e.g., only after two consecutive red intervals). This turns "we'll try" into "we decided."

3) Intraday playbook (one page). Three micro-moves in order: (i) reclaim one task, (ii) shift two breaks by five minutes, (iii) unlock a flex pool. Include the guardrail that *keeps coaching unless* SL is below target for two intervals and occupancy is above band. Small, consistent moves beat heroic improvisation.

4) Interval variance log (one page). At day's end, record two intervals where reality deviated: "10:30 SL 74%, occ 91% — volume +7%; noon SL 86% — AHT +0:40." This is the fuel that makes next week's forecast smarter.

Turn tacit habits into SOPs (lightweight, lived, and local)

Level 1 doesn't need a binder; it needs clarity. Each core process gets a one-page SOP that answers five questions: *why, who, when, how, handoff*. Boxes are *breakable* so long SOPs paginate cleanly.

SOP — Weekly Forecast   v1.0 | 2024-01-15

Why — Give Scheduling a believable 15–30 minute picture they can build around.
Owner — Forecast lead (name/role)
Cadence — Publish Thu 15:00 for next week
Inputs — Last 4 comparable weeks by day/skill/channel; known events (campaigns, outages, holidays); current AHT trend.
Steps

1. Pull interval arrivals and AHT; smooth obvious anomalies.
2. Annotate known events (e.g., "Tue 12:00 email drop").
3. Set AHT assumption and note change vs. last week ($\pm$ mm:ss).
4. Compute *required staff* via Erlang-C for the service promise (e.g., 80/30) (Section 7.6).
5. Write two uncertainties (e.g., "Mon AHT may +0:20; Fri volume may -5%").

Outputs — One shared source-of-truth tab: Arrivals, AHT, Required Staff; plus a one-paragraph forecast note (events, assumptions, uncertainties).
QC — Spot-check two peak intervals; confirm metric definitions; verify no missing intervals.
Handoff — Tag Scheduling owner; attach note; archive as `/Forecasts/Weekly/v#.date`.

SOP — Build the Roster   v1.0 | 2024-01-15

Why — Turn the forecast into seats and time *with protections* (breaks, coaching, training).
Owner — Scheduling lead (name/role)
Cadence — Post Fri 17:00
Inputs — Shrinkage policy (components + rates); coaching/training priorities; agent availability/preferences.
Steps

1. Apply shrinkage to *required* staff to get *scheduled* staff by interval (Section 7.4).
2. Place breaks away from forecast peaks; stagger lunches across the crest.
3. Block coaching/training windows; guardrail: keep unless two red intervals *and* occupancy above band.
4. Resolve conflicts; document any overrides and rationale.
5. Publish roster + "what changed vs. forecast" summary.

Outputs — Final roster (shared drive) + 7-day glance heatmap (coverage vs. required).
QC — Two peak intervals hit SL with occupancy inside band; breaks don't stack; protected windows visible.
Handoff — Tag Real-time owner with protected windows and flex options.

SOP — Intraday Control	v1.0 | 2024-01-15

Why — Steer the *next* interval, not judge the last.

Owner — Real-time lead (name/role)

Cadence — Every 15–30 minutes

Inputs — Live SL and occupancy; roster/protections; micro-moves playbook; thresholds (e.g., SL < target two intervals; occupancy > band).

Steps

1. Read interval SL + occupancy.
2. If SL low *and* occupancy high, apply micro-moves in order:

   a. Reclaim one back-office task (pre-named agents).
   b. Nudge two breaks by five minutes.
   c. Unlock a small flex pool (pre-approved).

3. Keep coaching/training unless both thresholds trip; if canceled, re-book within 48h.
4. Log two variance intervals (what moved: arrivals, AHT, staffing) for the end-of-day review.

Outputs — Quick action log in the shared variance sheet (time, move, reason, result).

QC — No "break cliffs"; micro-moves precede cancellations; occupancy remains within band over the hour.

Handoff — Post end-of-day variance notes for the forecaster; tag Scheduling if protections were used.

Quality without bureaucracy

A process exists when two things happen the same way in a row. Level 1 quality is simply *visible checkpoints* at the points of highest leverage: (i) *before* the week (are the assumptions written?), (ii) *before* the day (are breaks placed to protect peaks?), and (iii) *after* the day (did we learn anything we will use tomorrow?). Keep reviews to ten minutes; look for drift from *definitions*, not sinners to blame.

What changes tomorrow

When the board turns amber, you will still improvise—but now on purpose. The forecaster left a reason for AHT; the scheduler left guardrails; real-time has three small moves that preserve coaching before sacrificing it. At day's end, two intervals go into the variance log, and the loop closes. That is what "process" means at Level 1: *the same people, making better decisions, sooner.*

Bottom line. Processes do not make the work rigid; they make it repeatable. Start with the rhythm (week → day → interval), the four backbone artifacts, and three one-page SOPs. When the tool arrives in Level 2, you will already be operating like a team that knows what it wants the tool to do.

7.9 Sample SOPs for Level 1

This packet turns the rhythm from Section 7.8 into three one-page SOPs you can run on Monday. They are *instruments*, not paperwork: light, repeatable, and written in the language of the floor. Map them directly to the cadence—*week → day → interval*—so the same work happens the same way twice.

SOP 1 — Weekly Forecast   v1.0 | 2024-01-15

Purpose — Give Scheduling a believable 15–30 minute picture they can build around.
Owner — Forecast lead (name/role)
Cadence — Publish Thu 15:00 for next week
Inputs — Last 4 comparable weeks by day/skill/channel; known events (campaigns, outages, holidays); current AHT trend.
Steps

1. Pull interval arrivals and AHT; smooth obvious anomalies.
2. Annotate known events (e.g., "Tue 12:00 email drop").
3. Set AHT assumption and note change vs. last week ($\pm$ mm:ss).
4. Compute *required staff* via Erlang-C for the service promise (e.g., 80/30) (Section 7.6).
5. Write two uncertainties (e.g., "Mon AHT may +0:20; Fri volume may -5%").

Outputs — One shared source-of-truth tab: Arrivals, AHT, Required Staff; plus a one-paragraph forecast note (events, assumptions, uncertainties).
QC — Spot-check two peak intervals; confirm metric definitions; verify no missing intervals.
Handoff — Tag Scheduling owner; attach note; archive as `/Forecasts/Weekly/`

SOP 2 — Build the Roster   v1.0 | 2024-01-15

Purpose — Turn the forecast into seats and time *with protections* (breaks, coaching, training).
Owner — Scheduling lead (name/role)
Cadence — Post Fri 17:00
Inputs — Forecast tab (required staff); shrinkage policy (components + rates); coaching/training priorities; agent availability/preferences.
Steps

1. Apply shrinkage to *required* staff to produce *scheduled* staff by interval (Section 7.4).
2. Place breaks away from forecast peaks; stagger lunches across the crest.
3. Block coaching/training windows; guardrail: keep unless two red intervals *and* occupancy above band.
4. Resolve conflicts and coverage gaps; document any manual overrides.
5. Publish the roster and a "what changed vs. forecast" summary.

Outputs — Final roster (shared drive) + 7-day glance heatmap (coverage vs. required).
QC — Two peak intervals meet SL with occupancy inside band; breaks do not stack; protected windows visible.
Handoff — Tag Real-time owner with protected windows and flex options.

SOP 3 — Intraday Control   v1.0 | 2024-01-15

Purpose — Steer the *next* interval, not judge the last.

Owner — Real-time lead (name/role)

Cadence — Every 15–30 minutes

Inputs — Live SL and occupancy; roster/protections; micro-moves playbook; thresholds (e.g., SL < target two intervals; occupancy > band).

Steps

1. Read interval SL + occupancy.
2. If SL low *and* occupancy high, apply micro-moves in order:

    a. Reclaim one back-office task (pre-named agents).
    b. Nudge two breaks by 5 minutes.
    c. Unlock a small flex pool (pre-approved).

3. Keep coaching/training unless both thresholds trip; if canceled, re-book within 48h.
4. Log two variance intervals (what moved: arrivals, AHT, staffing) for the end-of-day review.

Outputs — Quick action log in the shared variance sheet (time, move, reason, result).

QC — No "break cliffs"; micro-moves precede cancellations; occupancy remains within band over the hour.

Handoff — Post end-of-day variance notes for the forecaster; tag Scheduling if protections were used.

How to adopt (one hour, no new tools). You can copy these templates from the WFM Labs wiki at `https://wiki.wfmlabs.org/wiki/Level_1_Process_Templates`, or build your own with the steps below. For context and updates, see the WFM Labs Companion in Appendix A and the landing page `https://wfmlabs.org`. Resources evolve; the wiki is the authoritative source.

- Create (or copy) the three one-page SOPs; assign owners and cadences.
- Add a single "variance log" sheet with columns: interval; lever moved (arrivals/AHT/ staffing); action taken; outcome.
- Agree guardrails once (SL threshold, occupancy band, abandon treatment) and reference them in each SOP.
- Version and archive: if it changed, increment the version; if it repeats, keep it in the SOP.

Governance in one line. If it changed the plan, it goes in the variance log; if it keeps happening, it becomes an SOP; if an SOP is ignored twice, fix the SOP or the goal.

7.10 Interpersonal (I) — People as Process

When the queue tightens, the floor changes in subtle ways: side conversations pause, eyes move to the wallboard, a supervisor hovers between pods. Agents adjust without being asked—one shortens wrap, another delays a coffee. None of that shows on a dashboard, yet it often decides whether a wobble becomes a slide. In a contact center, *people* absorb variance first. The task of Workforce Management (WFM) at Level 1 is not to squeeze harder; it is to design the day so people do not pay for instability with their energy.

The Service–Profit Chain (Section 4.2) frames this simply: engaged employees create better customer outcomes, which sustain the business. WFM often enters as "coverage and cost," but the moment you protect coaching, place breaks on purpose, and give agents a say in their schedules, you are engineering the employee experience. The numbers follow.

From control to partnership

Level 1 organizations often inherit assembly-line habits: rigid rosters, adherence as policing, occupancy celebrated without context. These keep the lights on, but they also teach agents to brace for the day rather than shape it. A small stance shift—*from controlling to partnering*—changes the conversation:

> *Control says:* "Be in the right place at the right time."
> *Partnership adds:* "Here is why this interval matters, here is your voice in how we get there, and here is the time we protect so you stay great at the job."

Partnership does not lower goals; it clarifies and co-owns them. It ties the **Goals** in Section 7.4 to the **Roles** in Section 7.7 and the **Processes** in Section 7.8 so the day feels designed, not improvised.

Four promises that turn intent into trust

In Level 1, technology is light and time is tight. Trust grows from four interpersonal promises you can deliver immediately:

1) Predictability.   Post schedules on time. Place breaks to protect peaks *and* keep them stable. If something must move, use a small, pre-agreed nudge (five minutes, not fifty) and explain why. Predictability lowers cognitive load and makes adherence feel fair.

2) Fairness.   Publish simple rules for PTO, shift bids, swaps, and overtime. When exceptions happen, record them once and apply them the same way next time. Fairness beats generosity—it lets agents plan their lives.

3) Voice.   Capture preferences (start times, days off, training interest) and show where they shaped the roster. Even at Level 1, a basic preference form and a monthly review create visible influence without promising what you cannot deliver.

4) Development. Protect coaching and training with guardrails. If variance forces a cancellation, re-book within 48 hours. Nothing signals priorities more loudly than whether development survives a busy day.

What this looks like on the floor (a short vignette)

The forecast note and AHT assumption are pinned in the team channel before opening. Two agents swapped lunches using the posted rules; the roster already reflects it. When SL dips and occupancy runs hot, the real-time owner applies the first micro-move from the playbook (pull one back-office task) and posts a one-line update: "Pulled Casey from email for a short window; training stays." Agents see the *why*, not just the ask. Later, a supervisor thanks the team for holding the peak and calls out a clean save from a new hire. The variance log captures two red intervals to inform tomorrow's forecast note. No heroics—just a designed day.

A lightweight working agreement (fits on half a page)

> **Team Working Agreement — Level 1**
>
> **Our promise to customers:** We will meet our interval service goal (e.g., 80/30) with stable performance.
> **Our promise to each other:**
> 1. **Predictability:** Schedules posted by Fri 17:00; breaks move in five-minute nudges only, with reason.
> 2. **Fairness:** PTO, swaps, and OT follow posted rules; exceptions are logged and reused.
> 3. **Voice:** Preference capture quarterly; where used is shown in the roster note.
> 4. **Development:** Coaching blocks protected; if canceled, re-book within 48h.
>
> **How we'll talk:** One-line updates for intraday changes (time, move, why). End-of-day: two-interval variance note; no blame, just inputs for tomorrow.

Making adherence humane

Adherence matters most when it is least comfortable. Treat it as a *support mechanism*: a way to keep promises to customers and protect time for development, not a surveillance tool. Share the occupancy band openly (e.g., 78–88%) and the reason behind it—high, sustained occupancy predicts fatigue and quality drift; very low occupancy signals waste. When someone misses a window, start with context ("what blocked you?") before consequence. Coaching first, policy second.

A short huddle exercise: Power of One for people

Numbers land when they become personal. Once per month, run a ten-minute huddle:

1. Show last Tuesday's tightest interval and the effect of "+1 / –1 agent" on SL (see Figure 7.2).

2. Ask two agents to narrate how a five-minute break nudge or a quick channel swap felt in the moment.
3. Close with one concrete commitment (e.g., "we'll pre-name two flexes for Wednesdays").

This connects staffing math to lived experience and turns compliance into shared craft.

Why this belongs in Level 1

You do not need new software to keep these promises. You need steady goals (Section 7.4), named roles (Section 7.7), and simple processes that honor people when the plan bends (Section 7.8). As technology arrives in Level 2, these interpersonal foundations multiply its value: preference capture becomes automated bidding, humane adherence becomes real-time nudges, and protected coaching becomes scheduled capacity, not an afterthought.

Bottom line. Interpersonal design is not a "soft add-on" to WFM; it is how the plan becomes a day people can sustain. Build predictability, fairness, voice, and development into Level 1, and the system will carry you when the queue does what queues do.

7.11 Technology (T) — Foundational Tools

Before the first call connects, the systems are already shaping the day: routing rules decide who will see which demand, messages set expectations, and wallboards translate traffic into signals. A scheduler compares today's forecast to yesterday's reality and wonders if there is a cleaner way to keep those views in sync. Level 1 runs on people and improvisation; technology becomes the lever when we want the day to feel *designed* instead of lucky.

This section is not a shopping list. It is a map. We name the core technology categories, show how they support the work you already do, and define a lightweight Level-1 "starter stack" that respects manual realities while preparing you for Level 2.

Why technology matters at Level 1 (and what it does not do)

Tools will not replace judgment in a volatile queue; they make judgment faster, more consistent, and more shareable. The point at Level 1 is *minimal instrumentation*: one place to see the plan, one way to speak about performance in intervals, and one path to turn variance into a small, timely move. As maturity grows, these same categories add automation and prediction, but they pay off only if the goals, roles, and processes from Sections 7.4, 7.7 and 7.8 already exist.

Eight core categories (what they are and how they help)

1) Telephony & Channel Management (ACD/IVR/digital). Routes demand to capacity and shapes the first seconds of customer experience. At Level 1, ensure queues/skills reflect reality and IVR messages match today's truth; avoid orphaned skills and stale prompts.

2) WFM/WFO Platforms. Purpose-built for forecasting, scheduling, adherence, and (in WFO) quality/coaching. Level 1 can live without it briefly, but this is the anchor investment for Level 2; until then, mirror its logic in a single source-of-truth workbook.

3) Real-Time Monitoring & displays. Surface interval SL/ASA/abandon and occupancy so the next move is obvious. A "Resource Optimization Center" can be one screen and a ritual before it is a room with video walls.

4) WFM automation. From consistent micro-moves (break nudges, channel flex) to automated intraday re-optimization. Once you've reached Level 2, automation is a natural progression. Design the playbooks first (Section 7.8), then automate its execution.

5) Advanced Forecasting & Decision Support. Erlang, time-series methods, and simple simulations make plans resilient; advanced algorithms arrive later to detect patterns and anomalies. Level 1 needs *clarity of inputs* first.

6) Reporting & Analytics. Turn raw exports into interval-level narratives your team can act on. Start with a daily "three intervals to learn from" view; grow toward dashboards when definitions are stable.

7) Employee Engagement & Development. Scheduling preferences, coaching delivery, feedback loops. At Level 1, a form and a rule beat an app and confusion; by Level 3, off-phone development can be placed dynamically.

8) Data Plumbing & Integration (ETL/warehouse/connectors). The quiet enabler: consistent definitions and repeatable loads from ACD/WFM to your workbook or BI tool. Even a small, well-labeled folder structure with scripted exports is a Level-1 win.

A compact view (purpose $\rightarrow$ Level-1 minimum)

Category	Primary purpose	Level-1 minimum that works
ACD/IVR/digital	Route demand; set expectations.	Clean queue/skill map; current IVR; weekly check that skills match roster.
WFM/WFO	Forecast/schedule/adherence; in WFO, quality/coaching.	Single shared workbook mirroring WFM logic; interval plan + shrinkage; posted rules.
Real-time	See & steer intervals.	One live wallboard + 10-min cadence; three pre-agreed micro-moves.
Automation	Execute small changes fast.	None required yet; document triggers so automation can be added later.
Forecasting/DS	Predict and test scenarios (Erlang, smoothing, simple sims).	Erlang-C sheet; simple smoothing; written assumptions and two uncertainties.
Reporting/BI	Explain what happened; reveal patterns.	End-of-day "two intervals that moved" note; weekly trend snapshot.
Engagement/dev	Voice, coaching, growth.	Preference capture; protected coaching blocks; re-book within 48h if canceled.
Data plumbing	Reliable definitions/flows.	Named exports; versioned folders; one "read me" with field definitions.

Level-1 starter stack (so you can start tomorrow)

> ### Minimal, manual, and real
>
> **One workbook as the system:** tabs for Forecast (arrivals, AHT, required staff via Erlang-C), Roster (scheduled staff with shrinkage), Live Read (copy/paste from wallboard), and Variance Log (two intervals/day, what moved and why).
> **One Real-Time screen:** SL/ASA/abandon and occupancy by interval; a 10-minute huddle cadence; three micro-moves in order before canceling development (Section 7.8).
> **One rule file as governance:** SL definition (incl. abandons), occupancy band, shrinkage components, PTO/shift-swap rules, and how intraday changes are communicated.

How this scales into Level 2

When the workbook starts to creak—too many skills, channels, or sites—use that pain to specify your first WFM platform. Your readiness signals:

- **Stable definitions** (SL/ASA/abandon, occupancy band, shrinkage policy) already in use.
- **Cadence discipline** (weekly forecast, daily roster, intraday huddles, variance log) observed for at least 6–8 weeks.
- **Volume/complexity** (multi-skill, multi-site, blended channels) now outgrows manual edits.

At Level 1, focus on understanding the tech you already run. Your routing/telephony platform—and its data—is the anchor: map channels → IVR/skills → queues → reports/exports, and lock metric definitions in one workbook/BI view. Then expand by need: tighten scheduling if coverage hurts, stabilize wallboards/BI if visibility lags, and formalize micro-moves before any automation.

A note on adjacent systems

Recording, speech analytics, knowledge, and CRM are outside WFM's direct remit but shape workload and quality. Treat them as signal sources: if knowledge gaps drive AHT up, that belongs in the forecast note; if CRM latency spikes, the team should see it next to SL/ASA so the day can be defended, not endured.

Bottom line. Technology at Level 1 is less about features and more about *fit*: one place for the plan, one view of reality, one path for action. Get those three right and the move to Level 2 is an upgrade, not a reboot.

7.12 Advancing from Level 1 to Level 2

Two views shape tomorrow's operation: what *actually* happened (yesterday's intervals) and what we *intend* to happen (today's roster and rules). Moving up a level is not a tool purchase—it is a set of agreements the team can keep. The GRPIT frame from this chapter gives those agreements a place to live: **Goals**, **Roles**, **Processes**, **Interpersonal**, and **Technology**. We use it to turn manual reality into a durable foundation.

What "moving up" actually means

Level 2 does not mean perfect forecasting or zero volatility. It means your service promise is explicit and measured in intervals; roles are named with clean handoffs; processes run the same way two days in a row; people see fairness and development in the plan; and technology makes those habits faster instead of fragile.

A map you can put on the wall by tomorrow

GRPIT Area	What Level 2 expects	What to start at Level 1 (this week)
Goals (G)	Interval SL defined (incl. abandons), occupancy band, shrinkage policy; daily read at interval granularity.	Publish SL (e.g., 80/30), how you treat short abandons, an occupancy band (e.g., 78–88%), and shrinkage components; pin to the roster note (Sections 7.4 and 7.5).
Roles (R)	Named owners for forecast, scheduling, and real-time with written handoffs.	Name the hats; write a half-page role charter and a handoff time (Thu 15:00 forecast; Fri 17:00 roster) (Section 7.7).
Processes (P)	Weekly forecast → roster → intraday control → variance loop.	Stand up the workbook tabs; run the three one-page SOPs; log two variance intervals per day (Sections 7.8 and 7.9).
Interpersonal (I)	Predictability, fairness, voice, development visible in the plan.	Post schedules on time; apply swap/PTO rules consistently; protect coaching or re-book within 48h; run a 10-min "Power of One" huddle monthly (Section 7.10).
Technology (T)	Core ACD platform + stable definitions into reporting.	Map technology layout; understand call routing and data flows; lock definitions in one workbook/BI; keep one rules file; defer automation (Section 7.11).

Your first 90 days: small, durable wins

A 30–60–90 that survives busy days

Days 1–30 (Make the promises visible). Publish SL definition (incl. short-abandon policy), occupancy band, and shrinkage components. Name owners for Forecast, Scheduling, Real-Time. Launch the three SOPs from Section 7.8. End each day with two variance intervals and a one-paragraph note.

Days 31–60 (Tighten the handoffs). Move break placement off habit and onto the forecast. Protect coaching with a guardrail (only cancel after two red intervals *and* high occupancy). Start a weekly 15-minute review that checks definitions before numbers.

Days 61–90 (Instrument and specify). Stabilize a simple real-time data cadence (one screen, 10-minute rhythm). Replace one high-pain manual step with a scripted export/import. Write a one-page WFM platform spec focused on *one* pain (e.g., schedule generation or real-time adherence), not ten features.

The three levers that move everything else

1) Make the math trustworthy. Erlang-C turns your promise into seats; use it at the interval level and write the assumptions you changed (arrivals, AHT, target). The goal is not perfect precision—it is *repeatable translation* from goal to staffing and back (Section 7.6).

2) Protect development as capacity, not charity. If coaching always loses to variance, variance will always win. Use the intraday guardrail from Section 7.8: micro-moves first; cancel only after thresholds; re-book inside 48 hours. Quality follows the time you actually protect.

3) Read intervals, not averages. A green daily SL can hide red intervals that customers actually lived. Pair SL with ASA and occupancy; decide the next interval's move, then log what you learned for tomorrow (Section 7.5).

Readiness signals that you're crossing into Level 2

You will feel the shift before you sign a software contract:

- Definitions (SL/ASA/abandon, shrinkage, occupancy) are posted and used in daily talk.
- The weekly forecast, roster, intraday cadence, and variance log run for 6–8 weeks without collapsing during peaks.
- Pain concentrates: manual schedule edits, real-time adherence visibility, or multi-skill coordination is now the bottleneck, not confusion.

Building the case for your first WFM platform (one page, not a novel)

Keep it concrete: *today's failure mode, tomorrow's capability, measurable effect.*

Problem. "Manual edits consume 6 hours/week; late changes create two red intervals most days."

Capability. "Auto-generated schedules from interval forecast + real-time adherence visibility."

Effect. "Reduce manual edits by 75%; cut red intervals by 40%; reallocate 4 hours/week to coaching."

Vendors can help model ROI; your job is to anchor the math to *your* intervals, shrinkage policy, and occupancy band so the savings aren't imaginary.

Bottom line. Advancing from Level 1 to Level 2 is less a leap than a cadence. Make the promises visible, name the hats, run the rhythm, and let technology scale the habits you can already keep. When the board goes amber tomorrow, the plan will bend—and the team will not break.

What to read while you build

Use references to sharpen the practices you are already running, not to delay them. Two books operationalize the foundations this chapter introduces.

Koole's *Call Center Optimization* translates queueing theory into accessible Excel tools and online calculators at gerkoole.com/CCO. His treatment deepens the Erlang–C foundations from Section 7.6 and addresses interval staffing with the occupancy-service level tradeoff that prevents the fantasy of simultaneously high service and high efficiency. Test the calculators before investing in WFM software—theory becomes immediate capability.[116]

Cleveland's *Contact Center Management on Fast Forward* is the definitive foundation for running contact centers—broader than WFM and the handbook to keep at your side as you climb the maturity curve. It frames the whole system (strategy, customer experience, operations) and then delivers the practical mechanics: the 9-step planning process, clear base-staff calculations, and guardrails such as avoiding extended levels of high occupancy. Start here; return often.[117]

Both books balance mathematical rigor with operational humanity. Together, they ground the GRPIT components—goal articulation, role clarity, process standardization, interpersonal effectiveness, and technology evaluation—in proven practice.

8 Level 2: Foundational – Structured Workforce Management

8.1 Introduction: Welcome to Your New Role

Sarah Chen stepped off the elevator at Midwest Mutual's main operations center eighteen months after stabilizing specialty lines. The contrast was immediate—where her 65-agent floor had whiteboards and Excel, this command center featured wall-mounted screens cycling through real-time metrics. Three thousand agents across four sites. Seven-figure SLA penalties. A dedicated Resource Optimization Center (ROC) behind glass walls.

"Welcome to the show," said David Kim, the COO who'd recruited her. "Let me show you what we've built."

The tour felt like stepping from a workshop into a factory. Where Marcus had juggled scheduling between supervisor calls, here sat fifteen dedicated WFM professionals. Where specialty lines had one Excel master file, this operation ran on an enterprise platform with modules for forecasting, scheduling, and real-time adherence.

"Impressive," Sarah said, and meant it. After months of making Excel do gymnastics it was never designed for, seeing actual workforce management software felt like a revelation.

David's expression shifted. "It is impressive. So why did I call you?"

Meeting the Forecasters

"We've got three years of patterns built into the platform," explained Jennifer Liu, lead forecaster, showing Sarah trending graphs and seasonal curves. "Every marketing campaign, every product launch, every holiday impact—it's all modeled."

Sarah studied the forecast. Clean intervals, sophisticated patterns, confidence bands—light-years beyond the "last month plus gut feel" she'd inherited at specialty lines.

"How do you handle month-end if you're behind on service level?" Sarah asked.

Jennifer switched to Excel—dozens of tabs calculating daily targets needed to recover monthly SLA. "If we're at 78% on day 20 with a month target of 80%, we calculate exactly what each remaining day needs to achieve. Usually means overtime and canceled training."

"How often do you need catch-up math?"

"Four of the last six months," Jennifer admitted. "The platform handles interval forecasting beautifully. But monthly SLA targets, penalty thresholds, the compound effect of being behind—that all lives in spreadsheets."

Sarah recognized the pattern: sophisticated tools solving part of the problem while Excel filled the gaps, just like Level 1 but with better infrastructure.

Sitting with the Schedulers

Tom Rodriguez ran scheduling from a bank of monitors showing shift patterns and coverage charts. "The platform optimizes and publishes thousands of individual schedules weekly, across all sites and channels."

The Tetris blocks of shifts were beautiful—perfectly aligned to forecasted demand, breaks distributed optimally, training and coaching slotted into predicted lulls.

"Show me yesterday," Sarah said.

Tom pulled up the actual executed schedule. Red marks everywhere—moved training, canceled coaching, shifted breaks. "By Tuesday, maybe 60% of the published schedule survives. By Thursday..." He scrolled through pages of manual adjustments.

"The platform builds a perfect schedule for the forecast," Tom explained. "When reality shows up different, we scramble. Yesterday alone: forty-seven manual schedule changes, eighteen training sessions moved, twelve coaching sessions canceled."

Sarah thought of her simple rule triggers at specialty lines—if X happens, do Y. Here, with all this technology, they were still moving blocks by hand, just with better visibility of which blocks to move.

Observing the Real-Time Analysts

The Real-Time command center hummed with controlled urgency. Eight analysts monitored performance across channels, screens showing queue depths, handle times, and service levels by interval.

"Red interval coming in claims," called out an analyst. "Need six more."

Sarah watched the response: messages to supervisors, skill changes in the platform, emails canceling training. Twelve minutes to execute what should have been automatic.

"When multiple queues need help?" Sarah asked.

Mike Chen, the lead analyst, didn't look up from his screens. "Biggest SLA penalty wins. By the time we've made the moves, we're usually fighting the next fire."

The irony struck her—they could see problems forming with precision but could only respond with manual coordination. Like having radar to spot storms but only buckets to catch rain.

The Afternoon Reality Check

Sarah found Patricia Washington in the break room—her former supervisor from specialty lines who'd transferred six months earlier.

"How does it compare?" Sarah asked.

Patricia laughed. "Remember when we thought Excel was the enemy? This place has every tool imaginable, but we're still playing the same game—scrambling when reality doesn't match the plan. We just scramble with better dashboards."

"Training completion?"

"Below 50%. The platform schedules it perfectly, then we cancel it perfectly when queues back up. My agents now joke that 'scheduled development' means 'available for emergency deployment.'"

The same problem Sarah had solved with protected minimums at specialty lines persisted here, just hidden behind professional tools.

The Three O'Clock Summit

David called Sarah into his office. "First impressions?"

"You've built something remarkable," Sarah began. "Compared to where I came from, this is sophisticated beyond measure. Professional forecasting, optimized scheduling, real-time visibility—"

"But?"

"But it's three strong teams working in sequence, not a system. Forecasters build beautiful models. Schedulers create perfect plans. Real-time tries to force reality back into those plans. When that fails—which is daily—everyone scrambles."

She pulled up the morning's performance. "This morning at 9:15, claims volume spiked 30%. It took twenty-three minutes to adjust—messages, approvals, manual changes. By then we'd missed service level for two intervals. The technology saw it instantly; the response was still human-speed."

David nodded slowly. "We've automated planning but not adaptation."

The Pattern Recognition

That evening, Sarah mapped what she'd observed against the monthly metrics:

- Service Level: 82.3% (target 80%)—achieved through heroics
- Overtime: 12% of hours—double the budget
- Training completion: 47%—half the goal
- Adherence exceptions: 1,847 monthly—hours of supervisor time
- Agent satisfaction: 3.2/5.0—declining quarterly
- Attrition: 42% annually—millions in replacement costs
- Catch-up months: 4 of last 6—perpetual emergency mode

The story was clear: Level 2 worked through extraordinary effort. Every monthly SLA achievement came with hidden costs—burned-out agents, perpetual catch-up math, and a constant background anxiety about the next variance.

Monday Morning Mission

Sarah gathered her new team. "Let me be clear—what you've built is genuinely impressive. Coming from Excel chaos, this infrastructure is remarkable. You've solved problems I was still discovering a year ago."

The room relaxed slightly.

"But we're optimizing parts instead of the whole. We have solid forecasting feeding into excellent scheduling that real-time has to constantly break apart. We meet monthly SLAs by sacrificing everything else in the final week."

"We've asked for automation—" Mike began.

"And we'll get there," Sarah said. "But first we need to strengthen what we have. We can't automate our way out of unclear definitions, missing handoffs, and monthly fire drills. We need to make Level 2 truly foundational."

She drew a simple diagram:

Current State: Forecast → Schedule → Reality Hits → Scramble → Catch-up Math → Monthly SLA (barely) → Exhaustion → Repeat

Target State: Clear Definitions → Protected Minimums → Simple Rules → Consistent Execution → Predictable Outcomes → Sustainable Performance

"Our mission for the next six months: Make this operation boring in the best way. Every term defined. Every handoff documented. Every common situation having a pre-decided response. Protection for development that doesn't vanish under pressure."

The Path to Stability

Sarah outlined the plan:

Month 1: Define and Align

- What exactly is "shrinkage"? (Three teams, three definitions currently)
- When exactly do we authorize overtime? (Currently: "when it feels bad")
- How much development is truly protected? (Currently: "depends on the day")

Month 2: Connect the Loop

- Forecasters own accuracy and document assumptions
- Schedulers own feasibility and flag conflicts early
- Real-time owns execution and feeds back variance patterns
- Everyone sees the same numbers the same way

Month 3: Build the Rules

- Common situations get standard responses
- Thresholds trigger actions without meetings
- Catch-up math becomes exception, not routine

"Once this foundation is truly solid," Sarah continued, "then we talk automation. Level 3 will let us harvest variance instead of fighting it. But it only works if Level 2 is stable first."

Tom raised his hand. "So we're not starting over?"

"Not at all. We're completing what you started. You built the rooms—forecasting, scheduling, real-time. Now we're building the hallways between them."

The Vision Beyond

As the team filed out, energized by clarity, David lingered.

"You could have pushed for automation immediately," he said. "Budget's there if you want it."

Sarah shook her head. "At specialty lines, I made Excel work through discipline and clear rules. Here, you have the tools but not the discipline. Automation without foundation just fails faster."

She looked at the ROC through the conference window—sophisticated, professional, perpetually reactive.

"Six months from now, this place runs predictably. Simple rules, clear triggers, protected development. Then we add automation that turns variance into value instead of fighting it. But first, we make Level 2 actually foundational."

David smiled. "That's why I hired you. You see what's missing, not just what's next."

As Sarah walked the floor that evening, she saw both the achievement and the opportunity. Level 2 was impressive—compared to Excel chaos, it was revolutionary. But impressive wasn't the same as effective. The foundation needed strengthening before they could build higher.

The real transformation wouldn't come from new technology. It would come from making the current technology work as a system. Then, and only then, would they be ready for Level 3's promise of harvesting variance instead of just surviving it.

8.2 What Defines Level 2?

Level 2 is where most large centers live: a WFM platform is in place, roles are named, interval goals are tracked, and schedules publish on a cadence. Planning remains mostly deterministic (often in exported spreadsheets), intraday adjustments are manual, and no automation executes real-time moves. The result is structure that works under predictable conditions and strains when variance appears.

Scope and scale. Centers span hundreds to tens of thousands of agents, often multi-site and multi-channel (voice, chat, email). The WFM tool supports short-term forecasting, scheduling, and adherence, but capacity planning and scenario work frequently "lift and load" to Excel where assumptions are fixed and slow to refresh.

Roles that exist—but don't yet close the loop. *Forecasters* maintain seasonality, event calendars, and interval views in-tool, yet rely on manual overrides and external models to manage hiring lead times and proficiency ramps. Mid-month SLA slip often triggers "catch-up" math for remaining days—precise, but brittle without fast feedback. *Schedulers* generate schedules aligned to the plan, then spend the week moving blocks: defending SL by rescheduling coaching/training and calling OT when forecasts misalign with reality. *Real-time analysts* protect intervals by reallocating skills and logging adherence exceptions, but act through tickets and chat threads rather than system-assisted micro-moves.

Metrics and limits. SL/ASA/abandon are formalized and visible; consistency is the struggle. Small movements in arrivals, AHT, or absenteeism create bottlenecks the platform surfaces but cannot resolve quickly. A "green" daily rollup can still mask red intervals customers actually lived. Multi-channel adds friction: voice holds SL while chat/email queues grow because cross-channel shifts are slow and policy-bound.

Culture and agent experience. Adherence is emphasized; schedules optimize fixed time slots. Without clear guardrails (e.g., an occupancy band and protected development), coaching loses to demand and flexibility is scarce. Over time, rigidity drives fatigue and attrition—especially for agents seeking predictable rules *and* some preference influence.

The ROC at Level 2. Many organizations form a Resource Optimization Center to colocate forecasting, scheduling, and real-time. The ROC improves visibility and cadence (reading intervals together, naming variance), but without automation it remains largely tactical—strong at incident management, slower at prevention. Alerts are faster; actuation is still manual.

Sarah's read. Walking the loop with the team, Sarah sees a solid foundation: credible interval forecasts, posted schedules, and a real-time function watching the right dials. She also sees the gap: abandonment-blind staffing when tight, rigid templates in blended channels, and slow intraday corrections that push coaching aside. Advancing from Level 2 is less about buying features and more about making the loop faster and tighter—definitions aligned, handoffs explicit, and small moves executed with less friction.

Operational profile (summary)

- **Tech:** WFM platform in place; capacity planning often external and deterministic; no real-time automation.
- **Roles:** Dedicated forecasters, schedulers, and RTAs; collaboration present, closed-loop learning inconsistent.
- **Process:** Schedules publish on time; intraday still manual; coaching/training frequently rescheduled to defend SL.
- **Metrics:** SL/ASA/abandon visible; interval stability uneven; multi-channel rebalancing is slow.
- **Risk:** Narrow SLA wins, development erosion, agent fatigue, and siloed channel experiences.

This is Level 2—*foundational*, not fragile by default, but prone to lag when conditions shift. The next sections specify mechanics and limits so we can strengthen the loop before introducing automation in Level 3.

8.3 Key Challenges at Level 2

Level 2 feels organized: a ROC screen is up, interval targets are set, and WFM roles are named. The loop—forecast → schedule → real-time—runs on time. Yet beneath the order sits a single weakness: plans are mostly *deterministic and reactive*. When demand holds, the machine hums. When variance arrives, the same machine strains—manual edits multiply, coaching slips, and end-of-month math takes over. Walking the floor, Sarah can see both truths at once: structure that helps, and latency that hurts.

The challenges below cut across GRPIT. Sequence them by your STaRS context (Startup, Turnaround, Realignment, Sustaining) so effort matches situation, not fashion.

1. Static plans vs. dynamic planning. Forecasts, schedules, and adherence targets exist but sit on fixed assumptions. When arrivals, AHT, or absenteeism move, the response is manual edits—OT calls, break shuffles, rescheduled development. Variance is treated as something to suppress, not steer. Turnarounds feel this as missed SL and cost spikes; Sustaining orgs feel a ceiling on growth.

2. Limited real-time adaptability (no automation). Real-time sees interval shifts but acts through tickets and chat, not system-executed micro-moves. Cross-skill/channel adjustments are slow; canceling training becomes the default relief valve. The gap is not visibility; it is actuation speed and consistency in the *next* interval. Startups may tolerate this briefly; Turnarounds cannot.

3. Operational fragility from manual workarounds. Processes exist yet break under stress: adherence exceptions pile up, last-minute changes proliferate, and "catch-up SL" math dominates late-month behavior. Documentation aids coordination, but without fast feedback loops and pre-agreed intraday rules, resilience doesn't materialize.

4. Rigid adherence models and engagement drag. Schedules optimize fixed slots; adherence is policed more than supported. Without guardrails (e.g., an occupancy band and protected development), flexibility is scarce and coaching loses to demand. Over time, rigidity drives fatigue and attrition—especially for agents who expect predictable rules *and* some preference influence.

5. Multi-channel allocation without a unifying mechanism. Voice, chat, and email run side-by-side, not as one system. Metrics and staffing live in silos; reallocation is policy-bound and slow. One channel's spike becomes another's backlog, yielding uneven CX and missed guarantees. Realignment scenarios surface this most clearly as digital volumes grow.

6. Documented processes that still react. Capacity planning, standards, and SOPs may exist, yet much work "lifts and loads" to spreadsheets with deterministic assumptions. Without a path from written rules to timely, repeatable intraday moves, the org remains precise on paper and late in practice.

The defining challenge: turn variance into an asset. Level 2 stalls when variance is treated as noise to average out rather than signal to instrument. Advancement means shifting from *the Plan* to *Planning*: read intervals, protect development with clear guardrails, and prepare the loop for automation (Level 3) so small, consistent corrections happen quickly.

Sarah's read. From the ROC, Sarah sees the strength—visibility and roles—and the gap: slow actuation, rigid templates in blended channels, and catch-up behaviors. Her next steps: align SL/ASA/abandon treatment; publish occupancy bands and a shrinkage policy; codify Rule→Trigger→Action at the interval level; and remove manual delays that keep the ROC reactive. These fixes set up the "how" in Sections 8.4 to 8.6 and point the way to Level 3.

8.4 Goals (G) — KPI Integrity and Relevance

At Level 2, the metrics exist; the risk is drift. Your first job is integrity: clear definitions, stable calculations, and one source of truth. Use the AQEE lens—**Availability**, **Quality**, **Efficiency**, **Expense**—to keep scope broad enough to be useful and narrow enough to steer the next interval. Governance comes before cleverness.

Define the few that run the day (AQEE)

Availability.   Service level (e.g., 80/30), with **ASA** and **abandon rate** as context. Read SL at 15–30 minute intervals, not just daily averages; decide and document how short abandons are treated (Sections 7.4 and 7.5).

Quality.   CSAT and FCR; add **forecast accuracy** as WFM's quality signal—better accuracy reduces avoidable strain on customers and agents.

Efficiency.   AHT and an **occupancy band** (e.g., 78–88%) to avoid "green SL, burnt people." Track **adherence** as a support mechanism, not a policing tool.

Expense.   Cost per contact and **actual vs. budget**. In revenue queues, **revenue per contact** adds context.

Metric integrity and governance (make it boring on purpose)

- **Definitions are explicit.** Publish SL/ASA/abandon treatment; what counts in AHT; what "engaged" means for occupancy.
- **One source of truth.** Interval calculations come from a shared, versioned dataset; labels match across WFM/ACD/BI.
- **Stability with change control.** KPIs do not shift mid-quarter; proposed changes carry a written rationale, test window, and effective date.

Forecast accuracy: set goals the math can support

Inherited targets (e.g., "≤5% MAPE everywhere") often ignore volume-driven variance. Use two tools: the *Minimal Interval Error Rate* and *WAPE*.

Minimal Interval Error Rate (baseline).   Smaller queues fluctuate more; even a perfect model cannot beat this floor:

$$\text{Minimal Interval Error Rate} = \sqrt{\frac{2}{\pi FC}},$$

where FC is forecasted contacts in the interval. Example: $FC=100 \Rightarrow \approx 8\%$; $FC=250 \Rightarrow \approx 5\%$; $FC=400 \Rightarrow \approx 4\%$. Targets below this floor are noise-chasing.

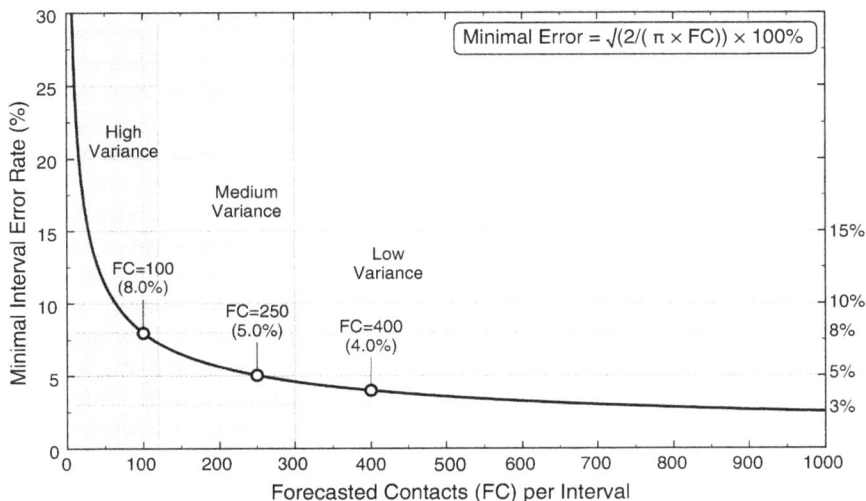

Figure 8.1: Minimal Interval Error Rate vs. interval volume (FC): smaller queues have higher irreducible error due to mathematical constraints, not forecast quality.

WAPE over MAPE (for uneven volumes). Weighted Absolute Percentage Error normalizes intervals by size:

$$\text{WAPE} = \frac{\sum |\text{Actual} - \text{Forecast}|}{\sum \text{Actual}} \times 100.$$

WAPE prevents low-volume intervals from dominating the story and better reflects operational impact. Use WAPE for weekly rollups; keep interval error for intraday learning.

A short exercise Sarah runs with the team

1. Compute the minimal error floor per interval using FC; flag intervals where the target sits below the floor.
2. Compare current targets to floors; adjust goals by band (e.g., $FC<120$, $120 \leq FC < 300$, $FC \geq 300$).
3. Produce weekly WAPE and a top-5 interval list with biggest absolute misses; annotate "volume vs. AHT vs. staffing."

This shifts debate from opinion to math and keeps improvement tied to intervals, not monthly averages.

Why broader quality metrics show up here (forward look)

At Level 2, WFM may not act on CSAT/FCR day to day. As Level 3 arrives, these metrics feed *dynamic coaching/training*: low FCR on a topic informs micro-training during natural lulls; CSAT patterns influence who gets nudged for coaching windows. Introduce visibility now so the loop is ready later.

What to standardize this quarter (checklist)

- SL/ASA/abandon definition (incl. short-abandon threshold) published and used in interval reads.
- Occupancy band documented and visible on ROC (Resource Optimization Center) screens; adherence framed as support.
- Forecast accuracy policy: interval error-floor bands + weekly WAPE in the scorecard.
- One-page metric governance: owner, data source, formula, change-control steps.

Bottom line. Level 2 wins come from *trusted numbers.* Get definitions and governance right, set accuracy goals the math can support, and you will spend less time arguing metrics and more time improving the day—while preparing the loop for Level 3 automation.

With definitions pinned, the platform work is mostly plumbing and visibility: mirror the same labels in WFM/BI, put SL/ASA/abandon+occupancy on a single ROC pane, and codify the Rule→Trigger→Action ladders so the smallest fixes repeat (Sections 8.8 to 8.10).

8.5 Roles (R) — Building Core WFM Practices

Level 2 solidifies WFM into distinct functions—forecasting, scheduling, and real-time, supported by a platform and interval targets. The work now is to make these roles *clear, connected, and growing* so the loop runs the same way twice today and is ready for automation tomorrow.

Principles that make roles work

1) Document the job and the handoff.   Write what each role owns and how work moves: inputs, outputs, and escalation paths. Update when rules change, not during a crisis. Clear handoffs reduce latency and set the stage for system-executed micro-moves later.

2) Collaborate on a cadence.   Short, regular touchpoints—weekly look-ahead, daily pre-shift, intraday huddles—keep assumptions aligned and decisions timely. Cross-role presence (forecaster in pre-shift; scheduler in the ROC) turns silos into a loop.

3) Build skills on a ladder.   Give each role a basic and an advanced tier: fundamentals now, next-level skills that anticipate Level 3 (data literacy, scenario thinking, rule design). Tie learning to real artifacts (forecast notes, roster protections, variance logs) rather than slides.

4) Prepare roles for evolution.   Real-time changes fastest at Level 3; scheduling becomes rule-driven; forecasting adds abandonment awareness and simple simulation. Start light pilots and cross-training so responsibilities can shift without drama.

Role charters (one page each, living documents)

Sarah asks each owner to publish a half-page charter—tight and operational.

Forecasting (owner: Name/Role). *Purpose:* believable interval view with assumptions. *Inputs:* last four comparables (the previous four same-day patterns, adjusted for events/policy), events, AHT trend. *Outputs:* interval arrivals/AHT, required staff (Erlang-C baseline), two uncertainties. *Handoff:* Thu 15:00 to Scheduling; variance notes returned daily.

Scheduling (owner: Name/Role). *Purpose:* turn intent into seats/time with protections. *Inputs:* forecast tab + shrinkage policy + preferences. *Outputs:* roster with protected coaching/training and break placement. *Handoff:* Fri 17:00 to Real-time; summary of changes vs. forecast.

Real-time (owner: Name/Role). *Purpose:* steer the next interval. *Inputs:* live SL/ASA/ abandon, occupancy, roster protections. *Outputs:* micro-moves log; two variance intervals/day. *Handoff:* end-of-day notes to Forecasting and Scheduling.

Targeted training (tiered, practical)

- **Forecasting.** Basics: interval stats, event tagging, assumptions. Advanced: abandonment awareness (Erlang-A context), simple simulation or scenario bands; WAPE reporting (Section 8.4).

- **Scheduling.** Basics: shrinkage application, break/coach placement vs. peaks, preference handling. Advanced: rule design for re-optimization, blended-channel templates, conflict resolution by policy not habit.

- **Real-time.** Basics: interval reads (SL+ASA+occupancy), escalation triggers, clean comms. Advanced: micro-moves playbook design, cross-skill/channel rebalancing rules, latency reduction.

Encourage external learning (WFM communities, conferences) and internal share-backs; WFM has few formal pipelines, so peer practice matters. Budget small but steady; tie spend to artifacts produced (playbooks, SOPs, dashboards).

Prepare for Level 3 (without jumping early)

- **Early L2.** Stabilize charters and handoffs; run the weekly/day/intraday rhythm; keep a clean variance log.

- **Mature L2.** Pilot small automations around the humans: alerting mapped to pre-agreed rules; scripted exports/imports; guardrails that preserve development unless thresholds trip. Cross-train real-time with scheduling.

- **Special focus on Real-time.** This role becomes "actuation design" at Level 3. Start documenting Rule→Trigger→Action with thresholds so buttons can be pressed by systems later.

A lightweight checklist Sarah uses with the team

- Each role has a one-page charter (purpose, inputs, outputs, cadence, handoffs).

- Handoffs occur at set times (Thu forecast; Fri roster; daily variance return) and are logged.

- Tiered training plans exist and tie to artifacts (forecast note, roster protections, ROC log).

- Real-time micro-moves are written as rules with thresholds; reschedules are exceptions, not the plan.

Bottom line. Level-2 role maturity is not headcount; it is *ownership with clean handoffs* and skills that anticipate automation. Document the work, practice the cadence, and grow the muscles you will need at Level 3.

8.6 Processes (P) — Traditional WFM Processes

The move from Level 1 to Level 2 is most visible in *process*. Heroics give way to defined workflows; spreadsheets give way to platforms. Yet the dominant pattern remains plan–then–defend: build a static blueprint and spend the week protecting it. That structure stabilizes the operation—and also creates fragility when variance is the norm.

The architecture of traditional processes (plan cascades)

Level 2 runs a familiar cascade that most practitioners can sketch from memory:

Long-range capacity (3–18 months). Finance shares envelopes, marketing shares calendars, operations sets service goals. WFM projects volumes, AHT, and staffing by month and quarter; leadership decides hiring classes, site footprints, and budget. The models are careful and documented—and brittle when product, policy, or market moves. Once requisitions and leases are set, course-correcting is slow and costly.

Mid-range forecasting (4–12 weeks). Monthly cycles refine the capacity picture with fresher data and event notes. These numbers anchor maintenance windows, training waves, and campaign coverage. In Level 2, mid-range outputs are treated as commitments; miss tolerance is low, judgment adjustments are high, and the learning loop is weak.

Short-term forecasting (1–4 weeks). Weekly processes produce interval targets by day and skill. Techniques vary—from seasonal indices to simple smoothing—but the logic is historical shape ± known events. The method works until it doesn't; variance is smoothed as noise rather than mined as signal.

The scheduling marathon (where control meets constraints)

Shift bids. Annual/semi-annual bids lock start times and days-off using performance, seniority and contract rules. The procedure is transparent and defensible—and locks rigidity into a world that will change.

Vacation planning. Yearly PTO bids balance preferences against min-staff rules. Good for fairness, hard on agility; policy debt accrues when business and life diverge from a calendar set months ago.

Schedule generation and publication. Engines optimize breaks and lunches to match net staffing to requirements. A precise roster emerges, then becomes sacrosanct: adherence enforces the plan; exceptions require frictions by design. The published artefact is optimized for yesterday's beliefs about tomorrow.

Change management.   Despite rigidity, changes proliferate: swaps, OT, VTO, same-day edits. Level 2 builds elaborate approval flows to contain this reality, inadvertently creating administrative load that steals time from improvement.

Real-time management (organized, but reactive)

Huddles and battle rhythm.   Morning reviews confirm risks, offline schedules, and contingencies. The ritual is crisp, the slides neat—and the situation has already moved.

Monitoring and adjustment.   Analysts watch SL/ASA/abandon and adherence; when thresholds break, they pull levers—cancel offline work, request OT, re-route, re-sequence breaks. Each lever requires permissions and updates; delays turn dips into slides. Tools show variance fast; processes act slowly.

Adherence management.   Systems track minutes; reports flag variance; exceptions are documented. The assumption is that the schedule is right and deviation is wrong. Valuable variance (finishing a complex fix, taking 60 seconds to reset after a hard call) is indistinguishable from drift. The result is compliance without context.

The documentation paradox

Level 2 replaces tribal knowledge with SOPs, maps, and guides—an advance over Level 1. But static documents calcify procedures and slow change: updates require approvals, retraining, reissue. As omnichannel work blurs boundaries, artifacts lag reality; the documentation that ensured consistency now enforces yesterday.

Why traditional processes create fragility

- **Predictability assumption.** Methods assume repeatable patterns; variance is treated as error to smooth, not information to use.
- **Hierarchical latency.** Decisions flow up; actions flow down. In fast-moving intervals, that latency is the loss.
- **Functional separation.** Forecasting, scheduling, and real-time specialize and hand off, impeding integrated optimization.
- **Perfection bias.** The goal is a "right" plan; energy then defends it rather than adapting to opportunity.
- **Control mindset.** Adherence enforces conformance, often at the expense of agent autonomy and quality.

Sarah's read (mini case thread)

Sarah inherits a clean cascade—capacity deck, mid-range packet, weekly forecast, and a polished roster. SL still wobbles mid-morning; training is first to fall; agents feel policed, not supported. Her diagnosis is not "work harder," it is "change where the process learns": move learning *into* the rhythm rather than after it.

Prepare processes for evolution (without skipping steps)

From plan to planning.   Keep the cascade, but add feedback at each seam: capacity $\rightarrow$ hiring classes validated against realized shrinkage; mid-range $\rightarrow$ a "delta ledger" that records event impact; weekly $\rightarrow$ interval variance notes that feed next week's shapes.

From control to guardrails.   Replace blanket adherence policing with *bands and rules*: occupancy bands, break "nudge" limits, training save/skip thresholds, and pre-approved micro-flex pools. Decisions become faster because the choices were made in advance (Sections 7.8 and 8.4).

From handoffs to loops.   Make each artifact carry assumptions forward and variance back: the forecast note lists two uncertainties; scheduling publishes protections and flex options; real-time returns two-interval learnings daily. The point is not new meetings but smaller loops.

From documents to living SOPs.   One-page SOPs with version tags live in the same workbook as the numbers. Change logs show what moved and why; monthly reviews retire rules that generate exception volume.

Practical packet (lightweight, Level-2 friendly)

- **Weekly source-of-truth tab:** arrivals, AHT, required staff (Erlang-C), shrinkage, scheduled, plus a one-paragraph assumptions note.
- **Shrinkage policy one-pager:** named components, rates, and application (required $\rightarrow$ scheduled) with training guardrails.
- **Intraday playbook:** three micro-moves in order (reclaim task, nudge breaks, flex pool) with thresholds.
- **Interval variance log:** two intervals/day—what moved (volume, AHT, staffing) and outcome; feeds next week's shapes.

Bridge to Level 3 (process lens)

Level 3 does not discard Level-2 discipline; it instruments it. Automation presses the same micro-moves, re-optimizes schedules within guardrails, and turns variance into planned work. The upgrade is from *defend a plan* to *continuously plan*.

Bottom line. Level-2 processes deliver order and also bake in delay. Keep the cascade, add loops, codify guardrails, and let artifacts carry assumptions and learning. Do that now, and Level 3 becomes an accelerator, not a rewrite.

8.7 Interpersonal (I) — The Triangular Tension

Level 2 professionalizes WFM and, paradoxically, makes it the lightning rod. Structure reveals tradeoffs that informal workarounds once hid. WFM now stands at the intersection of three forces with different definitions of "win": *Operations* (service), *Finance* (cost), and *Agents* (flexibility). The friction is structural, not personal.

The three forces (each reasonable from its seat)

Operations: the customer promise. Leaders in operations live inside interval reality. When queues lengthen, the answer feels obvious: add capacity, extend lunches, reclaim offline time, swap channels, open overtime. The request is urgent and tangible: protect SL, today. Those constraints—heads can't be conjured, and over-corrections degrade the afternoon—rarely soften the ask.

Finance: the cost envelope. Finance optimizes labor within plan: overtime down, idle time down, variance down. "Close enough to 80/30" reads rationally on a monthly roll-up and collides with the fact that interval misses are not fungible. Cost pressure is continuous, especially around budgeting and quarters close.

Agents: the human day. Agents seek predictability, fairness, voice, and development. Rigid bids, punitive adherence, and repeated training cancellations signal that numbers outrank people. Engagement dips; attrition rises; nesting load loops back into capacity risk.

Daily reality (the crossfire without the play-by-play)

In a single morning, WFM can be told to cut OT, raise coverage, and approve emergency PTO—simultaneously. WFM explains constraints and guardrails; stakeholders hear "no." The result is escalation, exception queues, and rework that steals time from improvement.

Ripple effects across partners

With HR (policy ideals vs interval math). Flex policies, expanded PTO, and development goals are healthy. When designed without interval views, they bottleneck coverage and force after-the-fact denials. Co-design prevents policy debt.

With Supervisors (being supportive vs keeping shape). Supervisors want to accommodate real people with real needs. Quiet swaps and soft adherence accumulate until WFM must reset the baseline, which feels punitive. Clear lanes for swaps and micro-flex reduce shadow processes.

With Senior Leadership (expectations vs constraints). Investment in a platform can create the belief that WFM can deliver perfect service at minimal cost with high engagement—simultaneously. WFM must translate tradeoffs in plain language and show interval consequences, not just monthly tiles.

Human cost (WFM and frontline)

Inside WFM. Analysts come for optimization and stay for arbitration. Emotional labor—delivering unpopular truths, defending thresholds, managing grievances—drives fatigue and churn inside WFM teams.

On the floor. Contact center work is intrinsically demanding; Level-2 rigidity amplifies it. When every minute is policed, when training is repeatedly sacrificed, and when schedules lack voice, the job becomes hard to sustain. Turnover lifts costs and erodes the very service the policies intended to protect.

Why the tension persists (the structural trap)

- **Misaligned metrics.** SL, cost, and flexibility peak at different operating points; maximizing one can degrade the others.
- **Information asymmetry.** Queueing constraints and shrinkage math can look like inflexibility to non-practitioners.
- **Ownership without authority.** WFM owns processes but not budgets, policies, or external promises.
- **Reactive positioning.** Plan-centric mechanics keep WFM on defense, narrating yesterday and firefighting today.

Perception problem (how WFM gets typecast)

When decisions feel opaque, WFM becomes "schedule police," "bureaucrats," "roadblock," or "blame target." Exclusion follows: marketing launches without volume planning; HR changes policy without interval modeling; ops commits SL without staffing validation—each creating later emergencies that reinforce the stereotype.

Seeds of evolution (patterns progressive L2 teams adopt)

- **Transparency that teaches.** Publish the SL definition (incl. abandons), occupancy band, and shrinkage policy with one interval example—what changes and what doesn't. Replace anecdotes with math narrations (Section 8.4).
- **Collaborative guardrails.** Monthly, put Ops, Finance, HR, and agent reps in the same room to set OT envelopes, PTO lanes, and training protections—on interval views. Decisions made together travel better.

- **Value demonstration.** Quantify: X% forecast-error reduction $\rightarrow$ Y% OT reduction; protected coaching $\rightarrow$ FCR/CSAT lift; micro-flex pools $\rightarrow$ fewer red intervals. Make wins visible.

- **Technology as mediator.** Self-service within constraints and rule-based alerts depersonalize "no" into "here's what fits."

Sarah's move: reposition WFM from enforcer to enabler

Sarah introduces a one-page *Tradeoff Card*: service, cost, and people guardrails with the math behind each (SL threshold and abandon treatment; occupancy band and why; PTO lanes by interval; training save/skip rule). In reviews, decisions are made against the card—not ad hoc. Language shifts from "can't" to "can, within these bands."

Bridge to Level 3 (relationship lens)

Level 3 reduces interpersonal strain by making fair choices visible and repeatable: from enforcing static plans to enabling dynamic optimization; from reactive exceptions to proactive variance harvesting; from siloed, conflicting metrics to integrated value. Some relief is possible now—through transparency, co-owned guardrails, and light self-service—but the durable fix is a system that acts on the rules we agree to.

Bottom line. Level-2 friction is systemic. Treat it as a design problem: align definitions, expose tradeoffs, co-own guardrails, and use simple mechanisms (rules, self-service, alerts) to mediate conflict. Do that, and technology in Level 3 becomes a relationship upgrade, not just a software change.

8.8 Technology (T) — Platforms That Help, Limits That Hurt

Level 2 has a WFM platform in the middle of the operation. It produces short-term interval level forecasts, generates "optimized" schedules, shows adherence, and supports interval reads. That's progress. The constraints are just as real: variance to plan is real and persistent, intraday actuation still happens by people, not rules; capacity planning "lifts and loads" to spreadsheets with fixed assumptions; and integrations are brittle. Technology helps you *see* faster than you can *move*.

What's in place (and what it actually buys)

- **WFM platform (forecast/schedule/adherence).** One system of record for rosters and interval targets. It standardizes inputs and cadences; it does not, by itself, execute micro-moves.
- **ACD/IVR & digital routing.** Queues, skills, and prompts reflect today's org chart more than tomorrow's variance. Hygiene matters: no orphaned skills, current prompts, clean mappings.
- **Wallboards/ROC views.** SL/ASA/abandon and occupancy are visible; alerts fire. Actuation is still manual (tickets, chats, calls).
- **Reporting/BI.** Exports flow to dashboards; definitions often diverge across ACD, WFM, BI, creating trust gaps when pressure rises.

The fatal flaws at Level 2 (name them so you can contain them)

- **Deterministic capacity planning.** Long-range plans run outside the platform, assume stability, and age quickly. Hiring classes lock before demand shifts are understood.
- **Abandonment-blind staffing.** Erlang-C everywhere yields optimistic staffing when queues are tight. Without an abandon treatment or Erlang-A context, plans misstate risk.
- **Manual intraday actuation.** Alerts without rules create latency: by the time a break is nudged or a back-office task reclaimed, the spike has moved.
- **Fragmented data plumbing.** Multiple "sources of truth," mismatched time zones, and silent transform steps produce reconciliation cycles that steal analyst capacity.
- **Rigid templates in blended channels.** Static voice-centric patterns starve chat/email when voice spikes; cross-channel shifts are policy-bound and slow.

What "good Level 2" looks like (before automation)

Keep the stack simple, the definitions shared, and the loop tight.

- **Shared definitions.** Publish SL/ASA/abandon treatment, the occupancy band, and shrinkage policy inside the platform and the BI layer (Section 8.4).
- **One stitched view.** A small, versioned pipeline from ACD → staging → WFM/BI with time normalization and field dictionaries. No one-off extracts.

- **ROC ritual, not a room.** A single screen with interval SL/ASA/abandon and occupancy; a 10-minute cadence; three pre-agreed micro-moves (pull task, nudge breaks, flex pool) executed consistently (Section 7.8).
- **Abandon-aware thinking.** Keep Erlang-C for baseline, but test sensitivity with simple Erlang-A scenarios where holds and patience matter (Section 7.6).
- **Compact governance.** A one-page metric sheet (owner, source, formula, change control) and a one-page rules sheet (Rule→Trigger→Action with thresholds).

Sarah's move (vendor-agnostic, doable now)

Sarah doesn't shop first; she instruments first.

1. **Normalize the data.** Stand up a light ETL (or scripted exports) to align intervals, time zones, and keys across ACD/WFM/BI. Publish a field *read-me*.
2. **Pin the definitions.** Embed SL/abandon treatment, occupancy band, shrinkage components in both platform labels and ROC overlays; remove duplicate tiles that disagree (Section 8.4).
3. **Codify micro-moves.** Add a rules tab in the WFM tool or ROC notes: which agents are pre-named for back-office reclaim, how many breaks can move by five minutes, when coaching holds vs. yields (Section 7.8).
4. **Add abandon sensitivity.** For two peak queues, run "tight queue" what-ifs (A-style) monthly; annotate risk bands on coverage views.
5. **Close the loop.** Variance log feeds a weekly change set: definitions that drifted, rules that didn't trigger, data fields that confused. Ship small fixes every Friday.

Starter stack checklist (works at Level 2)

- WFM platform as roster & interval single source of truth (SSoT); *one* BI layer with mirrored definitions.
- ROC screen with SL/ASA/abandon + occupancy; 10-minute huddle; micro-moves list visible.
- Scripted extracts (or light ETL) with versioned folders; no manual copy/paste chains.
- Abandon treatment documented; accuracy reported as weekly WAPE + interval error bands (Section 8.4).

Bottom line. Level 2 tech should make the loop faster and clearer, not heavier. Fix plumbing and definitions, expose rule-based micro-moves, and add abandon-aware reads. Save automation for Level 3—your goal here is a platformed operation that *sees* the same picture and moves the same way twice.

8.9 The ROC Model: Reframing Real-Time Management

Real-time management shifts here from schedule policing to *operational intelligence*: the ROC reads variance, coordinates the smallest effective move, and remembers what worked so the loop tightens next week (Section 8.4 KPI integrity & governance, Section 7.8 micro-moves).

Level 2 often treats real-time as schedule policing—watch adherence, process exceptions, send reminders. The **Resource Optimization Center (ROC)** reframes that work as operational intelligence: read variance, coordinate a response, and document what was learned. Same screens, different mandate.

From adherence police to operational intelligence

Adherence still matters, but it becomes one signal among many (SL/ASA/abandon, occupancy, routing state, offline plans). The question shifts from "Who's out of adherence?" to "What variance matters most *now*, and what is the smallest action that stabilizes the next interval?" The ROC optimizes resources under constraint rather than enforcing a static plan.

Command-center posture (physical or virtual)

Presentation influences behavior. A ROC is a focal point—shared displays, a single queue of incidents, clear communications. It need not be a room with video walls; a disciplined virtual space with the same rituals works. What changes is *stance*: coordinated, time-boxed decisions with documented outcomes, not scattered chats and ad-hoc pings.

Incident management: the ROC heartbeat

Borrowing from IT Service management (ITSM), the ROC treats material deviations as *incidents* with owners, states, and closures. This creates speed and memory.

Trigger. A variance threshold trips (e.g., two consecutive intervals below SL *and* occupancy above band; absenteeism spike on a skill; chat backlog breaches policy). An incident ticket opens automatically with timestamp, queue/skill, and current metrics.

Triage. The ROC confirms scope (volume vs. AHT vs. staffing), checks protected windows (coaching/training), and selects the smallest move likely to work.

Response (micro-moves first). Follow a pre-agreed ladder: (1) reclaim a named back-office task; (2) nudge two breaks by five minutes; (3) flex a small pool or temporary reroute; (4) only then unlock overtime or cancel protected time. Each action is logged with time and expected effect.

Closure & learning.   When metrics recover or the window closes, the incident is closed with cause and impact notes. Two closures per day roll into the variance log feeding forecasting/scheduling changes. Over time, repeatable playbooks emerge.

Making variance visible (to change behavior)

The ROC's value compounds when others can see variance and the response:

- **Executive pane.** A simple view: current incidents, state, ETA to recovery, and what tradeoffs were made (e.g., training held vs. skipped).
- **Ops updates.** Short, structured comms during major incidents ("Marketing drop +15% on Q2; ROC applied surge step 1–2; recovery in 30–45 min").
- **Story of the day/week.** A one-page summary: top incidents, root patterns, and which rules worked. Visibility reduces second-guessing and funds improvements.

How ROC builds the case for Level 3

Every manual incident is a data point for automation. The ROC quantifies:

- frequency by incident type (e.g., "break-cliff after 11:30"),
- average manual response time vs. target,
- impact of delay (lost SL minutes, abandons, OT triggered),
- repeatability of the winning move.

This turns "we need automation" into "automating steps 1–2 on these three incident types cuts time-to-stabilize from 18 minutes to under 60 seconds." It is a bridge to Level 3 grounded in the center's own intervals.

Cultural shift the ROC enables

- **From defensive to proactive.** Less post-mortem, more pre-agreed moves at defined thresholds.
- **From isolated to integrated.** Forecasting, Scheduling, and Real-time share the same incident feed and language.
- **From "plan compliance" to "outcome under constraints."** Decisions reference guardrails (SL/abandon policy, occupancy band, protected development) rather than personalities.
- **From cost center to value.** Documented incident handling prevents churn, keeps development on the calendar, and reduces OT—value you can show.

Sarah's implementation (vendor-agnostic, Level-2 ready)

1. **Define guardrails.** Publish SL/abandon treatment, occupancy band, and the training "save/skip" rule (Sections 7.8 and 8.4).
2. **Stand up a light incident queue.** Use your ticketing tool or a shared sheet with required fields: trigger, owner, moves, result. Time-box updates.
3. **Codify micro-moves.** Write Rule→Trigger→Action ladders per major queue/channel; pre-name flex pools; cap how many breaks can shift.
4. **Wire basic alerts.** Threshold alerts that open incidents automatically; align to interval timing to avoid thrash.
5. **Close the loop weekly.** Review top incident types, update thresholds and playbooks, feed changes to forecasting (events/AHT) and scheduling (break placement, protection windows).

Operating metrics (beyond adherence)

Track measures that reflect ROC effectiveness:

- **Time-to-stabilize** (trigger → recovery) by incident type.
- **Incident avoidance rate** (proactive moves that prevented threshold breach).
- **Protected-time retention** (percent of coaching/training preserved during incidents).
- **Rule hit-rate** (share of incidents resolved by step 1–2 vs. escalations).
- **Variance reuse** (incidents that produced a rule change or schedule tweak).

ROC Incident Management Flow

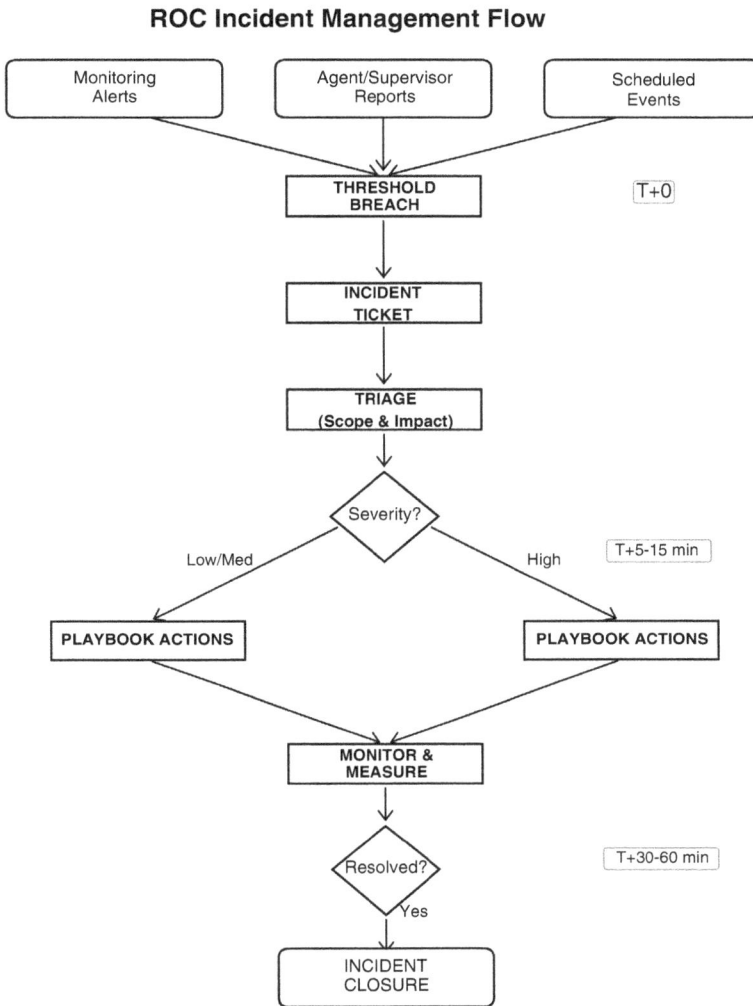

Figure 8.2: ROC incident flow

What a good Level-2 ROC is *not*

- **Not** a wall of TVs with no rules behind the alerts.
- **Not** a permission gate for every break change; micro-moves should be pre-approved within bands.
- **Not** an automation promise. At Level 2, the ROC standardizes *manual* control so you know what to automate in Level 3.

Bottom line. The ROC makes variance actionable. It formalizes small, fast, rule-based responses and captures learning so the loop gets tighter each week. Done well, it upgrades real-time from schedule enforcement to resource optimization—and builds the evidence you'll need for automation in Level 3.

8.10 The Path to Level 3: From Reactive to Proactive

Moving from Level 2 to Level 3 is less a tooling upgrade than a change in how the operation treats variance. Level 2 *sees* and reacts (often via a ROC); Level 3 *harvests* variance as an asset. The shift spans three fronts: technology, organization, and philosophy—built on Level-2 foundations but pushing past their limits.

Technology: from monitoring to automation

Level 2 excels at visibility—dashboards, adherence, reports, ROC views—but still relies on humans to press the buttons. Level 3 adds an automation layer that executes pre-agreed micro-moves at machine speed: deploy training into safe lulls, nudge breaks, flex small pools, adjust routing within guardrails. Existing WFM systems remain the source of truth; automation *acts* on them. Required capabilities: real-time integrations, a rules engine that balances objectives, safe dispatch to agent desktops, and feedback loops that learn. Properly designed, automation increases control by making responses consistent and fast.

Organization: from silos to integrated optimization

Forecasting, Scheduling, and Real-time keep their craft but share outcomes and rules. Cross-functional teams design automation ladders together; planning assumes intraday adaptability from the start. The ROC becomes the hub for rule design and review—not just incident response—while Quality, Training, and HR co-own policies that automation will enforce (e.g., protected coaching rules, swap lanes). The work moves from "my metric" to *our outcome*.

Philosophy: from fighting variance to harvesting it

Level 2 treats variance as failure against "the plan." Level 3 assumes variance and monetizes it:

- **Planning**: build flexible frames with embedded adaptability, not brittle precision.
- **Staffing**: plan small overhead bands that automation can deploy dynamically.
- **Development**: modular training/coaching delivered opportunistically.
- **Management**: optimize outcomes under constraints, not adherence for its own sake.

"Overhead" becomes capacity for adaptation; "variance" becomes optimization opportunity.

Cultural prerequisites

Trust in automation (transparent rules, clear ownership, visible wins), an **experimentation mindset** (iterate rules; learn fast), and **employee partnership** (automation removes nuisance work—exceptions and rebooking churn—so supervisors can coach and agents can grow). The ROC's documented incident history helps prove that automation simply executes what humans already do, faster and more consistently.

What to lock in at Level 2 (GRPIT snapshot)

Goals (G). Publish interval definitions for SL/ASA/abandon (incl. short-abandon policy), an occupancy band, and a shrinkage policy. Use WAPE for weekly forecast accuracy and enforce change control on KPI formulas (Section 8.4).

Roles (R). Keep charters to one page each; formalize handoffs (forecast → schedule → real-time → variance notes). Tier skills so each role is learning the next-level muscle (rule design, scenario thinking) (Section 8.5).

Processes (P). Run the week/day/interval rhythm; standardize micro-moves and log them. Treat documentation as a living system, not a binder—optimize for speed of correct action, not paperwork (Section 8.6).

Interpersonal (I). Make tradeoffs visible. Pair SL with ASA and occupancy; protect coaching unless thresholds trip; enable fair self-service within posted rules. Use transparency and co-owned guardrails to reduce "schedule police" dynamics (Section 8.7).

Technology (T). Let the WFM platform be the source of truth; keep capacity planning assumptions versioned (even if external). Re-position the existing ROC as the operational hub; instrument an incident register with time-to-stabilize, and use the cadence to promote/retire micro-moves. (Sections 8.8 and 8.9).

Sarah's Level-2 readiness checklist (lightweight)

- One-page metric governance: owner, data source, formula, and effective date.
- Role charters published; fixed handoff cadence; variance log returned daily.
- Intraday playbook with Rule→Trigger→Action; reschedules are exceptions, not the plan.
- ROC incident register: frequency, response steps, time-to-stabilize, outcome.
- Forecast accuracy policy: interval error floors by volume band + weekly WAPE.

Why Level 2 stalls (and how to unstick it)

- **Deterministic planning.** Precise on paper, slow in practice. Remedy: bake adaptability into guardrails and micro-moves.
- **Manual actuation.** Visibility without speed. Remedy: design rules now so automation can execute later.
- **Rigidity costs.** Training canceled; adherence policed. Remedy: occupancy bands and protected development with clear thresholds.

- **Channel silos.** Voice stable, digital backlogs. Remedy: cross-channel rules and ROC-led rebalancing standards.

The business case catalyst (built in the ROC)

Incident data quantifies frequency, response time, impact of delay, and the repeatable move that worked. That turns "we need automation" into "automating steps 1–2 on these incident types cuts time-to-stabilize from minutes to seconds, preserves X% of coaching, and reduces OT by Y%." Service, cost, and EX improvements combine for near-term ROI.

Point of no return

Once teams experience automatic adherence protection, preserved coaching, and interval-level stability, going back to manual exception handling is unthinkable. Executives see variance converted from liability to asset; supervisors refocus on coaching; agents see flexibility with guardrails. That irreversibility is the signal you have crossed into Level 3.

Bottom line. Make Level 2 boring in the best way—tight mechanics, clear handoffs, simple rules—then let Level 3 press the buttons and make it fast.

What to read while you build

Level 2 broadens your horizon—forecasting accuracy drives every downstream decision, and connecting with the broader WFM community accelerates learning beyond any single book. One resource and two networks solidify the foundations this chapter introduces.

Hyndman and Athanasopoulos's *Forecasting: Principles and Practice* is the modern standard for time series forecasting, freely available at otexts.com/fpp3. Their treatment moves from exploratory analysis through ARIMA, exponential smoothing, and advanced methods, all implemented in R with reproducible examples. The clarity makes sophisticated techniques accessible—you understand *why* a method works before applying it. Test the models on your historical data before committing to vendor modules—open-source rigor becomes immediate capability.[118]

Community engagement matters at Level 2. Cleveland's handbook [117] referenced in Section 7.12 remains essential, but the field evolves through shared practice. The Society of Workforce Planning Professionals (SWPP) offers training and practitioner networks that ground concepts in real operations. WFM Labs serves as companion to this book—a community inventing next-generation practices around employee-first principles, simulation, and automation. Join us at https://wfmlabs.org - the questions your peers ask surface challenges you haven't encountered, and their solutions save months of trial and error.

9 Level 3: Progressive – Real-Time Variance Harvesting

9.1 Introduction: From Fighting Variance to Harvesting It

Sarah Chen stood before Midwest Mutual's executive team, six months after taking over workforce management. Behind her, a slide showed two trend lines—one declining, one rising. Service levels had stabilized at 85%. Training completion had climbed from 47% to 62%. The foundation she'd promised was solid.

"Level 2 is stable," she began. "Definitions are clear. Handoffs work. Rules execute consistently. We no longer scramble daily or play catch-up monthly. But we're still fighting reality instead of working with it."

She clicked to the next slide—a net staffing chart from yesterday, annotated with red marks. "Every red mark is canceled training. Every gap is unharvested capacity. Every spike is overtime we could have avoided. We've built a disciplined system, but it's still rigid. Today, I'm proposing we make it adaptive."

CFO Margaret Peterson leaned forward. "More technology spending?"

"Different thinking," Sarah corrected. "Eisenhower said 'Plans are worthless, but planning is everything.' We've been perfecting plans. I'm proposing we perfect planning—continuous, intelligent, adaptive."

The Morning That Changed Everything

Sarah pulled up a specific example from the previous week. "Tuesday, 9:47 AM. Claims volume dropped unexpectedly—a system issue upstream. Six agents sat idle for twelve minutes while we confirmed it was safe to act. Meanwhile, three agents had training canceled that morning due to an earlier spike."

She zoomed into the interval view. "Those twelve minutes of unexpected capacity? Gone. Vanished. While agents who needed training sat on phones. This happens dozens of times daily—micro-gaps we can't harvest manually."

"What if," she continued, "when those six agents became free, the system automatically offered the next training module? What if supervisors got alerts about long calls before they became escalations? What if breaks self-adjusted when calls ran long, eliminating hundreds of adherence exceptions?"

The room was listening now.

The Vision: An Ecosystem of Micro-Automations

Sarah unveiled a framework showing not one automation but an ecosystem of small, intelligent adjustments:

Development Optimization

- Dynamic training delivery when capacity appears
- Micro-learning in 2-3 minute availability windows
- Automated coaching schedule optimization
- Just-in-time knowledge reinforcement

Operational Flexibility

- Intelligent break sliding within windows
- Automatic adherence protection
- Voluntary time off auto-offers when overstaffed

Support Automation

- Long-call assistance alerts
- Escalation prediction and preemptive support
- Automated post-call work optimization

Wellness and Engagement

- Fatigue monitoring and micro-breaks
- Automated achievement recognition
- Stress-break recommendations after difficult calls

"Each automation is simple," Sarah explained. "Together, they transform how we operate. We stop fighting variance and start harvesting it."

The Math of Micro-Moments

Tom Rodriguez from scheduling had run the analysis. "We mapped every interval for the past month. On average, we have 847 micro-gaps daily—moments where 2-5 agents are temporarily available for 30 seconds to 5 minutes. That's 42 hours of capacity we can't capture manually."

Sarah built on this. "Currently, we plan 5.5% shrinkage for training. But we only deliver 3.8% because we cancel it under pressure. What if we could plan just 2% scheduled training but deliver 6% by harvesting variance? Less planned overhead, more actual development."

Margaret was doing math. "That's essentially adding FTEs without hiring."

"Exactly. One industry study showed 0.8 FTE equivalent per 100 agents just from smarter training delivery. At our scale, that's 24 FTE worth of capacity."

The Human Element

David Kim, still COO, raised the critical question. "How do agents react to constant system decisions?"

Sarah had anticipated this. "The key is agency and transparency. Agents can defer training offers. They see why decisions are made. They influence their preferences. It's not the system controlling them—it's the system enabling them."

She shared feedback from a small test they'd run with Patricia Washington's team. "Agents said it felt like having a smart assistant, not a supervisor. Quote: 'Finally, the system works with my reality, not against it.'"

The Roadmap: Crawl, Walk, Run, Fly

Sarah presented a phased approach spanning 18 months:

Phase 1 - Pilot (Months 1-3): Prove the Concept

- 200 agents in life insurance division
- Three simple automations: dynamic training, break protection, long-call alerts
- Rigorous A/B testing with control group
- Success metrics: training completion, SL stability, agent satisfaction

Phase 2 - Rollout (Months 4-9): Scale the Winners

- Expand to 1,000 agents across two divisions
- Add five more automation rules based on pilot learnings
- Build governance structure and rule management processes
- Establish ROC as automation command center

Phase 3 - Expansion (Months 10-15): Departmental Coverage

- Full deployment across 3,000 agents
- Customize rules by line of business
- Integrate with quality, learning, and performance systems
- Add predictive agent attrition functionality

Phase 4 - Evolution (Months 16+): Continuous Innovation

- Monthly rule competitions—frontline ideas become automations
- Quarterly hackathons for new use cases
- Cross-industry automation exchange program
- Building toward Level 4 - expanded predictive capabilities

Change Management: The Make-or-Break Factor

"Technology is 20% of this," Sarah emphasized. "Change management is 80%."

She outlined the approach:

- **Co-creation:** Agents and supervisors design rules with us
- **Transparency:** Every decision is explainable and visible
- **Control:** Opt-out options and preference settings throughout
- **Celebration:** Public recognition for automation successes
- **Evolution:** Regular feedback loops to refine rules

"We're not implementing technology. We're evolving our culture to be adaptive rather than rigid."

The Philosophical Shift

Sarah returned to her opening theme. "For decades, workforce management has been about creating the perfect plan. Level 3 abandons that quest. Instead of a perfect plan executed imperfectly, we have an imperfect plan that continuously perfects itself."

She showed a visual of two loops:

Old Way: Plan → Execute → Fail → Scramble → Replan → Repeat

Level 3: Sense → Decide → Act → Learn → Adapt → Continuously

"We stop treating variance as failure. We treat it as information. We stop scheduling training and hoping it happens. We deliver training when reality allows. We stop fighting the universe. We dance with it."

The Decision Moment

The executive team exchanged glances. They'd approved many technology initiatives. This felt different—not just an upgrade but a philosophy change.

David spoke first. "Six months ago, you stabilized our chaos. You're now proposing we weaponize that chaos?"

"I'm proposing we stop calling it chaos," Sarah replied. "It's just reality. The question is whether we keep fighting it or start using it."

Margaret, who'd been reviewing the business case appendix, looked up. "You're projecting over 300% ROI within the first year. That's aggressive."

"It's conservative," Sarah responded. "Those numbers only include direct, measurable impacts—capacity gains, overtime reduction, attrition improvement. They don't capture improved customer satisfaction, reduced supervisor burden, or the compound effects of better-trained, more engaged agents."

Michael Harrison, CEO, who'd been quiet, finally spoke. "If we say yes, what's your first move?"

"Tomorrow, I gather twenty frontline agents and supervisors. We design the first three rules together. Not for them—with them. We build trust before we build automation."

Michael nodded slowly. "You stabilized Level 2 as promised. The business case is compelling—300% return in under a year is worth the risk. More importantly, you're not promising magic—you're promising disciplined evolution. Approved."

Walking Out With Purpose

As Sarah left the boardroom, her phone buzzed with messages from her team—they knew today was pitch day.

"Well?" Jennifer texted.

"We're go for Level 3. All hands tomorrow at 8 AM."

Patricia's response captured it: "Finally. We stop pretending the plan is reality and start making reality the plan."

Sarah looked at her notebook where she'd written Eisenhower's quote months earlier, with her addition: "Plans are worthless, but planning is everything. And continuous planning? That's transformation."

Level 3 wasn't just about automation. It was about accepting that perfection was impossible while making improvement inevitable. The perfect plan that never was would be replaced by something better—a system that thrived on imperfection and turned variance into value.

The real journey was about to begin.

9.2 The Journey to Automation: A Personal Perspective

Sarah's story at Midwest Mutual wasn't unique. Across the industry, WFM leaders were discovering a counterintuitive truth: efficiency comes less from perfect plans and more from systems that *use* variance. My own path to that realization crossed multiple industries and scales, each revealing a piece of the puzzle.

Learning Through Consolidation: The CLEC Years

I started in a fast-moving, acquisition-heavy telecom environment (CLECs), wearing every hat: ACD/IVR configuration, WFM parameters, QA, training, and KM. Each acquisition brought a new contact center with different tooling and habits. Some prized precision without flexibility; others ran hot on improvisation. Integrating them forced objectivity: keep what works, drop what doesn't. The best performers weren't the most complex—they were the most adaptable. Patterns emerged that later shaped my view of WFM's purpose.

Scale and Visibility: Building ROCs at a National Cable Provider

Next came scale: supporting thousands of agents across many sites and outsourcers. Small changes meant millions. We stood up a Resource Optimization Center (ROC): shared wallboards, enterprise visibility, and incident management borrowed from IT. With one view, variance became obvious—morning training cancellations echoing as afternoon coverage gaps, queues spiking in one site while capacity sat idle elsewhere. The ROC improved detection and response and pushed standardization (routing, rate codes, partner alignment) so the network behaved like one system. But the limitation was clear: the ROC still relied on human-speed actuation. By the time decisions were made and communicated, many "micro-moments" had passed.

The Automation Breakthrough: Fortune 100 Insurance

Armed with ROC experience, I joined a Fortune 100 insurer to take WFM to the next level. We built another ROC—and added an *automation layer*. Where previous ROCs saw variance and responded manually, rules now executed changes instantly: dynamic training during micro-lulls, long-call assist prompts to supervisors, and automatic adherence protection when calls ran into breaks.

The effect was immediate: more training delivered with *less* planned shrinkage, steadier service because the system reacted faster than people could, and higher agent satisfaction as exception policing faded. The ROI topped 300%: doing more with less by converting idle micro-moments into value instead of letting them evaporate.

From Practitioner to Evangelist

That experience made the shift feel inevitable. The technology wasn't a minor upgrade—it enabled a different operating model. Helping other enterprises repeat the journey, the pattern was consistent: skepticism, pilot proof, scaled adoption. It also revealed a gap in the math and language we used to plan. Two contributions followed:

- **Erlang-O.** A formalization of planning with operational overhead as a designed input—extending classic Erlang logic for dynamic, automation-ready operations.
- **The WFM Labs Maturity Model™.** The five-level framework in this book, placing automation squarely at Level 3 as the hinge from reactive to proactive.

The Vision Realized

Looking back—from CLEC integrations to enterprise ROCs to automation at scale—the thread is consistent: variance, when instrumented, becomes an asset. The insurance implementation wasn't just another command center; it was proof that dynamic delivery beats static reservation: more training, steadier SL, lower cost, and a better agent experience, achieved *because of* variance, not despite it.

This is the roadmap, not an anomaly. The capability to adopt Level 3 now exists for any operation willing to trade pre-booked activities for real-time placement driven by variance. The question is not *if* you move to automation-driven WFM, but *how quickly*—before competitors turn the same variance you fight into capacity they harvest.

What follows in Chapter 9. We detail how large organizations operationalize this at scale: rule design, safety guardrails, measurement, and change management—so automation presses the right buttons, at the right time, for the right reasons.

9.3 STaRS Framework Application: When Level 3 Makes Sense

Not every organization is ready for Level 3. The STaRS frame—*Startup, Turnaround, Realignment, Sustaining Success*—adds needed context for when (and how aggressively) to pursue real-time automation. Sarah's success at Midwest Mutual wasn't just technology; it fit the org's situation. Use STaRS to answer: *Should we do Level 3 now? How fast? Where will resistance/support appear?*

Startup: build right, not fast

Level 3 is attractive but premature without foundations. Risks: little historical data to shape rules, unstable processes that automation would "freeze," small-scale economics that dilute ROI, and gaps in L2 basics (forecasting, scheduling, real-time).

Path for startups (prepare the ground):

- Install solid L2: interval definitions, cadence, variance log.
- Pick a WFM platform with APIs and automation integration capabilities.
- Capture variance patterns early; hire RTAs who embrace tooling.
- Set a trigger: e.g., implement at ≥200 agents or ≥18 months of data.

Turnaround: use automation as accelerant

When metrics slip, costs climb, and morale dips, L3 can catalyze recovery if sequenced well. Benefits: visible wins in weeks, cost relief without layoffs, objective rule-based decisions, and a signal of committed change.

Turnaround playbook (90 days to momentum):

1. **Start with pain relief:** automate high-friction work (adherence protections, break nudges).
2. **Over-communicate:** position as job-preserving competitiveness, not headcount reduction.
3. **Measure everything:** publish incident counts, time-to-stabilize, and outcome deltas.
4. **Move fast:** pilot → prove → expand; perfection later.

Realignment: the sweet spot

Performance is okay but momentum stalls; competition pressures rise. Foundations are stable, data is rich, resources exist. This is ideal for systematic L3 adoption.

Realignment advantages (methodical transformation):

- Comprehensive current-state + variance mapping before rule design.

- Cross-functional rule stewardship (Ops, WFM, QA, Training, HR).
- Link to strategy (e.g., CX consistency, growth efficiency).
- Measured pacing: multi-iteration pilots, 6–18 month rollout.

Sustaining success: innovate at the edge

Leaders ask, "Why change?" Because advantage decays. L3 deepens the moat, attracts talent, expands margin, and lets you learn safely from strength.

Approach for leaders:

- Position as innovation leadership, not fix-it work.
- Start with volunteer high-performers; let pull beat push.
- Benchmark against the possible, not just peers.
- Embed rules into existing excellence rituals and reviews.

The STaRS decision snapshot

- **Startup:** build toward L3; 12–18 month runway.
- **Turnaround:** L3 as catalyst; 3–6 month aggressive timeline.
- **Realignment:** systematic L3; 6–18 month paced rollout.
- **Sustaining:** selective L3 for edge; 6–12 month targeted deployments.

Sarah's context

Midwest Mutual sat in *Realignment*: stable enough to invest, pressured enough to change. That shaped the pilot scope, rule selection, and rollout cadence—and explains why L3 stuck. Your STaRS position won't decide the *if*, but it should govern the *how fast, where first*, and *how to message*—all decisive for Level 3 success.

9.4 Understanding Level 3: The Automation Revolution

Level 3 is more than an upgrade—it is a shift in operating philosophy. Plans still matter, but *continuous planning* becomes the system: the operation senses variance and acts, turning micro-moments into value at scale. Technology enables this; the transformation is ultimately organizational.

The automation landscape (and why contact centers are different)

General automation (DPA/RPA/BPA) excels at predictable, linear workflows—claims, forms, back-office steps. ETL jobs, scripts, and no/low-code tools move data and trigger tasks on schedules. Contact centers face a different problem: thousands of micro-decisions per minute under changing conditions. Traditional platforms that thrive on batch logic and exports struggle here; Level 3 requires a real-time layer that reads the ACD/WFM heartbeat and executes small, safe actions without delay.

An origin story (illustrative, not prescriptive)

A pioneer that began as a training company, Knowlagent, founded by Matt McConnell, saw scheduled training repeatedly sacrificed to protect SL and shifted to *intraday* delivery. By 2013 it rebranded as Intradiem to reflect that mission: harvest variance in real time rather than fight it.

What makes intraday automation distinct

- **Placement in the stack.** A real-time "nervous system" between ACD and WFM, vendor-agnostic to major telephony and WFM platforms.
- **Low Latency.** Real-time reads and actions capture the fleeting availability windows that 5- to 15 minute refresh cycles miss.
- **Rule stewardship by WFM.** Analysts author and iterate rules without code, closing the loop daily instead of via IT tickets and release cycles.

Goodbye monolith; hello integrated ecosystem

Level 3 favors best-of-breed components connected by live integrations: WFM for short-term forecasting and scheduling, a real-time automation layer for actuation, and specialized tools for capacity planning (Level 4) and enterprise orchestration (Level 5). The value lies in orchestration—not in any single platform.

Core characteristics of Level 3 operations

- **Automation as the nervous system.** Variance generates signals; rules choose and execute the smallest effective move.
- **Dynamic activity queues.** Training, coaching, comms, and project work sit in priority queues and deploy when queue health allows.
- **Instant variance response.** Spikes defer non-critical work; lulls trigger development; long calls surface assists—within seconds.
- **Planned overhead, lower than before.** Build a modest buffer, then convert micro-idle into development—often reducing planned shrinkage while *increasing* completed training.

- **Leaders shift from firefighting to configuration.** Attention moves from chasing exceptions to refining rules and guardrails.

What this looks like in practice (no clock, just flow)

Early arrivals create small availability pockets—micro-modules deploy before lines open. If arrivals run light, queued coaching and compliance launch automatically and are tracked back to WFM. A marketing surge hits; the system pauses non-critical items, nudges eligible early breaks, and surfaces long-call assists. When demand normalizes, deferred items resume and missed learners receive re-offers. The ROC monitors and tunes; the system does the pressing.

The spectrum of automation use cases (representative, not exhaustive)

Employee development. Dynamic training; supervisor "available for coaching" pairing; just-in-time knowledge refreshers.

Communication that lands. Priority comms during cognitive slack; urgent updates with completion tracking; cultural moments woven into the day.

Wellness & support. Microbreak intelligence after tough sequences; fatigue flags from extended ACW; recognition prompts during positive windows.

Operational optimization. Automatic break/lunch adjustments; fluid voice–chat–email switches for multi-skilled agents.

On-call assistance. Long-call prompts that route contextual help; ACW interventions that ask before escalating; tech-issue detection that pulls IT proactively.

Flexible work at scale. Real-time VTO/VOT, attendance adjustments, and bite-sized project work when coverage permits.

A day—end to end

Mid-shift, lunch windows smooth automatically; post-lunch dips get short wellness content; minor overstaffing triggers VTO for opted-in agents; shift end trims overtime via early-release nudges; the evening team inherits a stable, well-documented state. Every action is rules-based, auditable, and reversible; every outcome feeds next week's rule tuning.

Why this sets up Levels 4 and 5

Level 3 creates a living dataset of *signals → actions → outcomes*. That closed loop fuels Level 4 predictive models and Level 5 autonomous optimization. Getting Level 3 right still depends on GRPIT: *clear goals*, *role stewardship of rules*, *process guardrails*, *interpersonal trust*, and the *technology* wiring to act safely. The next sections apply GRPIT so automation scales without surprises.

9.5 Goals (G) — From Plan Defense to Outcome Optimization

Automation only scales what you can see. Tie every rule to a concrete measure—*Automation Acceptance Rate (AAR)* for adoption, *Variance Capture Efficiency (VCE)* for realized value, *Service-Level Stability (SLS)* for steadiness of delivery, and *Supervisor Coaching Ratio (SCR)* for manager focus—and keep one source of truth for formulas. Treat these as representative options you may adopt; a simple starter set works too—e.g., track weekly *hours of training* and *hours of coaching* delivered versus a pre-automation baseline—then expand as automation rules mature. This turns "pilot" into weekly portfolio management.

Level 3 shifts success from *forcing reality to match the plan* to *optimizing outcomes whatever reality delivers*. Where Level 2 guarded the plan, Level 3 treats variance as fuel: better service stability, *more* development, and *lower* cost—simultaneously—through automation.

Evolving the classic metrics (don't drop them—upgrade them)

Service level stability, not just attainment. Monthly 80/30 with wild daily swings is customer whiplash. Track interval stability (e.g., stdev or coefficient of variation of SL across the day) and aim to flatten the curve as automation harvests variance. Stability improves experience and reduces pressure swings.

Training hours: planned vs. harvested. Planned hours may fall while delivered hours soar. One insurer cut planned training from 3% to 1.8% and delivered 360% more hours by capturing micro-lulls. Report *both*: planned vs. harvested, and celebrate when harvested exceeds planned.

Handle time intelligence. AHT stays, but becomes actionable. Use controlled tests (e.g., long-call assist on/off) to isolate impact by call type and tenure; a 5–15s reduction at scale is material. Shift the metric from blunt average to targeted intervention evidence.

Overtime transformation. Goal evolves from "minimize OT" to "eliminate *unintentional* OT and deploy *planned* OT strategically." End-of-shift rules, early-break nudges, and dynamic VTO/VOT reduce waste OT while preserving coverage.

New metrics for the automation age

Automation Acceptance Rate (AAR). When prompts fire (training, break adjust, assist), what % are accepted?

$$\text{AAR} = \frac{\#\ \text{accepted prompts}}{\#\ \text{total prompts}} \times 100$$

Slice by rule, time of day, tenure. Healthy rules clear 85%+; low AAR flags timing, content, or trust issues.

Variance Capture Efficiency (VCE).   How much positive variance becomes value?

$$\text{VCE} = \frac{\sum \text{minutes of harvested activities}}{\sum \text{minutes of available variance}} \times 100$$

Where available variance per interval measures the surplus capacity you could potentially harvest—calculated as the number of surplus agents multiplied by the interval length:

$$\text{available variance} \approx \max(0, \text{staffed} - \text{required}) \times \text{interval minutes}$$

The $\max(0, \ldots)$ ensures we only count positive surplus; if you're understaffed, there's no variance to harvest. For example: 50 agents staffed with 45 required in a 15-minute interval yields $(50 - 45) \times 15 = 75$ minutes of harvestable capacity.

Employee Experience Index (EEI).   A composite, read as dynamically as CX:

- perceived schedule control,
- development cadence (training/coaching touchpoints),
- stress signals (adherence exceptions, escalations),
- growth velocity (new skills, AHT improvements),
- engagement markers (voluntary participation, peer assists).

Weight locally; trend weekly, not just annually.

Supervisor Coaching Ratio (SCR).   Quantify the time shift from admin to development/coaching:

$$\text{SCR} = \frac{\text{time on coaching/development}}{\text{total supervisor time}} \times 100$$

Use calendar tags, workflow logs, and ROC tickets to instrument it. Level 3 should flip the Level-2 ratio (e.g., from 30/70 to 60/40+). Direction and magnitude matter more than a universal target.

Building the measurement framework (make it drive the day)

- **Balance leading and lagging.** AAR and VCE predict; Service-Level Stability and delivered training confirm. Use both.
- **Tie every rule to a metric.** Long-call assist → AHT tail reduction; break automation → adherence exceptions; dynamic training → completion and time-to-complete. No orphaned automations.
- **Evolve with maturity.** Early: adoption (AAR). Mid: efficiency (VCE by rule). Late: second-order effects (CSAT/FCR lift from better training cadence).
- **Make it visible.** Put VCE and SLS on ROC panes; show SCR in manager forums; share EEI pulse weekly. Visibility creates momentum.
- **Govern the math.** Keep one source of truth and change control on formulas (Section 8.4); document rule→metric mappings so improvements are attributable.

Sarah's Level-3 dashboard (weekly, one screen)

- SLS index (intraday stdev) by Lne of business.
- VCE overall and top/bottom 5 rules by capture minutes.
- AAR by rule, tenure band, and hour of day.
- Delivered training: harvested vs. planned; avg time-to-complete.
- Adherence exceptions per 100 agents (should crater vs. Level 2).
- SCR: % supervisor time on coaching vs. admin ratio.

Bottom line. Level 3 success is measured by *how well you turn variance into value.* Keep the classics, add AAR and VCE, and wire metrics directly to rules. Do that, and "plan defense" gives way to outcome optimization—daily, visibly, and at scale.

9.6 Roles (R) — Evolution of WFM Functions

Level 3 does not remove roles; it *elevates* them. Automation (Section 9.4) shifts effort from manual actuation to rule design, measurement (Section 9.5), and cross-functional optimization. The same three pillars from Level 2 (Section 8.5) remain—forecasting, scheduling, real-time—but the work tilts from *defending plans* to *improving outcomes* in the ROC environment (Section 8.9).

Real-time analyst → automation orchestrator

At Level 2, RTAs fought fires; at Level 3, they architect automated responses and tune the system.

Core responsibilities.

- **Rule design & optimization.** Map incident patterns to Rule→Trigger→Action logic (e.g., long-call assist, break protection, dynamic training). Start small, pilot, measure AAR/VCE (Section 9.5), then scale.
- **Experimentation cadence.** Run A/B toggles, threshold sweeps, and holdouts; retire low-value rules. Maintain a changelog with owner, hypothesis, guardrails, and rollback.
- **Pattern recognition.** Mine acceptance, timing, and tenure effects (e.g., "Fri 3–5pm training AAR dips; nudge after breaks works better"); feed insights to L&D, QM, and Knowledge.
- **Proactive interventions.** Design early-warning rules (fatigue, ACW overrun, repeated escalations) that escalate from self-help to supervisor assist.
- **Narratives with numbers.** Publish weekly "top value rules," "silent cost rules," and "next hypotheses," tying rule impact to Service-Level Stability (SLS), AHT tails, adherence exceptions, and training completion.

The RTA rule lifecycle (lightweight).

1. *Spot* a repeatable variance pattern in the ROC log (Section 8.9).

2. *Draft* the rule with guardrails (SL floor, occupancy band from Section 8.4).

3. *Pilot* with a small cohort; collect AAR, VCE, AHT/SL changes.

4. *Decide*: scale, tweak, or retire based on effect size and trust.

5. *Document*: owner, intent, metrics, change history, rollback.

Skills that matter. Applied data literacy (interval reads, causal sanity checks), rule-builder fluency, experiment design, concise stakeholder comms, and cross-functional facilitation.

A new role emerges: the *Automation Strategist*

Often grown from senior RTAs, this role steers the portfolio and bridges WFM and tech.

- **Bridge & translate.** Align operational constraints (SL, occupancy, shrinkage policy) with platform capabilities; ensure rules serve outcomes, not the tool.
- **Rule library & templates.** Curate proven patterns (e.g., "new-hire 90-day pack," "seasonal surge set"); provide safe defaults and guardrails.
- **ROI & governance.** Tie rules to *owned* metrics (AAR, VCE, SLS, SCR from Section 9.5); run change control with test windows and rollback criteria (Section 8.4).
- **Change management.** Design pilots that create early wins; seed champions in Ops, L&D, and QA; keep "how it works" transparent to build trust.

Supervisor focus (from policing to coaching)

Automation removes exception churn; supervisors return to people leadership.

- **No more schedule policing.** Break/lunch protection and auto-adjustments erase most adherence tickets; supervisors stop approving minutiae.
- **Higher-quality coaching.** Dynamic training/coaching delivery keeps sessions; one-on-ones focus on skills and CX outcomes, not exceptions.
- **Intelligent alerts.** Intervene where humans add value (e.g., contextual long-call assist); avoid random walk supervision.
- **Measure the shift.** Track the *Supervisor Coaching Ratio* (SCR, Section 9.5) to show time moving from admin → coaching.

Forecasters and schedulers at Level 3

Forecasters. Use stable SL to reduce "catch-up" games; publish risk bands and event tags the automation can consume (e.g., thresholds for defer/protect rules). Feed back variance learnings to improve arrival/AHT assumptions; maintain the adaptability budget that rules will harvest.

Schedulers. With significant training and coaching moved out of pre-bookings, schedulers gain capacity to improve the fundamentals: sharper vacation and shift bids, better preference windows, and tighter VTO/VOT analysis. Pull schedulers into the automation journey: publish a rolling two-week outlook that flags interval over/under on the plan, highlight risk lanes, and validate that rules acted as intended (defer/protect/adjust) against the roster. Design *for* flexibility—fewer static blocks, more micro-windows the engine can use, blended-skill templates, and protections encoded as rules/flags; the system does the nudging.

Team operating model (cadence and artifacts)

- **Daily (15 min).** ROC "rule health" huddle: yesterday's AAR/VCE, any guardrail hits, today's watchlist.
- **Weekly.** Rule review: top/bottom value, pilots to promote, candidates to retire; share two insights with L&D/QA.
- **Monthly.** Portfolio tune: refresh thresholds for seasonality, audit guardrails, update templates; republish role charters with Level-3 duties (Section 8.5).
- **Artifacts.** Rule registry (owner, hypothesis, guardrails, metrics), playbooks (by scenario), and a living governance page (formulas, data sources, effective dates).

Sarah's Level-3 role checklist (ready-to-run)

- RTAs trained on the rule lifecycle; each owns ≥ 2 pilots with defined AAR/VCE targets.
- Supervisor enablement: "no-exceptions" policy for protected adjustments; coaching time goal with Supervisor Coaching Ratio (SCR) tracking.
- Forecast handoff includes risk bands and event tags consumable by rules; scheduler templates expose micro-windows.
- Automation strategist named; rule library and change board active; rollback is rehearsed.
- Dashboards show SLS, VCE, AAR, adherence exceptions, delivered training, and SCR side-by-side (Section 9.5).

Bottom line. Level 3 roles trade keystrokes for levers. RTAs design and tune rules, supervisors coach, forecasters and schedulers design for adaptability, and an automation strategist curates the portfolio. The organization spends less time enforcing the plan and more time improving the system that meets reality on its own terms.

9.7 Processes (P) — Dynamic Execution

At Level 3, automation (Section 9.4) doesn't just speed work; it rewrites the playbook. The safest path is evolutionary: *each new rule triggers a mini process review* rather than a big-bang rewrite. Tie those reviews to the ROC cadence (Section 8.9) and to the measurement model you set in Section 9.5. Document changes as living artifacts, not binders (Section 8.6).

Process transformation: schedule adherence

Level 2 treats adherence as a top-line performance metric with heavy admin load.

Traditional (Level 2) — a typical flow:

1. Call overruns a break → agent messages supervisor.
2. Supervisor validates and files exception in WFM.
3. WFM reviews, approves/denies; reports roll up weekly.
4. Repeat for lunches/meetings; escalate repeat "violations."

Level 3 — automation handles the physics:

1. Overrun detected in real time; break/lunch auto-adjusted within guardrails.
2. WFM platform updated; agent notified ("Your break was shifted after the call.").
3. No tickets, no approvals, no retro reports—audit trail lives in the rule log.

So what: most "adherence exceptions" disappear. Many Level 3 shops retire adherence as a scored KPI and replace it with outcome metrics: Service-Level Stability (SLS), AAR (acceptance), fatigue indicators, and wellness (Section 9.5). Keep an audit view for compliance; drop the punitive loop.

Process transformation: training delivery

Level 2 assumes predictability and pre-schedules; cancellations abound. Level 3 splits *what* to automate from *what* to schedule.

Decision tree (own once, reuse often; see Figure 9.1).

1. L&D defines need and content.
2. **Dynamic eligibility?**
   - ≤30 minutes, interruptible, no special equipment ⇒ dynamic.
   - Long workshops, labs, or compliance with proctors ⇒ scheduled.
   - Hard-deadline compliance ⇒ hybrid (dynamic first, mop-up scheduled).
3. **If dynamic:** chunk to 5–15 min modules; set prerequisites, priorities, targeting; load into the automation queue; measure AAR/VCE and completion (Section 9.5).
4. **If scheduled:** block only what cannot be chunked; automation *protects* those blocks unless critical guardrails trip.
5. Track completions for both paths; use analytics to re-chunk or retarget low-AAR content.

Two more quick evolutions

Break/lunch orchestration.

- **L2:** fixed placements; manual shuffles at risk; exception backlog.
- **L3:** early/late nudges within occupancy band; auto-protection on overruns; supervisor freed from approvals. Measure: adherence tickets ↓, SL variance around meal windows ↓ (Section 9.5).

VTO/VOT & end-of-shift.

- **L2:** emails/chats, late decisions, accidental OT.
- **L3:** rules offer VTO ahead of overstaffed blocks; suppress new calls in last n minutes; offer micro-OT when beneficial. Measure: unintentional OT ↓, agent NPS on flexibility ↑.

Process evolution principles

- **Incremental documentation.** Update SOPs when a rule goes live; link each step to Rule→Trigger→Action and its guardrails.
- **Question necessity.** Don't just automate old steps; remove them. If breaks auto-adjust, retire exception queues.
- **Design for exceptions.** Define "automation defers to human" criteria (e.g., regulatory blocks, customer harm risk, edge-tech failures) and who decides. Capture learnings back into rules.
- **Measure outcomes, not paperwork.** Swap "exceptions processed" for SLS, VCE, delivered development, fatigue reduction (Section 9.5).
- **Cross-functional by design.** Processes span WFM, Ops, L&D, QA, HR, IT; make owners explicit and handoffs lightweight (Section 8.5).

The living process framework (what you keep current)

- **Rule registry:** owner, hypothesis, guardrails (SL/occupancy), metrics (AAR/VCE), change history, rollback.
- **Playbooks:** by scenario (surge, outage, weather, marketing drop) mapping who-to-alert and which rules to bias.
- **Cadence:** daily ROC "rule health" (10–15 min), weekly portfolio review, monthly audit of guardrails/templates (Section 8.9).
- **Stop-doing list:** legacy steps retired this month (and the risk they removed).

Sarah's lightweight process audit (quarterly)

- For each high-volume SOP, mark steps now automated, steps still human, and why.
- Verify every human step has a *timer* (SLA) and an *owner*.
- Confirm guardrails align with Section 8.4 (SL definition, short-abandon policy, occupancy band).
- Check dashboards show outcomes tied to the process (SLS, AAR, VCE, exceptions avoided).
- Publish a one-page delta: "what changed," "how to act," "who to call if it misfires."

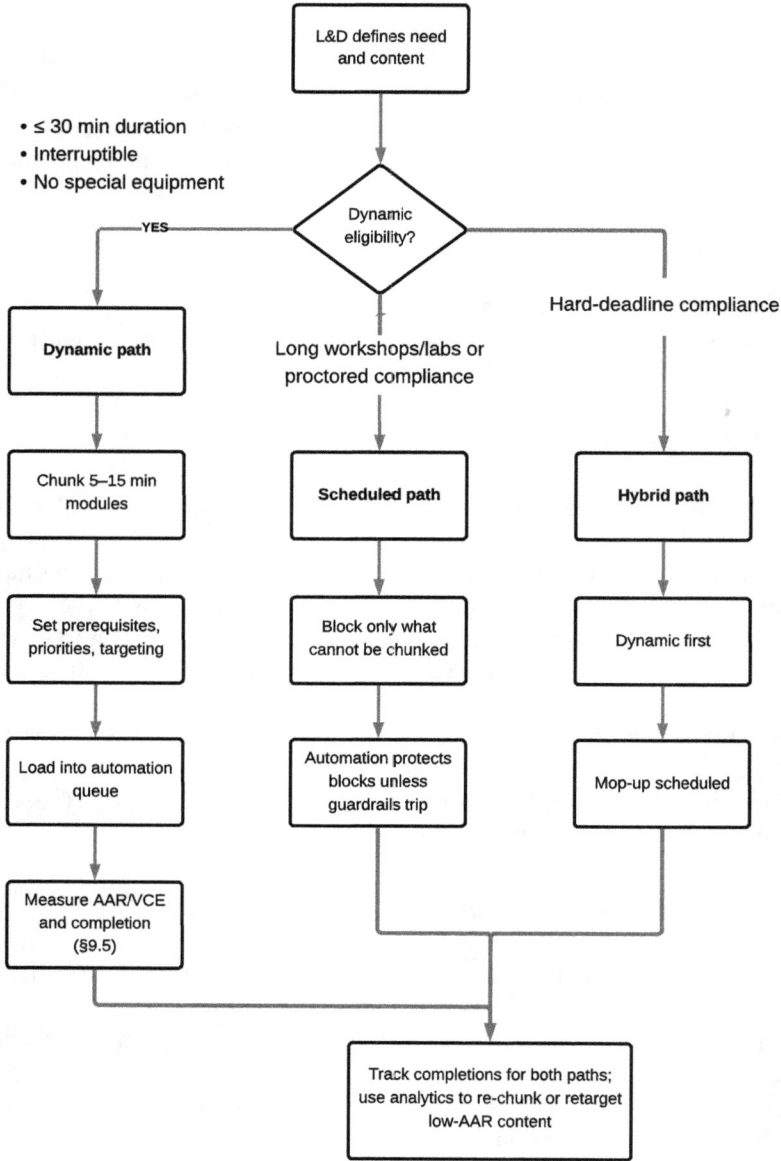

Figure 9.1: Sample decision tree for automation.

Bottom line. Level 3 replaces static, pre-planned workflows with condition-based execution. Keep processes alive, trim what automation makes obsolete, and wire outcomes into the ROC rhythm. The work shifts from *following steps* to *tuning the system* that meets reality on its own terms.

9.8 Interpersonal (I) — Trust and Partnership

The best automation fails without *trust*. Level 3 stands or falls on relationships—agents with tech, supervisors with systems, WFM with operations. Tooling rarely fixes a trust problem. Process and metric upgrades help (Sections 9.5 and 9.7), but the interpersonal shift is what makes them stick—especially where Level 2 tensions ran hot (Section 8.7).

A short trust equation for automation

$$\text{Trust} \propto \frac{\text{Transparency} + \text{Benefit} + \text{Control}}{\text{Risk}}.$$

Transparency. Explain *what* fired and *why*. Black boxes breed suspicion; short, plain-language reasons build confidence. *Example:* "Your break moved because your call ran over; adherence protected and customer served." Tie explanations to published guardrails.

Benefit. Make value personal and immediate (fewer exceptions, protected breaks, faster help), then show the org lift second. Rising acceptance/acknowledgement rates validate perceived benefit (Section 9.5).

Control. Options beat mandates. Let agents defer/decline training, snooze nudges, or request help on long calls. Optionality typically *raises* acceptance and reduces pushback (Section 9.5).

Risk. Name fears—jobs, surveillance, loss of flexibility—and answer plainly. Align words with actions (e.g., redeploy time to coaching, manage staffing via attrition, not layoffs). Keep an audit trail without turning it into a cudgel.

Partnering with agents (co-design, not sell-to)

Involve early, not after. Stand up a mixed agent council (new hires, veterans, high performers, skeptics) to co-design the pilot. Use early listening to tune the timing and copy of prompts before scaling.

Communicate like adults. Skip spin. "Automation will handle routine schedule adjustments so you can focus on customers; most prompts are accept-or-defer; this is about better jobs, not fewer."

Close the loop fast. Make changes visible: "Based on feedback, training offers now wait until post-ACW." Publish small A/Bs (acceptance, completion time, CSAT deltas) so people *see* impact (Section 9.5).

Use champions *and* skeptics. Convert a respectful skeptic and you gain your strongest advocate.

Supervisor empowerment (from cop to coach)

Automation removes the exception treadmill; supervisors reclaim time for development (Section 9.6).

Reframe the role. Share peer stories: "My first uninterrupted coaching in months." Provide coaching playbooks aligned to dynamic delivery (who, when, what).

Tech as power tool. Involve supervisors in selecting signal views, validating alert useful-ness, and proposing rule tweaks through a clear review path—ownership without everyone driving the car.

Collaborate across teams. Dynamic sharing (skills, channels) works when supervisors optimize the whole, not just "my team." Use shared metrics and joint huddles to reinforce system thinking.

WFM & Operations: from service provider to partner

The ROC (Section 8.9) is the natural forum: shared boards, shared incidents, shared wins.

Shared accountability. Tie goals both own to outcomes (Service-Level Stability, variance capture efficiency, development delivered) (Section 9.5).

Co-create rules. Ops brings ground truth; WFM brings constraints and levers. Workshop Rule→Trigger→Action together; test small; publish results (Section 9.7).

Transparent logic. Expose rule rationales and postmortems. When a rule misfires, analyze together; turn blame into learning.

Extend the partnership network

L&D. Co-design microcontent (5–15 min), sequencing, and targeting so it fits dynamic windows; keep monoliths only where necessary (Section 9.7).

IT. Treat integrations/performance as an ongoing product, not a project. Hold regular tech reviews; maintain a rollback plan.

HR. Update policies as processes evolve (e.g., fewer adherence exceptions, new supervisor competencies). Align incentives to outcome metrics.

Quality. Route targeted refreshers from evals; measure downstream effects (FCR, AHT bands) (Section 9.5).

Make trust durable (cadence, not campaigns)

Celebrate. Share quick wins (exception queue down 90%, coaching hours up, prompt acceptance above 85%).

Own the misses. Acknowledge noise ("break nudges were too chatty; we tuned the cool-down"). Fix fast; show before/after.

Keep evolving. Run monthly retros on relationships as well as rules: Where is trust thin? Which partnerships need refresh? Feed findings into the ROC rhythm (Section 8.9).

A lightweight trust checklist

- Every prompt has a one-line "why" message tied to published guardrails.
- Agent council meets biweekly during pilots; changes and A/Bs published within the month.
- Supervisors have stake in alert thresholds and see impact on outcomes.
- Shared dashboards show rule fires, accept/decline rates, and outcome deltas (Section 9.5).

• Monthly ROC retro covers *people* signals (sentiment, feedback themes) alongside ops metrics (Section 8.9).

Bottom line. Level 3 is a relationship upgrade as much as a technology one. Make interventions explainable, benefits personal, choices real, and risks addressed. When trust and partnership take root, automation stops feeling like control and starts reading as support—and the culture changes with the metrics.

9.9 Technology (T) — Intelligent Automation Platforms

Sarah didn't sell software at Midwest Mutual; she sold a different way of operating. The platform mattered only as the nervous system that could sense, decide, and act in real time. In the first month, she told the team, "If this feels like a tool rollout, we've missed it. The point isn't buttons—it's what the buttons let us do at machine speed."

How she framed the mandate

In the ROC war room, Sarah drew three circles on the glass wall:

ACD — "This is our pulse: queue health, agent states, handle times."
WFM — "This is our plan: forecasts, schedules, adherence history."
LMS/Comms — "This is our content and messages."

"The automation layer," she said, sketching a thin ring connecting them, "lives between these circles. It reads the pulse, respects the plan, and delivers the right thing, right now." Heads nodded; suddenly "integration" wasn't an architecture diagram—it was a promise of flow.

From demo theater to proof

Vendors promised "real time." Sarah didn't argue; she tested. A two-week proof of concept used a small life-insurance pod, three rules (break protection, dynamic training, long-call assist), and one hard constraint—*bi-directional* schedule updates into the WFM system. Day one, the platform nudged two breaks; the WFM calendar reflected both within seconds. Day two, an 18-minute death-claim call triggered a discreet assist offer; the supervisor joined with context, AHT fell, agent stress fell further. Day three, early arrivals received 3-minute modules pulled from the LMS queue, logged automatically to learning records. The demo was over. They had a working loop.

What the platform actually *does* all day

At 8:07 AM, five agents clear simultaneously in Claims. The platform has already evaluated queue health (*green band*), checked agent calendars in WFM (*no meetings, breaks 20+ minutes away*), pulled next-priority micro-modules from the LMS (*eligible, interruptible*), and delivered two without touching the other three (one declined—system logs the declination for later timing). No tickets, no pings, no "are we good to send training?" chatter. By 8:09, two completions are written back to the LMS and WFM.

At 11:42, an annuities call crosses the long-call threshold for its *type* (not a blanket 15 minutes—context-aware). A subtle prompt asks the agent if help would be useful. "Yes" routes a snapshot to the supervisor: call intent, customer tenure, agent tenure, recommended KB article. If the supervisor joins, the platform pauses any pending training for that agent and reschedules without penalty. Adherence exceptions never enter the chat, because the platform has already moved the lunch block in WFM.

At 4:55, end-of-shift protection activates. New calls won't hit agents inside the 5-minute window; a few available agents receive early-release offers. Overtime quietly evaporates. The ROC monitors, but the system does the moving.

Why Level 2 tech wasn't enough

Traditional WFM ran on intervals and uploads. It could *see* a lull; it could not *harvest* it before the lull ended. RPA could push a form; it could not weigh queue risk, agent readiness, prerequisites, and break proximity in under a second. Intraday automation brought three capabilities the team had never had at once:

1) *Continuous signal ingestion* from ACDs (agent states, skills, wrap codes) and WFM (current schedule, adherence) without 5–15 minute polling.
2) *A rules engine* analysts could author themselves—nested conditions, soft/hard constraints, priorities—without opening IT tickets.
3) *Closed-loop writes* back into systems of record so changes were audited and trustworthy.

The difference wasn't a faster report. It was a platform that could act while humans were still noticing.

Trust by design (not decree)

Week one of the pilot almost derailed on culture, not code. Sarah used the platform's transparency to repair trust: every intervention showed its "why." When an agent asked, "Why did my break move?" the audit panel showed: *Call overran by 3:11, queue risk low, adherence protected, lunch shifted +6, WFM updated at 12:31:07*. When a training prompt arrived at a bad moment, declination was a valid choice—and a signal. Acceptance rates climbed as the system respected control.

How Sarah chose without a spreadsheet beauty contest

She scored vendors against *her* first five rules, not generic feature grids:

- Could they *prove* real-time decisions with nested logic on her data? (She replayed Wednesday's traffic to simulate "what would have happened.")
- Would they write back to WFM and LMS cleanly, with human-readable audits?
- Could analysts build and A/B test rules without code and without IT?
- Did the APIs and webhooks look like something her team could live with?
- How quickly could they recover from a broken integration or version bump?

References mattered—but only where scale, stack, and complexity *rhymed* with Midwest Mutual. One peer warned about rule sprawl; that single comment birthed Sarah's lightweight governance in Section 9.11: version control, a weekly rule review, and a rollback playbook.

Security and scrutiny without drama

Compliance didn't slow them because the platform treated it as a first-class feature: role-based access so supervisors saw their teams, not the enterprise; immutable logs for every action; OAuth 2.0 and mutual TLS across integrations; data residency configurations for regulated lines. When Legal asked for a right-to-erasure workflow, the vendor showed it live. The conversation moved on.

Build or buy (and what they *did* build)

They *bought* the intraday automation platform. Building that core—real-time ACD/WFM integrations, versioning, latency/reliability, security audits—was not realistic for the enterprise timeline. What they *built around* it was theirs: a rule library (playbooks of proven patterns), a thin analytics layer blending automation data with CX/quality, and a small service that standardized agent attributes across HR, WFM, and ACD. They bought speed; they built differentiation.

Future-proofing without futurism

Eighteen months in, the platform still felt invisible—which was the point. Yet it was ready for what came next: event streams clean enough for ML features (Section 9.13), channel-aware rules that respected async work in chat/email, and hybrid deployment as telephony modernized. The stack didn't trap them at Level 3; it prepared the runway for Level 4.

The quiet test of good technology

On a Tuesday afternoon, a visiting VP asked to "see the tool." Sarah pointed at the floor. Agents were learning between calls, supervisors were coaching, the ROC was calm. "You're already seeing it," she said. Good Level 3 tech disappears into behavior: fewer cancellations, steadier service, lighter admin, better coaching, clearer audits. The story wasn't software; the story was everything the software made *boringly* reliable—so people could do the work only people can do.

9.10 The Business Case for Level 3

When Sarah briefed Midwest Mutual's executives, the pilot data did the heavy lifting: 360% more training delivered, a 15s AHT reduction, 94% fewer adherence exceptions, and agent satisfaction rising from 3.4 to 4.1. But strong numbers need a clear narrative. A complete case for Level 3 ties *why it works* (variance harvesting), *how it scales* (rules and ROC cadence, Sections 8.9 and 9.7), and *what you measure* (AAR, VCE, Supervisor Coaching Ratio (SCR, Section 9.5))—plus the cost of doing nothing.

The mathematics of variance harvesting

Classic cases chase cost-out; Level 3 shows *"more with less"* is real: less planned overhead, more development, steadier service.

Baseline (1,000 agents).

- Fully loaded cost/agent: $40,000 ⇒ $40M labor.
- Planned training/coaching shrinkage: 5.5% ⇒ $2.2M.
- Actual delivery at Level 2: 47% of planned ⇒ $1.034M; $1.166M effectively wasted.

With Level 3.

- Planned shrinkage reduced to 3.4% ⇒ $1.36M (budget *saves* $0.84M).
- Harvested delivery ≈ 360% of prior actual ⇒ $3.72M-equivalent activity.
- Net value: $0.84M budget + $2.686M incremental development "value"[1] ⇒ $3.526M/year.

The engine: micro-moments. Ten agents free for three minutes is 30 minutes of productive time; repeated across the day and population, it compounds into hours of development without pre-blocked shrinkage.

Direct ROI components (attribution you can defend)

AHT reduction. Pilot: −15 seconds via long-call assists and just-in-time knowledge (Section 9.4). For 3,000 agents at 100 calls/day:

$$3,000 \times 100 \times 15s = 4,500,000s/day \approx 1,250 \text{ hours/day.}$$

Annualized (250 days): 312,500 hours. That's ≈ 155–170 FTEs depending on assumed annual productive hours (2,000–1,850) ⇒ $6.2–$6.8M at $40k/FTE. Even half the effect funds the program.

Overtime reduction. Typical 5–8% OT drops to 2–3% with end-of-shift protection, dynamic VTO, and better balancing:

$$\Delta OT \approx 2\text{–}4\% \text{ of } \$40M \Rightarrow \$0.8\text{–}1.6M/\text{year (1,000 agents).}$$

Turnover reduction. If Level 3 trims annual attrition by 10 points (e.g., 50% → 40%):

$$100 \text{ fewer replacements} \times \$6,000 \approx \$600k \text{ (recruit+training)}$$
$$+ \text{ productivity lift} \approx \$400k \Rightarrow \sim \$1M.$$

---

[1]Valued at the same cost basis as planned shrinkage for apples-to-apples comparison.

Administrative efficiency. Supervisors reclaim ≥2.5 hours/day from exceptions and rescheduling; RTAs shift to rule design (Section 9.6):

$$100 \text{ supervisors} \times 2.5 \times 250 = 62{,}500 \text{ hours} \Rightarrow \$1.9M \text{ at } \$30/hr.$$

Putting the pieces together. These results roll up into four defensible value streams—*shrinkage budget saves, AHT reduction, overtime reduction,* and *administrative efficiency.* Figure 9.2 shows their *relative share* on a common 1,000-agent baseline; absolute amounts follow the modeled calculations above. Aim for *composition, not false precision*: what actually funds the Level 3 journey.

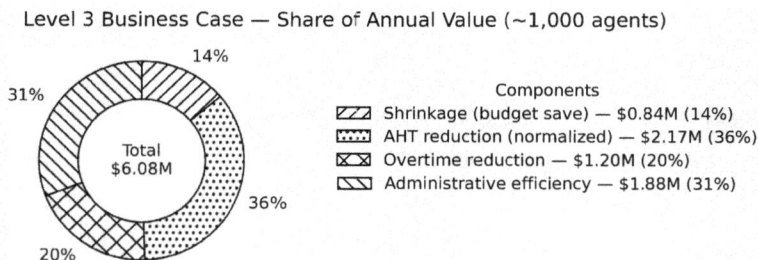

Level 3 Business Case — Share of Annual Value (~1,000 agents)

31% 14% 36% 20%

Total $6.08M

Components
- Shrinkage (budget save) — $0.84M (14%)
- AHT reduction (normalized) — $2.17M (36%)
- Overtime reduction — $1.20M (20%)
- Administrative efficiency — $1.88M (31%)

Figure 9.2: Business Case for Automation

Hidden value streams (often missed, material in scale)

Service level stability premium. Variance capture smooths SL (fewer 95/65 whiplashes), avoiding penalties where applicable and improving CX where not (Section 9.5).

Faster competency growth. Micro-learning accelerates cross-skill; scheduling flexibility improves FCR and reduces recontacts.

Quality lift. Just-in-time refreshers boost quality scores 5–15%, lowering repeat volume and escalations.

Created capacity. Combined effects (AHT, automation, fewer admin hours) yield 8–12% "phantom" capacity—fuel for growth without headcount.

Strategic advantages (beyond the spreadsheet)

Differentiated CX. Consistent SL and better-prepped agents are hard to fast-follow.

Talent magnet. Tech-forward, coach-first environments attract and retain top agents/supervisors.

Agility. Dynamic delivery enables faster launches, seasonal pivots, and multi-channel fluidity (Section 9.4).

Data flywheel. Rule fires, accept/decline, outcome deltas feed continuous improvement (Sections 9.5 and 9.7).

The cost of inaction (the gap widens)

Relative competitiveness. As peers adopt Level 3, your unit costs rise *relative* to theirs even if yours are flat.

Talent drain. The best people choose environments where tech removes friction.

Technical debt. Delay multiplies integration complexity and hardens resistance.

Margin squeeze. Without automation, the trade-off triangle (service–cost–people) bites harder each year.

How to build & position your case

Anchor to pain. Lead with the org's hot spots (penalties, attrition, OT, backlog). Map rules to pains.

Be conservative. Use pilot or benchmark results, then haircut them (e.g., model 7–8s AHT vs. 15s observed). Credibility beats exuberance.

Show phases. Pilot (200 agents) → expand (1,000) → scale (enterprise) with ROI at each step.

Quantify risk reduction. Compliance delivery, fewer exceptions, steadier SL—these are avoided-costs worth money.

Tell the human story. Pair tables with vignettes (Rodriguez finishing certs; Lisa coaching again; RTAs becoming rule designers, Sections 9.1 and 9.6).

Investment snapshot (typical ranges)

- Software: $15–$40/agent/month.
- Implementation: $50k–$200k (scale/complexity dependent).
- Internal resourcing: 2–4 FTEs for 6–12 months (WFM, Ops, IT).
- Change enablement: comms, training, supervisor upskilling.

For 1,000 agents, first-year all-in is often $400k–$700k, with 4–8 month payback and 3-year ROI ≥400%. Few investments touch those economics with this risk profile.

Bottom line. Level 3 isn't a feature buy; it's an operating upgrade. The math works, the metrics guide it (Section 9.5), the processes adapt (Section 9.7), and the ROC supplies the discipline (Section 8.9). The real question for executives isn't "Can we afford it?"—it's "How long can we afford not to?"

9.11 Implementation Roadmap: From Pilot to Scale

Sarah's path from skeptical conference attendee to enterprise changer followed a pattern now common among successful Level 3 programs: start small and real, prove value fast, then scale with discipline. The roadmap below balances speed with stability, and technology with human change. It leans on the ROC cadence (Section 8.9), the metrics that matter (Section 9.5), the role shifts (Section 9.6), and the process updates that keep reality in sync (Section 9.7).

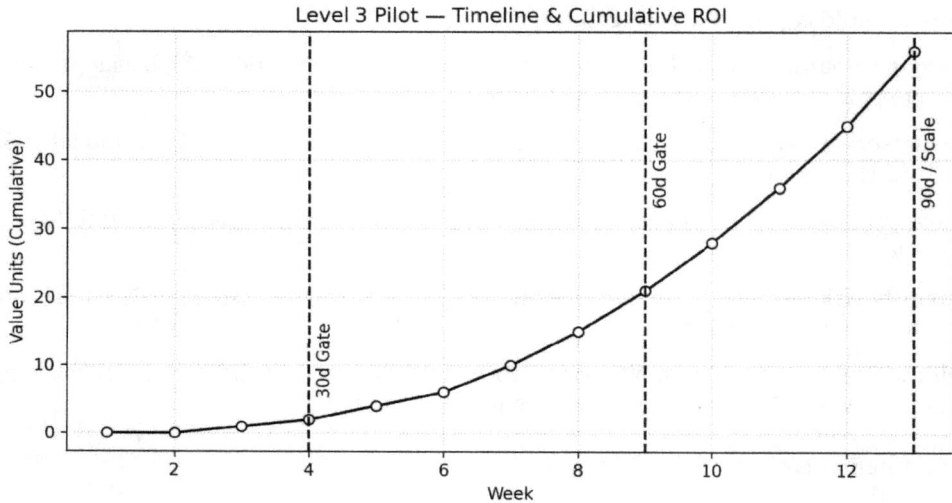

Figure 9.3: Implementation Roadmap: From Pilot to Scale

Phase 1: Pilot design & execution (60–90 days)

Scope (the Goldilocks rule). Big enough to be believable, small enough to be safe: typically 100–200 agents. Choose:

- *Representative ops*: reflect real variance and pain points.
- *Mixed performance*: include strong and average teams.
- *Supportive–skeptical leaders*: challengers who want success.
- *Stable tech baseline*: ACD/WFM integrations working first.

Rules (start simple, solve pain). Begin with 3–5 high-signal, low-debate automations:

1. *Break protection*: auto-adjust when calls run long.

2. *Dynamic training*: 2–3 short modules queued for delivery.

3. *Long-call assist*: alert supervisors past a threshold.

4. *End-of-shift protection*: no new calls in final 5 minutes.

5. *Dynamic VTO*: offer time off when overstaffed.

If you can't explain a rule in one sentence, it's not a pilot rule.

Measures (decide before you start). Establish clean baselines and a control group. Track:

* *Operational*: training hours, AHT deltas, adherence exceptions, OT.
* *Experience*: agent CSAT, supervisor time mix, acceptance rates (Section 9.5).
* *Technical*: rule fire accuracy, latency, reliability.
* *Financial*: cost/interaction, projected ROI.

Comms (overshare on purpose). Weekly stakeholder notes; daily pilot huddles; a live dashboard of rule fires and outcomes. Key messages:

* "This is an experiment; your feedback shapes it."
* "Nothing is permanent until it proves value."
* "We're improving jobs, not eliminating them."

Phase 2: Expansion & refinement (6–12 months)

Graduated expansion. Avoid a leap from 200 to 2,000. Grow in waves and learn each time:

* *Wave 1 (months 1–2)*: adjacent teams ($\approx$500 agents).
* *Wave 2 (months 3–4)*: new lines of business ($\approx$1,000).
* *Wave 3 (months 5–6)*: remote/outsourced sites ($\approx$1,500).
* *Wave 4 (months 7–9)*: approach critical mass ($\approx$2,500).
* *Stabilize (months 10–12)*: codify learnings and prep enterprise rollout.

Rule sophistication (only when it pays). Introduce:

* *Conditional chains*: queue health & availability & conflicts.
* *Skill-specific logic*: sales vs. service; novice vs. expert.
* *Personalization*: preferences, history, acceptance signals.
* *Predictive hints*: near-term risk forecasts to pre-act.
* *Cross-functional flows*: L&D/Quality/IT-triggered actions.

Complexity is a tax—spend it only where value is proven.

Build the capability.

* *Automation CoE*: rule design, governance, analytics (WFM, Ops, IT, HR).
* *Training paths*: creator/admin/change tracks; certify designers.
* *Governance*: intake, approval, test, versioning, rollback.
* *Performance management*: include automation KPIs in reviews (Section 9.5).

Harden the tech.

* *Integrations*: error handling, retries, failover.

- *Reporting*: exec, ops, and CoE views; self-serve drilldowns.
- *RuleOps*: dev/test/prod environments; change windows; audits.
- *Performance*: tune latency for scale; watch queue-to-action time.

Phase 3: Enterprise rollout & continuous optimization

Rollout choreography.

- *Graduated "big bang"*: complete in 8–12 weeks, not a day.
- *Support first*: help desk, floor champs, playbooks ready.
- *Comms blitz*: success stories, go-live calendars, "how to get help".
- *Contingencies*: rule-level and wave-level rollback plans.

Make optimization the job.

- Monthly rule reviews: retire, refine, or scale.
- A/B frameworks: test thresholds, audiences, and prompts.
- Frontline feedback loops: agents/supervisors propose and prioritize.
- Benchmarking: compare sites/LOBs; publish best-practice kits.

Advance the frontier.

- *ML assists*: predict long calls, next-best action triggers.
- *Omnichannel orchestration*: voice/chat/email flows as one.
- *Predictive interventions*: act before the spike lands.
- *Personalized experiences*: tailor rules to the individual.

Critical success factors (all phases)

- *Executive air cover*: visible support that survives the first bump.
- *Change investment*: fund comms, training, floor support—features don't adopt themselves.
- *Realistic pacing*: compress with experience, not pressure.
- *Vendor as partner*: leverage pattern libraries and lessons at scale.
- *Cultural integration*: when people say "our automation," you've arrived.

The journey continues

Level 3 go-live is not the finish line—it's the operating system. What starts as break protection becomes workforce orchestration; early efficiency becomes differentiating agility. Most importantly, this roadmap builds *transformation muscle*: the habit of experimenting, measuring, and improving. You'll need it as Level 4 introduces prediction and Level 5 pursues autonomous optimization.

9.12 Common Challenges and How to Overcome Them

Every Level 3 transformation hits turbulence. Sarah's week-one scare at Midwest Mutual—confused agents, wary supervisors, hiccuping integrations—wasn't failure; it was the syllabus. The difference between programs that stall and those that scale is not challenge-avoidance, but *challenge-readiness*: naming the patterns, preparing responses, and keeping momentum when the first frictions arrive. What follows are the most common obstacles and the field-tested responses, linked to earlier guidance on trust (Section 9.8), roles (Section 9.6), processes (Section 9.7), metrics (Section 9.5), and the roadmap (Section 9.11).

Challenge 1: The Trust Deficit

The pattern. Contact center teams have lived through tech that added pressure without relief—IVRs, rigid adherence, surveillance-heavy QM. Skepticism surfaces as low pilot volunteering, passive resistance, rumor mills, even attempts to "prove" automation won't work. (Section 9.8)

The response.

- **Radical transparency:** Share objectives, metrics, and tradeoffs—including the exec deck. Answer "Is this a headcount play?" with facts.
- **Small wins first:** Lead with agent-benefit rules (break protection, adherence relief). One avoided exception creates an advocate.
- **Own misses fast:** "Timing was wrong—we fixed it today." Visible repair builds more trust than flawless spin.
- **Ambassadors, not posters:** Put thoughtful skeptics on the design team; their conversion travels further than cheerleading.

Challenge 2: Technical Integration Complexity

The pattern. Heterogeneous stacks (ACD, WFM, QM, KM) plus vendor versions, API limits, security constraints, and scale-induced latency. Promises in slides, surprises in prod. (Section 9.4, Section 9.11)

The response.

- **Map first:** Document systems, versions, APIs, limits; decide with your real topology, not a reference diagram.
- **POC or pass:** Require working integrations during selection; two weeks now beats two months later.
- **Right team:** Name an integration squad that speaks both ops and APIs.
- **Crawl–walk–run:** Start with agent state and queue stats; add skills, context, and write-backs as stability grows. (Section 9.11)

Challenge 3: Middle-Management Resistance

The pattern. Supervisors fear loss of relevance ("If the system does adherence and training, what's my job?"). Resistance shows up as lukewarm support and selective focus on failures. (Section 9.6)

The response.

- **Reframe the role:** From timekeeper to coach; from exception processing to performance development.
- **Co-create rules:** Involvement → ownership → championship.
- **Skill up:** Invest ahead of go-live in coaching, data literacy, and performance conversations.
- **Measure what matters:** Shift supervisor scorecards from adherence policing to team growth, quality, and engagement.

Challenge 4: Rule Design Complexity

The pattern. Simple ideas meet messy reality. Edge cases explode; teams oscillate between underfit (bad UX) and overfit (unmaintainable), or stall in analysis. (Section 9.7)

The response.

- **Start simple, evolve by data:** Launch with clear assumptions; log edge cases; only generalize when patterns persist.
- **User stories drive logic:** "As an agent, I want break protection so I'm not penalized when calls run long."
- **Treat rules like code:** Versioning, change notes, test/rollback paths; prevent rule sprawl with a cadence.
- **Governance with voices:** Cross-functional reviews (WFM, Ops, IT, agent reps) to retire, refine, or scale.

Challenge 5: Change Fatigue

The pattern. Initiative overload breeds cynicism: "This too shall pass." Engagement dips, compliance is shallow, innovation antibodies activate.

The response.

- **Anchor to personal pain:** "Remember the adherence ding when your call ran long? This fixes that."
- **Quick, visible wins:** Tangible week-one benefits (protected breaks, finished modules, avoided OT).
- **Simplify the day:** Replace three hated manual steps with one automated flow.
- **Sustained focus:** Give automation 18–24 months of air cover; depth beats breadth.

Challenge 6: Scaling Governance

The pattern. Pilots are nimble; enterprises are not. As scope expands, decisions slow, rules proliferate, and ownership blurs. (Section 9.11)

The response.

- **Tier decision rights:** Team tweaks → lead approval; LOB rules → manager; enterprise changes → steering.
- **Cadence, not chaos:** Weekly rule reviews; monthly optimization; quarterly strategy resets.
- **Clear ownership:** WFM = rule performance; IT = stability; Ops = outcomes. Shared accountability ≠ no accountability.
- **Innovation pipeline:** Frontline ideas → triage → prototype → pilot—so governance enables, not just prevents.

The Meta-Challenge: Sustaining Momentum

Enthusiasm fades, champions rotate, budgets tighten. Keep the flywheel turning:

- **Ritualize celebration:** Regularly spotlight agent wins, coaching breakthroughs, and rule-of-the-month improvements.
- **Tell the story with numbers:** Dashboards that show cumulative impact—variance captured, hours redeployed, stability gained. (Section 9.5)
- **Make it "how we work":** From project to operating norm; from "the system" to "our automation."
- **Point to what's next:** Preview Level 4 prediction and Level 5 autonomy to sustain purpose.

From Challenge to Capability

Each hurdle builds muscle. Integration work hardens your architecture; trust-building strengthens change craft; rule governance becomes a reusable discipline. That is Level 3's quiet dividend: not only a better day *today*, but a smarter organization for *tomorrow*. Sarah's week-one "crisis" became the case study that unlocked adoption. Yours will, too—if you name the pattern, apply the play, and keep moving.

9.13 Key Takeaways and Path to Level 4

Eighteen months after that conference session, Sarah's command center looked different—and so did the work. The morning scrambles had given way to smooth flow. Agents served customers without clock-watching. Supervisors coached rather than policed. The ROC that once *revealed* problems now *orchestrated* solutions (Section 8.9). Level 3 delivered on its promise: variance became an asset; automation, a daily reality.

And yet, it felt like a beginning. If variance can be harvested in real time, what happens when we can *predict* it? If automation optimizes the present, can intelligence prepare the future? Level 3's success creates appetite for Level 4.

The Level 3 Transformation: Core Lessons

Lesson 1: Variance is an asset, not a liability. Traditional WFM treats variance as failure (forecast misses, adherence exceptions). Level 3 shows it as opportunity—micro-windows for development and stabilization. Stop forcing reality to match the plan; optimize outcomes *given* reality. (Sections 9.4 and 9.5)

Lesson 2: Automation amplifies human potential. Automation removes administrative friction so people can do human work—coaching, problem solving, connection. Supervisors become coaches; analysts become designers; agents become professionals. (Sections 9.6 and 9.8)

Lesson 3: Trust and technology must advance together. Tools don't transform organizations—*trusted* tools do. Invest as much in change management and transparency as in features. (Sections 9.8 and 9.12)

Lesson 4: Integration beats isolation. Level 3 breaks silos by necessity. Real-time decisions require real-time collaboration across WFM, Ops, L&D, Quality, HR, and IT. (Sections 9.4, 9.7 and 9.8)

Lesson 5: Continuous evolution wins. Small, steady improvements compound: rule refinements, process tweaks, governance rhythms. This cadence underpins the roadmap from pilot to scale. (Section 9.11)

Signs You're Ready for Level 4

Operational (system health):

- Automation runs with minimal intervention; rule reviews are rhythmic. (Section 9.11)
- Variance capture efficiency $\geq 60\%$ sustained; acceptance rates $\geq 85\%$. (Section 9.5)
- Integrations are stable at volume; latency is within targets. (Section 9.4)

Cultural (people health):

- Agents and supervisors ask for more sophisticated rules. (Section 9.8)
- Cross-functional collaboration occurs by default, not decree. (Sections 9.6 and 9.7)
- Frontline ideas routinely enter the automation pipeline. (Section 9.12)

Strategic (business pull):

- Level 3 value curves are flattening; competition pressures are rising. (Section 9.10)
- Leadership is asking "what's next?" not "is this enough?" (Section 9.3)

The Level 4 Promise: From Reactive to Predictive

Level 3 excels at acting on what *is*. Level 4 plans for what *may be* by treating uncertainty as a first-class input. The workflow is practical and repeatable: *forecast* with error bands, *simulate* outcomes under policy, then *optimize* decisions against objectives and constraints. Chapter 10 details this operations-research toolkit and how to use it without turning every team into a math department.

- **Forecast with ranges.** Predict arrivals, AHT, shrinkage, and mix with error bands (not single points); incorporate external signals only where they add skill.
- **Simulate to see risk.** Use Monte Carlo and/or discrete-event simulation to produce SL/ASA/abandon/occupancy *distributions* under proposed staffing and policies.
- **Optimize decisions.** Choose hiring cadence, FTE mix, templates, and policy guardrails via single- or multi-objective optimization, often using fast queueing/surrogate models and validating with simulation.
- **Validate and iterate.** Backtest against holdouts, monitor drift, and automate checks so models stay calibrated as behaviors change.
- **Make it usable.** Package results as bands, trade-off frontiers, and "what-if" scenarios managers can act on; leverage modern tooling so scale and speed are accessible.

In short, Level 4 replaces brittle, single-number plans with *risk-aware* ranges and policy choices proven in simulation—so you can staff and steer *ahead* of impact, not just react to it.

Preparing for Level 4 (while you scale Level 3)

- **Data foundation:** Persist granular intraday data—signals, decisions, outcomes—for model training. (Section 9.5)
- **Analytics muscle:** Grow ops-aware analysts; partner with data science early. (Section 9.11)
- **External feeds:** Inventory candidate signals (weather, sentiment, promotions) and access paths. (Section 9.4)
- **Pilot predictions:** Small tests (e.g., Monday volume from Fri sentiment; attrition risk flags) to build confidence. (Section 9.12)
- **Probabilistic culture:** Normalize ranges and likelihoods over absolutes across planning forums.

Your Level 3 Action Plan (by starting point)

If you're at Level 2:

1. Use STaRS to time the leap; pick the right context. (Section 9.3)

2. Target painful variance moments for first rules; build the conservative ROI. (Section 9.10)

3. Scope a 100–200 agent pilot with 3–5 simple rules. (Section 9.11)

If you're early Level 3:

1. Prioritize adoption and trust over feature count. (Section 9.8)

2. Stand up governance before complexity arrives. (Sections 9.11 and 9.12)

3. Celebrate quick wins; publish rule-of-the-month impact. (Section 9.5)

If you're mature Level 3:

1. Check readiness indicators; design Level 4 pilots.

2. Extend automation into adjacent workflows (QM nudges, KM reinforcement). (Section 9.7)

3. Codify playbooks and libraries; share patterns enterprise-wide. (Sections 9.6 and 9.11)

Bottom line. Level 3 is the inflection: from plan defense to outcome optimization; from firefighting to orchestration. Make the numbers trustworthy (Section 9.5), the roles elevated (Section 9.6), the processes living (Section 9.7), the partnerships real (Sections 9.8 and 9.9), the case undeniable (Section 9.10), and the rollout disciplined (Sections 9.11 and 9.12). Then look up—Level 4 is not a leap of faith; it's the next sensible step.

What to read while you build

Level 3 demands organizational transformation and philosophical reorientation—from fighting variability to leveraging it, from rigid plans to continuous planning. Two books and one accessible companion guide this 12–18 month journey through cross-functional change.

Kotter's *Leading Change*   remains the definitive roadmap for enterprise transformation. His framework addresses every Level 3 challenge: building cross-functional coalitions before technology decisions, creating pull through compelling vision rather than mandate-driven push, sustaining momentum through the difficult middle months when enthusiasm wanes, and anchoring changes in culture so they outlast implementation teams. The approach treats trust as something earned through leadership actions—transparent communication, obstacle removal, early wins—not requested through speeches. Published by Harvard Business Review Press (2012, 187 pages), this book transforms temporary behavior change into permanent cultural shift. Test the framework's coalition-building and vision-setting steps before launching technology initiatives.[119]

For broader team engagement, Spencer Johnson's *Who Moved My Cheese?* offers an accessible 96-page fable about adapting to change. While too simplistic as a primary guide, it provides common language for discussing change anxiety across all organizational levels. Use it to open conversations, not replace substantive change management.[120]

Taleb's *Antifragile* I draw on Taleb's ideas to argue that WFM should evolve from static plans to continuous planning. Things that are antifragile don't just resist shocks—they gain from disorder, volatility, and stress. His core insight challenges traditional WFM: prediction errors aren't failures to eliminate but realities to design around. Systems become antifragile through optionality, decentralization, and small failures that prevent catastrophic ones. Note on style: Taleb writes in a forthright, opinionated style; the tone isn't for everyone, but the concepts are durable and practical. The payoff is clear for contact centers: stop fighting variance and start leveraging it as competitive advantage. Level 3 builds systems that strengthen from volatility.[121]

Level 3 transformation requires both organizational machinery (Kotter) and philosophical reorientation (Taleb). Leading Change provides the structure for building coalitions and sustaining momentum. Antifragile provides the intellectual foundation for why continuous planning beats static plans. Together, they turn the principle that trust and technology must advance together into operational reality.

10 Level 4: Advanced – The Ecosystem Revolution

10.1 Introduction: The Last Manual Frontier

Sarah Chen arrived at 6:30 AM for the quarterly capacity planning ritual. Eighteen months after Level 3's rollout, Midwest Mutual's operation hummed with automated precision. Training delivered itself in micro-gaps. Breaks self-adjusted. The ROC responded smoothly rather than scrambled. By every operational measure, they'd transformed.

Yet here she sat, watching Tom Rodriguez and Jennifer arrange printouts like archaeological artifacts.

"Morning, Sarah," Tom said, not looking up from his laptop. "Already pulled last quarter's actuals from five systems. Only took three hours this time."

Jennifer Liu added, "Marketing finally sent their campaign calendar. Of course, it doesn't match the format from last quarter."

Sarah surveyed the familiar scene: Excel files numbered in versions, printed reports highlighted in three colors, whiteboards covered in capacity calculations. It looked exactly like her planning sessions five years ago at specialty lines—just with bigger numbers.

"We've automated how we execute perfectly," Sarah said. "But we still plan like it's 1995."

The Monthly Marathon

Every month, the same three-week sprint:

Week 1: Data Archaeology
The team extracted data from everywhere—ACD for volume and handle time trends, CRM for channel mix, HR for attrition, WFM for shrinkage. Each system had its own format, own definitions, own export quirks.

"Remember when marketing changed 'campaign' to 'initiative' in their system?" Tom muttered. "Broke every lookup for two days."

Week 2: The Excel Olympics
Jennifer opened `CapPlan_Master_v74.xlsx`. Sixty-three tabs. Four thousand formulas. Links to seventeen other workbooks.

"What if attrition increases by 2%?" Finance had asked yesterday.

"Give me three hours," Jennifer had replied, knowing she'd need to manually adjust assumptions across every line of business, every month, every skill.

Week 3: The Single-Number Fiction
They'd present: "We need exactly 312 agents for Q2."

Finance would ask: "What if volumes are 10% higher?"

They'd return to Excel, rerun everything, present: "Then we need exactly 343 agents."

No ranges. No confidence levels. No acknowledgment that their "exact" number was built on dozens of assumptions, any of which could be wrong.

The Variance They Couldn't See

"Look at this," Tom pulled up last year's projections versus actuals. "Q1: Missed by 15%. Q2: Over by 12%. Q3: Under by 18%. Q4: Somehow over by 1%, but only because higher variances in volume and lower in handle time canceled out."

Sarah studied the patterns. "We learned to harvest variance in real-time with Level 3. But we're still planning as if variance doesn't exist beyond today."

Jennifer laughed bitterly. "Level 3 treats variance as an asset to harvest. Our capacity plans treat it as something to ignore until it bites us."

The Missing Signals

Marketing interrupted with an urgent email: "Launching surprise campaign next week. How many agents do we need?"

Tom sighed. "I'll need to rebuild the entire model. Again."

"Wait," Sarah said. "Marketing spends millions on digital ads. That data exists in real-time. Weather patterns affect insurance claims. Economic indicators drive call types. Product launches have predictable curves. Why aren't we using any of this?"

"Because our Excel models can barely handle the data we have," Jennifer admitted. "Adding more variables would collapse the whole thing."

The Acquisition Catalyst

That afternoon, David Kim, COO called an emergency meeting. "Board is evaluating acquiring Southeastern Mutual. Two thousand agents, different systems, overlapping products. I need three scenarios by Monday: conservative integration, aggressive consolidation, and optimal mix."

Sarah looked at her team. Monday was four days away.

"Aside from workload projections, we'll need to model skill overlap, facility optimization, and system migration timing..." Tom was already overwhelmed.

"And run it three different ways, with sensitivity analysis on each," Jennifer added.

They'd done this before—barely. It had taken three weeks and nearly broken the team. Now they had four days.

The Conference Connection

Sarah remembered a presentation from last year's conference: "Forecast-Simulate-Optimize: Modern Operations Research for Capacity Planning." The speaker, Dr. Howard Stewart, had shown how other industries approach complex planning with three distinct but connected models.

"Every other industry uses OR for complex planning," she told her team. "Airlines don't schedule fleets in Excel. Supply chains don't run on spreadsheets. Why do we?"

Tom pulled up the conference proceedings. "He breaks it into three steps: First, forecast what demand will look like. Then simulate how different staffing levels perform under that demand—like Erlang but capturing real variability. Finally, optimize to find the best staffing decision given multiple objectives."

"And look at this," Jennifer added, reading further. "They validate their models against actual results. When was the last time we checked if our capacity plans matched reality? We just blame 'variance' when we're wrong."

"It's not just better math," Sarah realized. "It's acknowledging uncertainty exists, quantifying it from actual data, then making the best decision anyway. Not pretending we know exactly what will happen."

The Ecosystem Vision

Sarah sketched on the whiteboard:

Current State:

- Core WFM Platform (Level 2): Handles scheduling and real-time
- Automation Engine (Level 3): Harvests variance dynamically
- Capacity Planning: Manual Excel gymnastics, disconnected, deterministic

Future State:

- Core WFM Platform: Still the operational backbone
- Automation Engine: Still harvesting variance
- **NEW - OR Planning Layer**: Connected ecosystem component that:
  - Continuously ingests data from all systems
  - Runs probabilistic forecasts with confidence bands
  - Simulates thousands of scenarios automatically
  - Optimizes across multiple objectives
  - Refreshes weekly, not monthly
  - Handles what-ifs in minutes, not days

"We don't replace what's working," Sarah emphasized. "We extend our ecosystem. Just like Level 3 added automation to Level 2's foundation, Level 4 adds science to our planning."

The Comparison Study

Over the weekend, while Tom and Jennifer built the Excel scenarios for Monday, Sarah researched what Level 4 could provide. She reached out to Dr. Stewart and spent Sunday afternoon understanding the fundamental difference.

"Look at this," she told the team Monday morning, before the board presentation. "Our Excel model says we need exactly 5,142 agents for the merged entity. One number. Based on averaging last year's volumes and adding 10% for 'safety.'"

She pulled up a mockup based on Stewart's methodology. "With OR-based planning, we'd show this: 80% confidence we need between 4,800 and 5,400 agents, with the variance driven by three key factors—integration timing, customer retention, and system migration delays."

"But here's the real difference," she continued. "Our Excel what-if takes three hours per scenario. An OR platform could test a thousand scenarios in minutes. Want to know the impact if customer retention drops 5% but integration happens faster? Instant. What if we phase the integration over six months instead of three? Immediate answer with confidence bands."

Tom stared at the comparison. "We're giving them false precision with our single numbers."

"Worse," Sarah said. "We can't even tell them which assumptions matter most. The OR approach would show that integration timing drives 60% of the variance, while the skill mix we're obsessing over only accounts for 8%."

The Board Decision

That afternoon, Sarah presented both approaches to the board. The Excel version was familiar—precise numbers implying certainty. The comparison to Level 4's approach was revelatory—ranges, probabilities, trade-offs made visible.

"If we had Level 4 today," Sarah explained, "we could show you not just one answer but the full distribution of outcomes. We'd identify which variables actually drive risk. We'd test hundreds of integration strategies to find the optimal path."

David leaned forward. "The acquisition isn't moving forward—regulatory concerns. But there will be others. We need to be ready."

The CFO, Margaret Peterson, nodded. "Every acquisition we've evaluated has taken weeks of modeling. By the time we have answers, the opportunity has often passed. You're saying Level 4 changes that?"

"From weeks to hours," Sarah confirmed. "And instead of three scenarios, we could evaluate the entire decision space. Find strategies we'd never discover manually."

The Path Forward

Board approval came within the hour—not for this acquisition, but for the capability to handle the next one properly.

Sarah gathered her team that afternoon. "We're not replacing our planning," she told them. "We're making it scientific. Tom, you'll stop wrestling with Excel and start defining business rules. Jennifer, you'll stop copying formulas and start validating models. We'll all stop pretending we can predict perfectly and start preparing intelligently."

Tom looked relieved. "No more data archaeology? No more Excel Olympics?"

Sarah looked at the whiteboard where she'd extended their ecosystem diagram. Level 2 had built the foundation. Level 3 had automated execution. Level 4 would now revolutionize planning.

"When the next acquisition comes—and it will—we'll be ready," she said. "Not with one answer, but with understanding."

As the team dispersed to begin the pilot, Sarah reflected on the journey. Each level hadn't replaced the previous—it had extended it. The ecosystem was growing, each component making the others stronger. And somewhere in those probability distributions and optimization curves lay something more valuable than certainty: preparedness.

The journey to Level 4 had begun.

10.2 The Broken Foundation: Why Traditional Capacity Planning Fails

Level 3 modernized execution; capacity planning often remains pre–digital. We apply deterministic spreadsheets to a probabilistic problem, producing plans that look precise and age instantly.

Point estimates in an uncertain world

Saying "we need 287 agents next quarter" asserts certainty that does not exist. In reality there may be a small chance of needing exactly 287, a much larger chance of needing a range (e.g., 260–310), and nontrivial probability outside that range. The issue is not analyst effort but method: single–output formulas for multi–uncertainty inputs.

Four structural flaws

1) Isolation from drivers. Traditional plans extrapolate history and add a growth factor. Actual demand is shaped by intertwined drivers:

- Marketing campaigns and spend shifts.
- Product launches that alter contact reasons.
- Competitor outages or offers shifting share.
- Macroeconomic and regulatory changes.
- Technology deflection that underperforms.
- Social media events that spike volume.

Spreadsheets may footnote these, but rarely *model* their uncertainty, timing, or interaction.

2) Brittle assumptions. Inputs are treated as fixed and independent: volume $+x\%$, AHT $-y\%$, attrition $=z\%$. In reality they couple:

$$\text{attrition} \uparrow \Rightarrow \text{experience} \downarrow \Rightarrow \text{AHT} \uparrow \Rightarrow \text{staffing} \uparrow \Rightarrow \text{hiring} \uparrow \Rightarrow \text{experience} \downarrow \dots$$

Small changes propagate nonlinearly; static sheets seldom capture the loop.

3) The time–horizon trap. The longest–lead decisions carry the most uncertainty:

- Hiring: 12–16 weeks from requisition to production (and longer to proficiency).
- BPO: 3–6 month commitments with volume guarantees.
- Facilities: multi–year footprints.
- Technology: license counts and capacity sized ahead.

Annual plans freeze assumptions months in advance; reality evolves weekly. What's needed is a *living* capacity plan that updates as drivers firm up (campaign calendars, attrition trend shifts, channel mix changes), guiding decisions like "accelerate hiring," "defer a class," or "extend BPO."

4) The static snapshot delusion. A typical cycle:

- Oct–Nov: collect data, build scenarios.
- Dec: finalize and approve.
- Jan 1: the plan is already stale.
- Jan–Sep: explain variances to a frozen baseline.

We spend a quarter producing a document the operation outgrows immediately.

Compound failure, not additive error

A 10% demand miss rarely yields a 10% staffing miss. It cascades:

1. Underforecast ⇒ understaffing.
2. Understaffing ⇒ overtime and burnout.
3. Burnout ⇒ higher attrition.
4. Higher attrition ⇒ lower experience, higher AHT.
5. Higher AHT ⇒ additional staffing need.

A modest initial miss can become a significant capacity problem within weeks or months.

The hidden costs

Beyond over/understaffing:

- Emergency hiring and accelerated training: $2–3M/year.
- Chronic overtime from gaps: $3–5M/year.
- Idle capacity from overage: $2–4M/year.
- Unused licenses/infrastructure: $1–2M/year.
- BPO penalties and surge cover: $2–3M/year.

For a 3,000–agent estate, total impact commonly reaches 15–20% of WFM spend.

Why spreadsheets persist

Familiarity. Everyone can open the file. *Flexibility theater.* Anything can be modeled (crudely). *Ownership.* Analysts "own" their workbook. *Diffuse accountability.* No single owner of the $~20M gap. *Norms.* When everyone does it, it feels acceptable.

A different foundation

Other domains solved this long ago:

- Airlines optimize to demand distributions, not points.
- Retail uses stochastic demand and inventory models.
- Manufacturing plans to robustness across scenarios.
- Finance prices risk by quantifying uncertainty.

Contact centers are the outlier. Level 4 replaces false precision with quantified uncertainty, static snapshots with dynamic, driver–linked models, and brittle plans with robust strategies. The task is not to make the old approach "better," but to adopt the right class of methods for an uncertain world.

10.3 Operations Research Enters WFM: The Theoretical Foundation

The missing discipline

Contact centers are queueing systems with uncertain inputs, coupled constraints, and human policies layered on top. Classical WFM made enormous progress with forecasting plus Erlang-style closed forms, but scaling modern complexity (multi-skill, interrupts, callbacks, messaging concurrency, work-from-anywhere) requires bringing the broader operations research (OR) toolkit to the fore. What follows is a practical, decision-maker's view: how OR pieces fit together, where they differ, and how to use them without turning every team into a math department.

A three–model workflow

In practice, WFM planning is a loop of *three distinct model classes* used in concert:

1. *Forecast* — predict drivers (arrivals, handle time, shrinkage, mix) with error bands.

2. *Simulate* — evaluate performance under uncertainty and policy ("pretend to be the operation").

3. *Optimize* — choose staffing and policy decisions given objectives and constraints ("pretend to be the decision-maker").

Forecast→simulate→optimize (and back again) is the rhythm of modern WFM. Each class solves a different problem; blurring them often leads to brittle plans or false precision.

Simulation & queueing (evaluate the system)

Purpose: given a proposed staffing/policy, estimate SL/ASA/abandon/occupancy distributions.

- **Erlang-class queueing.** Erlang-C/A/X and relatives provide fast, closed-form approximations under simplifying assumptions (Poisson arrivals, exponential service, steady state, single class). They are ideal as baselines or screening tools, and remain useful where assumptions are "close enough."
- **Stochastic sampling.** Replace point inputs with distributions and run many trials to produce outcome bands. A common technique is *Monte Carlo*, which samples empirical/parametric inputs (arrivals, AHT, shrinkage, patience) and tallies SL/ASA/abandon across runs.
- **Discrete-event simulation (DES).** Event-driven models explicitly represent queues, skills, priorities, abandon, retrials, routing/policy, and cross-channel interactions. DES is preferable when interactions and policies drive outcomes (e.g., skill prioritization, work interruptibility, callback policies).

Monte Carlo vs. DES. Monte Carlo samples inputs and tallies outputs with a simplified transformation; DES explicitly models the operational process and state transitions. When policy/network effects matter, DES provides higher fidelity; when structure is simple and speed is paramount, Monte Carlo or Erlang-class methods suffice.

Optimization (choose decisions)

Purpose: choose staffing/policy plans that best meet goals under uncertainty.

- **Single- and multi-objective optimization.** Formulate hiring cadence, FTE mix, overtime, outsourcing blocks, schedule templates, and policy levers as decision variables with constraints (budgets, SL/ASA bands, occupancy, fairness). Explore cost–service–risk trade-offs rather than over-optimize a single metric.
- **Using simulation inside optimization.** Common patterns include: (i) optimize against queueing or surrogate models for speed, then (ii) validate/tighten with DES or Monte Carlo. This respects the difference between "evaluate" and "choose" while keeping the loop tractable.

Are we optimizing the right metric?

The canonical service level (e.g., 80/20) often began as an *executive heuristic*. In a decision-science frame, teams validate the target against observed outcomes and optimize choices over *ranges* (hit-rate envelopes, cost/risk frontiers) rather than anchoring on a single point number.

Model validation (close the loop)

Simulation credibility rests on validated *inputs* and *outputs*. Good practice:

1. *Infer input distributions* from historical interval data (arrivals, AHT, patience/abandon, shrinkage, concurrency), preferring empirical distributions where data support them.

2. *Backtest outputs* by comparing simulated vs. observed SL/ASA/occupancy over holdout periods; monitor error bands and drift.

3. *Automate the checks* so models are continuously re-validated as operations and behaviors evolve.

This discipline reduces the "mystery variability" that is actually modeling error and keeps planning grounded in observed reality.

Monte Carlo: a practical entry to probabilistic planning

A pragmatic starting point for many teams is Monte Carlo with empirical inputs:

- Pull empirical distributions for arrivals, AHT, shrinkage (and where feasible, patience/concurrency).
- Run thousands of trials per scenario; summarize SL/ASA/abandon as bands (e.g., 5th/50th/95th percentiles).
- Use these bands to define *risk-aware* staffing ranges and "green/yellow/red" operating regions.

As policy complexity grows, swap in DES for the evaluation step while keeping the same forecast→simulate→optimize cadence.

Making OR usable

Adoption no longer requires custom code or advanced math on every team:

• Visual model builders and prebuilt components mask technical detail.

• Cloud compute handles large simulation sweeps and optimization runs.

• Outputs emphasize ranges, frontiers, and "what-if" scenarios that managers can act on.

The remaining shift is cultural: from defending a single number to communicating uncertainty; from static annual plans to living plans; from intuition-first to model-informed decisions.

A note on early pioneers

Vendors such as Bay Bridge Decision Technologies demonstrated that advanced OR can materially improve contact center planning. Ric Kosiba's work showed sound math paired with operational insight can outperform spreadsheet methods; adoption patterns varied with packaging, economics, integration effort, and data readiness. Many models proved robust in practice—particularly where inputs and outcomes were validated. With modern data pipelines, APIs, and compute, the conditions now exist to bring those ideas to scale within Level 4.

10.4 The Pioneers: Ric Kosiba and the Evolution of Capacity Planning

The Bay Bridge Decision Technologies story

In 2000, Ric Kosiba founded Bay Bridge Decision Technologies to bring modern OR methods to contact center planning. At the time, most organizations still relied on Erlang-C spreadsheets and single–point forecasts for multi–million–dollar staffing decisions—tools that assume no abandonment, exponential handle times, and static routing. Kosiba, with a background in operations research and airline optimization, applied discrete–event simulation and optimization to model real behavior: caller impatience, non-exponential handle times, skill routing, and policy effects.

Bay Bridge's "what-if" engine let planners vary drivers and see operational consequences before committing. Instead of "the plan is 287," teams could explore scenarios, sensitivities, and risk bands—an early, practical example of the probabilistic mindset outlined in Section 10.3.

Notable contributions

Bay Bridge helped mainstream several ideas that are now core to Level 4 practice:

- **Simulation at planning time:** replace closed-form simplifications with discrete-event models of queues, skills, priorities, and abandonment.
- **Scenario and sensitivity analysis:** move from single answers to families of outcomes with clear driver linkages (marketing, policy, product changes).
- **Risk-aware staffing:** express needs as ranges with confidence, not points without context.
- **Driver integration:** connect business inputs (e.g., campaigns) directly to capacity models, not only to narrative footnotes.

Acquisition and legacy

Interactive Intelligence acquired Bay Bridge Decision Technologies in 2012 and incorporated its models into a broader suite; Genesys later acquired Interactive in 2016. The Bay Bridge brand faded, but the methods persisted—both inside commercial platforms and through alumni who continued advancing OR-based planning.

What the market learned

Four pragmatic lessons stand out:

- **The math helped, the packaging mattered.** Simulation and optimization produced more robust plans, but adoption depended on accessible workflows, not on exposing raw models.
- **Adoption scale & economics.** Platform seat adoption was broad *(hundreds of thousands of seats industry-wide)*; the depth of advanced planning varied with *economics and packaging*: spreadsheets were effectively "free" and familiar, while commercial planning tools carried license, change-management, and integration costs.

- **Culture and data readiness were gating factors.** Many teams were organized around point forecasts and annual cycles; probabilistic thinking and driver feeds took time to institutionalize.

- **Integration was the hard part.** Models needed clean data flows and regular refresh; integration complexity shaped time-to-value and refresh cadence. *Notably, many deployed models proved robust for long periods*—even when distributions weren't frequently rebuilt—so fragility was not inherent to the modeling approach.

In short, Bay Bridge demonstrated that OR could be operationalized for contact centers: plan with distributions, test policies in simulation, and link staffing to business drivers. Those ideas set the stage for today's Level 4 ecosystem—API-first platforms, continuous data refresh, and risk-aware decisions—delivering at scale what early pioneers proved was possible.

10.5 The New Generation: Modern OR-Driven Capacity Planning

The seeds described in Section 10.4 have grown into a diverse ecosystem of OR-driven capacity planning platforms. Common threads run through the leading approaches: cloud delivery, API-first integration, probabilistic planning (not point estimates), and business-facing workflows that hide mathematical complexity without dumbing it down. Each entrant emphasizes a different angle—packaging, transparency, speed to value, or breadth of optimization.

Real Numbers & Strategies (Ric & Chris Kosiba)

Design focus. Informed by the Bay Bridge experience, Real Numbers is built as a cloud, API-first service intended to plug into contact center stacks without heavy custom ETL. The product language centers on planners and finance partners rather than modelers. *Terminology:* the engine uses *stochastic simulation* and *discrete-event simulation* (DES), and surfaces *risk bands* for decision-making.

Notable capabilities.

- **Living capacity plans:** automated daily refresh from ACD/WFM/CRM inputs with roll-forward re-baselining.
- **Scenario factories:** auto-generated "what-if" sets (demand shifts, staffing constraints, disruption cases) with side-by-side comparisons.
- **ML-assisted driver linkages:** supervised and exploratory ML discover and quantify business drivers (marketing calendars, product events) that feed the stochastic simulator and forecasts; impact bands update as drift occurs.
- **Risk views:** plan ranges with confidence levels and service/cost hit-rate projections to support risk-tolerance decisions.
- **Automatic model validation.** An AI layer infers operational input distributions from historical interval reports and assembles the simulation model ("models building models"). Continuous backtesting maintains accuracy bands as drivers change, preventing drift toward spreadsheet-math simplifications.

Cinareo (Dr. Mark Alpern)

Design focus. Cinareo emphasizes mathematical transparency for enterprises with multi-site, multi-skill complexity. Models and constraints are inspectable, supporting auditability and explainability.

Notable capabilities.

- **Multi-objective optimization:** surface the efficient frontier across service, cost, and workforce well-being targets.
- **Constraint orchestration:** concurrent handling of labor rules, policies, skills, and availability—no sequential "fix one, break another."
- **Skills-aware capacity:** explicit modeling of overlapping/specialized skills and routing structures.

- **Academic tie-ins:** methods stay current via research collaboration and documented formulations.

Datanitiv

Design focus. Datanitiv blends ML with OR in a self-service, data-pipeline-first package aimed at fast-scaling operations that need quick onboarding and iterative refinement.

Notable capabilities.

- **Automated data plumbing:** connectors and schema detection to ingest from WFM/ACD/CRM without bespoke ETL.
- **Pattern discovery:** ML-based detection of latent demand drivers and seasonal effects that feed stochastic planning.
- **Continuous learning:** models re-estimate as new data arrives; forecasts and optimizations co-evolve.
- **Accessible entry tiers:** pricing and setup designed for sub-enterprise footprints with a path to scale.

What this new wave has in common

Across vendors, several design choices mark the break from spreadsheet planning:

- **Distributions, not points:** plans expressed as ranges with confidence, plus playbooks for tails.
- **Continuous refresh:** capacity models update as drivers change; annual artifacts give way to living plans.
- **APIs as first-class citizens:** ingest/emit to ACD, WFM, LMS, CRM, HRIS, finance; no duplicate sources of truth.
- **Audience-appropriate outputs:** the same model drives executive ranges, planner scenarios, and finance bridges.
- **Governance hooks:** versioned assumptions, audit trails, and change logs to align planning with compliance.

No single platform is "best" in the abstract. Fit depends on your integration posture, the complexity of skills/routing, transparency needs, and whether you prize speed to value or depth of formulation. The common shift, however, is unmistakable: from static, point-estimate spreadsheets to continuously updated, risk-aware capacity models that connect directly to business drivers and operational systems.

10.6 Building the Modern WFM Ecosystem

Level 4 maturity replaces monolithic, all-in-one suites with an integrated ecosystem. The goal is simple: let each component excel at its core function, connect them cleanly, and keep the plan and the operation in sync. What follows is a reference architecture and the integration patterns that make it practical.

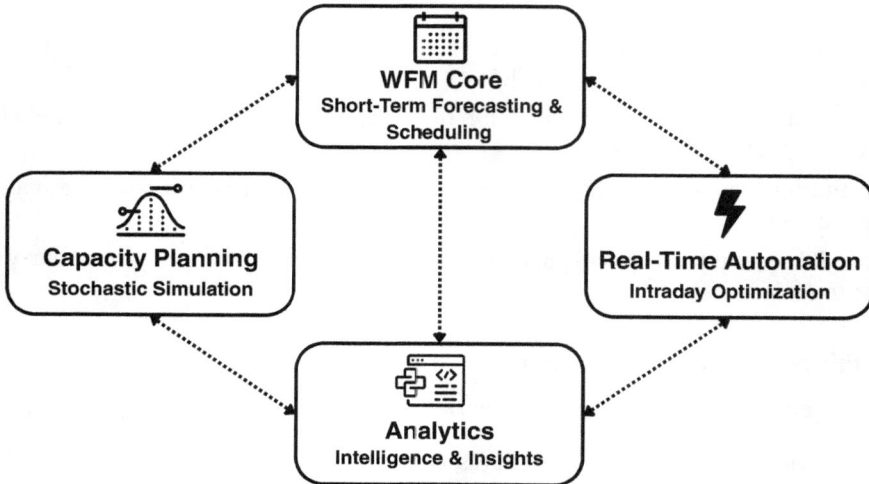

Figure 10.1: The Modern WFM Ecosystem

A four-part architecture

1) Best-in-breed WFM core. Choose a WFM platform that is API-first rather than API-available. The core should handle short-term forecasting, scheduling, adherence, and time-tracking, while exposing:

- read/write endpoints for schedules, activities, and forecasts;
- event hooks for changes (agent state, activity start/stop);
- bulk export for analytics without proprietary hurdles.

The differentiator is not a checklist of features but *integration readiness*: assume the core will coexist with dedicated automation, planning, and analytics tools.

2) Industrial-strength automation (Level 3 foundation). Real-time automation plat-forms (e.g., Intradiem-class tools) sit between ACD/CCaaS and WFM to convert small windows of availability into value and to protect service during spikes. They continuously ingest:

- *queue health* from the ACD (arrivals, backlog, SL);
- *schedules/coverage* from WFM;
- *agent states* from ACD/desktop.

They then execute micro-actions (training offers, break moves, VTO/VOT, long-call assists) and write completions back to WFM. Critically, this layer produces variance telemetry that becomes input to strategic planning.

3) Advanced capacity planning (the OR layer). Specialized *Operations Research (OR)* platforms combine historical patterns from WFM and business drivers (e.g., marketing calendars, product events) to produce *living* capacity plans: distributions with confidence ranges and scenario playbooks. Methods extend beyond Erlang-class queueing (Erlang-C/A/X) to Monte Carlo, discrete-event simulation (DES), and multi-objective optimization. Public, independent benchmarks may be limited; treat vendor claims as inputs to a structured evaluation, not settled fact.

4) Modern analytics workspace. Notebook- and BI-centric environments (e.g., Jupyter, Deepnote, or your enterprise BI stack) move teams from "running reports" to *doing analysis*. In notebooks, analysts use Python or R to join data across systems, test hypotheses, and build reproducible workflows. Paired with modern LLMs, notebooks can generate starter code, suggest checks, and explain outputs—accelerating insight without requiring a master's in data science (though statistical judgment and code reviews still matter).

- correlate drivers (weather, campaigns) with arrivals and AHT, and sanity-check with simple causal tests;
- quantify rule impact (acceptance rates, SL stability, OT drift) with versioned notebooks;
- build lightweight predictive features to feed planning models and simulations;
- create audience-specific dashboards with shared, governed definitions.

This does not replace vendor reporting; it unlocks exploration beyond it—code-backed, auditable, and integrated with your ecosystem.

Integration patterns that work

Event streaming for real-time. Prefer push over poll. When an agent completes training or a break shifts, emit an event (e.g., webhook, message bus). Consumers (WFM, planning, analytics) subscribe and update immediately.

Operational data lake for analysis. Keep systems of record separate, but land copies into a governed store (cloud object storage + warehouse). Benefits:

- cross-system joins without loading production databases;
- reproducible metrics with versioned transformations;
- one place to compute features for planning models.

Microservices and loose coupling. Expose small, purpose-built services: forecasting separate from scheduling; automation rule service separate from action executors. This allows selective scaling and vendor mixing (e.g., keep your forecaster, swap schedulers).

Bidirectional contracts. For each integration, document *who is source of truth* and *what gets written back*. Examples:

- WFM is the schedule authority; automation may request changes and records completions.

217

- Planning publishes capacity ranges; WFM consumes the staffing envelope and scenario triggers.

The network effect

Tight, well-governed connections compound value:

- Automation yields variance data → planning improves ranges and tail playbooks.
- Better ranges → schedules align more closely to demand.
- Better schedules → automation finds more safe windows for development.
- Analytics surfaces gaps → rules and plans iterate with evidence.

Over time, the ecosystem learns faster and adjusts with less manual effort.

Operating implications

Ecosystems change how teams work as much as how systems talk:

- **Vendor posture:** move from single-suite dependence to *specialist collaboration*.
- **Data ownership:** shared definitions and metric governance across tools.
- **Team skills:** basic API literacy, comfort with event logs, and fluency in interpreting distributions rather than points.

In practice, Level 4 organizations treat the ecosystem as a living platform: evolve one component at a time, protect interfaces, and let continuous feedback tighten the loop between plan and execution.

10.7 The STaRS Context: Where Your Organization Sits

Level 4 (OR-driven) planning is not a feature drop; it is a shift in how decisions get made under uncertainty. The STaRS lens—*Startup, Turnaround, Realignment, Sustaining Success*—helps determine *how* to introduce OR, at *what* pace, and *where* resistance or tailwinds will appear.

Why STaRS matters at Level 4

- OR changes the conversation from point estimates to probability ranges. Different contexts tolerate that change differently.
- Tooling is necessary but insufficient; readiness (data, skills, governance) varies by stage.
- The first wins should match the stage's incentives (survival, stability, growth, or edge).

Startup: build OR into the foundation *Profile.* Few legacy constraints, high pace, thin historical data. *Aim.* Simple, explainable models that scale; early habits around clean data and metric governance.

- **First moves:** hire at least one analyst with OR/statistics; implement lightweight Monte Carlo bands around core forecasts; stand up basic data collection with stable definitions (arrivals, AHT, shrinkage).
- **What to watch:** do not overfit sparse history; favor interpretable models over sophistication you cannot maintain.
- **Win condition:** leaders make staffing choices using ranges (P50/P80) rather than single numbers.

Turnaround: OR as crisis stabilizer *Profile.* Performance pain, limited time, urgent credibility gap. *Aim.* Rapid, measurable relief; objective decisions when politics heat up.

- **First moves:** deploy proven methods with short setup: percentile staffing bands, overtime/VTO playbooks tied to risk thresholds, scenario packs for the next 2–3 quarters.
- **What to watch:** resist bespoke experiments; document baselines and deltas weekly; keep the model small and auditable.
- **Win condition:** quick drops in OT and abandon variance; executives see a weekly *plan-vs-range* dashboard and act on it.

Realignment: side-by-side proof and gradual swap *Profile.* Operations work, but strain is visible; stakeholders are persuadable. *Aim.* Demonstrate superiority of risk-aware planning without disrupting what still functions.

- **First moves:** run OR pilots parallel to the current process; compare P80 staffing envelopes to legacy outputs; introduce *driver-aware* scenarios (marketing, product, seasonality).
- **What to watch:** change fatigue; ensure metric definitions match across tools (Section 10.2 on false precision).
- **Win condition:** governance adopts ranges as the official input; annual plan becomes a living model with monthly or weekly refresh.

Sustaining success: push the frontier safely *Profile.* Stable performance, room to invest, appetite for edge. *Aim.* Incremental gains and new capabilities (speed, resilience, optionality).

- **First moves:** multi-objective optimization (cost/SL/EX), multi-skill discrete-event simulation, external drivers (weather, macro) integrated into scenarios.
- **What to watch:** justify incremental ROI; keep models explainable for audit/regulatory review.
- **Win condition:** predictable SL with lower capital/OT buffers; faster scenario turnarounds for strategic moves (e.g., M&A, new channels).

Industry nuances

- **Contact centers.** Natural fit for queueing + Monte Carlo; typical path: Erlang → risk bands → simulation with driver inputs.
- **Healthcare.** Tight constraints and safety goals; start with nurse/clinic scheduling LP and ED capacity scenarios; bias toward conservative policies.
- **Retail.** Strong seasonality and labor rules; couple promotional calendars and weather to range forecasts; optimize multi-site staffing envelopes.
- **Financial services.** Regulatory scrutiny; adopt risk-adjusted capacity with documented model validation and audit trails.

Tailoring the approach (quick map)

- *Startup:* foundations first—data hygiene, simple Monte Carlo, metric governance.
- *Turnaround:* proven playbooks—percentile staffing, OT/VTO guardrails, weekly re-forecast.
- *Realignment:* dual-run & compare—replace point estimates with envelopes incrementally.
- *Sustaining:* advanced methods—multi-objective optimization, external-driver simulations.

What this unlocks for GRPIT

- **Goals (G):** adopt service *stability* and risk thresholds, not single SL targets.
- **Roles (R):** add an OR planner and analytics partner; upskill WFM on distributions.
- **Processes (P):** move from annual static plan to monthly refresh with scenario triggers.
- **Interpersonal (I):** teach "ranges not points"; build trust with transparent models.
- **Technology (T):** ensure API-first WFM, automation telemetry, and an analytics workspace (Section 10.6).

The right STaRS diagnosis sets scope and tempo. Pick the first win that fits your stage, prove it side-by-side, and let evidence—not bravado—pull the organization into Level 4.

10.8 Goals (G): Redefining Success in the OR Era

Level 4 reframes "what good looks like" from single targets to *explicit trade-offs under uncertainty*. Earlier levels emphasized metric integrity (L2), automation/variance harvesting (L3), and execution stability; Level 4 adds mathematical rigor so goals become *optimizable objects* rather than slogans (Section 10.2).

From single targets to multi-objective choices

- *Past framing:* "Hit 80/30 at lowest cost." One metric dominates; risk and experience are implicit.
- *Level 4 framing:* Optimize a *set* of objectives—service stability, cost, agent experience, and resilience—subject to hard constraints. Plans are chosen from a Pareto set, not a single point.
- *Probabilistic shift:* KPIs move from points to distributions (e.g., "P_{85} of meeting 80/30") with explicit tolerance for tail risk (Section 10.3).

A practical goal architecture

A three-tier structure that OR tools can solve and governance can review:

1) Primary objectives (continuous, optimizable):

- **Service stability:** maximize probability of meeting interval SL/ASA bands (or minimize expected delay).
- **Total cost:** minimize labor + premiums (OT/BPO) + risk buffers.
- **Agent experience:** maximize schedule quality (preference satisfaction, fairness, volatility limits).
- **Resilience:** maximize robustness across scenarios (small performance loss when inputs shift).

2) Hard constraints (must hold):

- Labor rules, break windows, tenure/skill coverage, union provisions, regulatory minima.
- Operating windows by site/channel; training/compliance completion by due dates.

3) Risk metrics (quantify uncertainty):

- Confidence bands on staffing demand (Monte Carlo ranges).
- Stress tests (high absenteeism, AHT spikes, campaign surges).
- Sensitivity indices (which inputs move outcomes most).

Combining goals: use (a) a weighted utility to select a single plan when priorities are stable, or (b) Pareto frontiers to present options when leadership must choose trade-offs. Both approaches produce auditable decisions.

Making it real: elicitation, validation, iteration

- **Preference elicitation:** capture leadership trade-offs via structured "A vs. B" scenarios (e.g., 84% SL at lower cost vs. 86% SL at higher cost). Calibrate weights from choices rather than debate.
- **Governance loop:** monthly review of ranges vs. actuals; adjust risk appetite, weights, and constraints as evidence accumulates.
- **Performance readout:** report not only target attainment, but (i) how efficiently objectives were balanced, (ii) robustness under realized variance, and (iii) model calibration drift.

Examples of Level 4 goal statements

- *Service:* "Maintain $P_{85} \geq 80/30$ by interval; minimize expected delay subject to cost cap C."
- *Cost:* "Minimize $\mathbb{E}[TCO] + \lambda \cdot VaR_{95}(TCO)$, with OT $\leq$ 3% of hours."
- *EX:* "Maximize schedule-preference score with fairness Gini $\leq$ 0.10 and week-to-week start-time drift $\leq$ 30 minutes."
- *Resilience:* "Select plans with $\leq$ 2 pp SL degradation across top five stress scenarios."

In plain terms: Hit 80/30 in most intervals ($\geq$ 85%), and among feasible plans pick the one with the shortest waits without breaking the cost cap. Keep costs low while avoiding expensive worst cases (penalize the 95th percentile) and hold overtime $\leq$ 3%. Match agent preferences fairly and stably (start-time drift $\leq$ 30 minutes), and choose plans that pass the top five stress tests with $\leq$ 2 percentage points of service-level loss.

Integration with planning and tech

- **Continuous planning:** goals live inside a model that refreshes with new drivers (marketing, attrition, AHT) and re-optimizes on change triggers (Section 10.6).
- **Execution link:** Level 3 automation supplies variance telemetry; Level 4 uses it to tighten distributions and reset buffers (Sections 9.10 and 10.6).
- **Dashboards:** expose ranges, trade-offs, and sensitivities; avoid "one number" summaries that imply certainty.

Cultural shift and enablement

- Train managers on distributions, percentiles, Pareto sets, and scenario reading.
- Standardize metric definitions to prevent "precision theater" (Section 10.2).
- Communicate in plain language: *what changed, why the model chose this plan, how risk is covered,* and *what would trigger a different choice.*

Level 4 goals turn success from a single bullseye into an explicit balancing act—quantified, explainable, and adjustable—so decisions reflect reality, not wishful precision.

10.9 Roles (R): New Positions for the OR Era

Level 4 adds an *analytical layer* on top of Level 3 execution. That layer requires new hybrid roles, clearer interfaces between analytics and operations, and upskilled incumbents. The goal is not to replace WFM; it is to augment it with Operations Research (OR) so planning becomes quantitative, explainable, and repeatable (Sections 10.2, 10.3 and 10.8).

Three net-new roles

1) Capacity Planning Data Scientist (CPDS). Brings statistical and optimization methods into capacity planning.

- *Accountabilities:* probabilistic demand models; scenario-based Monte Carlo ranges; discrete-event/queueing simulations; risk metrics (e.g., VaR on TCO) under uncertainty; model calibration vs. actuals with backtesting.
- *Typical tools:* Python/R, SQL, simulation/LP solvers; version control; notebook-driven analysis.
- *Deliverables:* staffing distributions (not points), stress-test packs, sensitivity reports, and model cards documenting assumptions.

2) OR–WFM Translator (Product Owner for Planning). Bridges math and operations; converts business rules to model constraints and back.

- *Accountabilities:* elicit trade-offs and weights (Section 10.8); encode labor/union rules as constraints; define acceptance criteria for models; own planning dashboards.
- *Typical background:* senior WFM analyst or planner with strong quantitative literacy; superb communication.
- *Deliverables:* requirement specs, constraint catalogs, Pareto-front option sheets with *plain-language* implications.

3) Automation Orchestrator (Level 3→Level 4 interface). Operates the runtime link between models and the floor.

- *Accountabilities:* convert staffing envelopes into executable rules for the automation platform (Sections 9.10 and 10.6); monitor algorithm drift; run controlled A/Bs; capture variance telemetry for model refresh.
- *Typical tools:* real-time automation console, feature flags, experiment frameworks, observability dashboards.
- *Deliverables:* rule sets keyed to forecast risk bands; weekly learning summaries feeding CPDS calibration.

Evolving core WFM roles

Forecaster → Probabilistic Forecaster. From single-number predictions to distributions with drivers and confidence bands; curates data quality and external drivers (marketing, weather, policy).

WFM Analyst → Strategic Workforce Planner. From schedule efficiency to *capacity strategy*: multi-horizon scenarios, option value of BPO/flex pools, and resilience constraints embedded in schedules.

Real-Time Analyst → Experimenting Operator. From firefighting to experiment design: early-warning thresholds, targeted interventions, and post-mortems that update model priors.

Supervisor → Data-informed Coach. Consumes plan ranges, understands why shifts move, and reinforces preference-aware scheduling; provides feedback on plan realism to Translators.

Operating model: who owns what

- **Model integrity (CPDS):** methods, code, calibration, and risk reporting.
- **Business fitness (Translator):** constraints, utilities/weights, and stakeholder sign-off.
- **Execution fitness (Orchestrator):** deployability, guardrails, and telemetry.
- **Governance (joint):** monthly range vs. actuals; weight/constraint updates; sunset criteria for rules/models that underperform.

Competency blueprint (by stream)

- **Math/OR:** probability, queueing basics, linear/mixed-integer programming, simulation, sensitivity.
- **Data/tech:** SQL, Python/R, APIs, version control, reproducible notebooks, dashboarding.
- **Domain:** multi-skill routing, shrinkage taxonomy, labor/union rules, BPO constructs.
- **Decision:** trade-off elicitation, Pareto interpretation, risk appetite setting, post-implementation review.
- **Communication:** executive narratives, "why this plan" explainer charts, change notes for the floor.

Sizing and structure (guidance)

- *500 agents:* 1 CPDS (shared), 1 Translator (0.5–1.0 FTE), 1 Orchestrator (embedded in RT).
- *3,000 agents:* 2–3 CPDS, 2 Translators (LOBs), 2 Orchestrators (shifts), plus a lead for model governance.
- Centralize methods (CPDS) and standards; federate Translators to business lines; keep Orchestrators near operations.

Career paths and upskilling

- *Bridges:* Senior Forecaster → Translator; RT Lead → Orchestrator; Analyst (with Python) → CPDS.
- *Curriculum:* foundations (distributions, queues), coding for analysts, constraint modeling, experiment design; capstone on a live scenario.
- *Credentialing:* internal "model owner" and "rule owner" certifications with peer review.

Integration risks & mitigations

- *Role overlap:* publish RACI for models, constraints, and deployments; review quarterly.
- *Precision theater:* ban point-estimate commitments; require ranges with risk cover (Section 10.2).
- *Black-box fear:* model cards, assumption logs, and explainer views owned by Translators.
- *Silo drift:* monthly "range vs. reality" forum (CPDS, Ops, Finance) with actions that update weights or constraints (Section 10.8).

Outcome With these roles and interfaces in place, Level 4 turns planning into a managed product: *models with owners, constraints with provenance*, and *deployments with feedback*. That structure is what enables continuous, risk-aware decisions at scale—and readies the organization for Level 5.

10.10 Processes (P): From Periodic to Continuous

Level 4 replaces calendar-driven planning with *continuous, model-driven* loops. Plans are maintained as probability distributions (Sections 10.2 and 10.3); objectives are multi-criteria (Section 10.8); and roles have clear ownership of model, constraint, and deployment change (Section 10.9). The result is a cadence that runs across multiple horizons, with explicit triggers, artifacts, and handoffs.

A multi-horizon operating cadence

Real-time / intraday (minutes–hours).   Purpose: keep execution within risk bands.

- *Inputs:* live arrivals, queue health, agent states; current schedule and rule sets (Section 10.6).
- *Logic:* guardrails and policies derived from the current staffing *range*, not a point; defer/non-defer rules by risk band.
- *Owners:* Automation Orchestrator (run), Probabilistic Forecaster (alerts), Supervisors (coaching pivots).
- *Artifacts: Intraday policy* by band (green/amber/red), exception playbook, telemetry feed to models.
- *Triggers:* breach of control limits (e.g., *Service Level (SL)* below 5th percentile for 3 intervals), drift in realized *Average Handle Time (AHT)* vs. prior ($\Delta > 2\sigma$).

Daily.   Purpose: refresh beliefs; carry learning forward.

- *Inputs:* prior-day realized arrivals/AHT/shrinkage, variance capture, intervention logs.
- *Logic:* Bayesian/Monte Carlo update of near-term forecast distributions; re-compute next 14–28 day staffing envelopes.
- *Owners: Capacity Planning Data Scientist (CPDS)* (model update), Translator (constraint changes), Orchestrator (rule adjustments).
- *Artifacts: Daily range update* (percentiles *P50/P80/P95* in *Full-Time Equivalent (FTE)*), *change note* (what moved and why), *model card* delta.
- *Triggers:* marketing/campaign change notice; external event flags (weather, policy).

Weekly.   Purpose: align decisions with business risk appetite.

- *Forum:* "Range vs. Actuals" review with Ops, Finance, Marketing.
- *Content:* service/cost outcomes by planned band; sensitivity to top drivers; scenario set for next 6–12 weeks.
- *Decisions:* hiring class go/no-go; *Business Process Outsourcing (BPO)* flex adjustments; training volume targets; risk band selection per LOB.
- *Artifacts: Pareto sheet* (efficient trade-offs), *constraint register* updates, *open risks*.

Monthly. Purpose: model refinement and governance.

• *Analytics:* backtest error (*MAPE*—Mean Absolute Percentage Error; *WAPE*—Weighted APE) and bias; residual diagnostics; recalibration; feature adds/removals.

• *Optimization:* re-tune weights for multi-objective goal function (Section 10.8); re-solve seasonal envelopes.

• *Controls:* retire underperforming rules/models; promote pilots with sustained lift.

• *Artifacts: Model release notes*, updated *assumption log*, experiment registry.

Quarterly. Purpose: strategy, options, and capacity posture.

• *Activities:* stress tests (P95–P99 demand, absentee spikes), option valuation for flex pools/BPO blocks, tech roadmap sync.

• *Decisions:* risk appetite statement for next quarter; structural levers (skills, cross-training, channel mix).

• *Artifacts: Capacity posture document* with confidence bands and contingency playbooks.

Core control loops (closed-loop by design)

Forecast→Schedule→Automation→Telemetry→Forecast. Executed continuously; telemetry (realized arrivals/AHT/shrinkage and intervention acceptance) updates priors and bands.

Scenario→Decision→Deployment→Outcome→Learning. Weekly and monthly; each decision links to an experiment ID; outcome deltas must update weights/constraints or be rolled back.

Process artifacts (make the math visible)

• **Staffing envelope**: P50/P80/P95 FTE by interval with notes on drivers and constraints in force.

• **Constraint register**: labor law, union/bid rules, business policies; versioned; mapped to model clauses.

• **Model cards**: scope, assumptions, training data windows, known failure modes, calibration history.

• **Intraday policy by band**: allowed actions, deferrals, supervisor messages, customer promises.

• **Experiment registry**: hypothesis, population, metrics, stop rules, results, action taken.

Integration points (enterprise alignment)

• **Finance:** risk-adjusted budgets (distributions, not points); *Value-at-Risk (VaR)* on *Overtime (OT)* and BPO; hiring cashflow under scenarios.

• **Marketing/Prod:** campaign APIs emit expected lift/uncertainty; auto-recompute envelopes; return *capacity feasibility*.

- **IT/Data:** streaming events for arrivals/state; nightly lake updates; reproducible pipelines; *Service-Level Agreement (SLA)* for data freshness (Section 10.6).
- **HR/TA:** *Human Resources / Talent Acquisition* lead-time curves and ramp profiles captured as constraints; hiring classes triggered by band thresholds.

Triggers and guardrails

- *Statistical drift:* residuals outside control limits for k days $\Rightarrow$ forced recalibration.
- *Policy drift:* constraint violations or repeated exemptions $\Rightarrow$ register review.
- *Event flags:* campaign delta >X%, outage advisories, macro events $\Rightarrow$ immediate scenario refresh.
- *Safety stops:* hard caps on deferments, max occupancy, and after-hours OT regardless of band.

Continuous improvement toolkit

- **Statistical Process Control (SPC):** control charts on SL, AHT, and occupancy; separate common vs. special cause variation.
- **Design of Experiments (DoE):** A/B and factorial tests on interventions (e.g., long-call assist thresholds, break policies); pre-registered metrics.
- **Sensitivity analysis:** one-at-a-time and global methods (e.g., Sobol variance indices—first order and total effect) to rank drivers.
- **Post-mortems:** blameless reviews for major misses; update model cards and the constraint register within 5 business days.

RACI (Responsible, Accountable, Consulted, Informed) — simplified

- **Capacity Planning Data Scientist (CPDS): R:** models, calibration, scenario packs. **A:** forecast distributions.
- **Translator: R:** constraints/utilities, stakeholder buy-in. **A:** decision packs.
- **Orchestrator: R:** rule deployment, telemetry quality. **A:** runtime adherence to bands.
- **Ops/Finance/HR: C:** trade-offs, hiring/funding gates. **I:** range updates and changes.

Anti-patterns to avoid

- Point-estimate commitments in executive forums (reintroduces false precision).
- Monthly "rebuild from scratch" (breaks learning loops); prefer incremental updates.
- Black-box deployments without model cards and rollback plans.
- Siloed change (marketing shifts with no capacity link; hiring waves with no model update).

Outcome With this cadence, plans become living artifacts: continuously updated ranges with explicit risk, constraints with provenance, and deployments with measured effects. That is the operational substrate Level 4 needs—and the on-ramp to Level 5.

10.11 Interpersonal (I): Breaking Down Silos

Level 4 elevates WFM from a specialist function to an *enterprise* partner. Because models at this level drive hiring, budget, campaign timing, and service posture, success depends as much on relationships and shared language as on algorithms. This section makes the interfaces explicit: who works with whom, on what cadence, using which artifacts—so that optimization in Sections 10.8 and 10.10 can operate without friction on the ecosystem in Section 10.6.

From handoffs to shared ownership

Principle 1 — Joint ownership of uncertainty. Finance, Marketing, Ops, and WFM co-own *ranges*, not point estimates (Section 10.2). Decisions are framed as: "At P80 we need $x \pm \Delta$; if campaign lift exceeds L, we trigger Plan B." Ownership is documented in decision packs, not email threads.

Principle 2 — One model, many views. The same underlying distributions feed multiple lenses: service risk (Ops), cost risk (Finance), demand drivers (Marketing). Views differ; the data and assumptions do not.

Principle 3 — Clear change pathways. Any change to drivers, constraints, or risk appetite has a named path: who proposes, who reviews, who decides, and how fast. These paths are as visible as the KPIs they influence.

Collaboration contracts (who/what/when/with-what)

WFM & Finance — Risk-adjusted planning.

- *Cadence:* weekly *Range vs. Budget* review; monthly risk posture refresh.
- *Inputs:* P50/P80/P95 staffing envelopes (Section 10.10); OT/BPO VaR; hiring lead-time curves; constraint register updates.
- *Decisions:* hiring class go/no-go; OT caps; BPO flex; where to carry buffer vs. buy options.
- *Artifacts:* a one-page *risk sheet* (cost bands, service bands, key drivers, open risks).

WFM & Marketing/Product — Demand shaping.

- *Cadence:* biweekly *campaign desk*; ad hoc 48h locks for late changes.
- *Inputs:* campaign lift priors (mean/interval), channel mix, creative test calendar.
- *Decisions:* launch window within capacity bands; channel steering targets; contingency if lift > threshold.
- *Artifacts: capacity feasibility note* returned via API (green/amber/red with limits and trade-offs).

WFM & Operations — Service posture and execution.

- *Cadence:* daily stand-up; weekly *range review*.
- *Inputs:* intraday policy by risk band; training backlog; skill pipeline.
- *Decisions:* band selection for each LOB; deferral allowances; training volume; cross-skill unlocks.
- *Artifacts: intraday playbook* (allowed actions by band) and *coaching plan* aligned to envelopes.

WFM & IT/Data — Data you can bet the business on.

- *Cadence:* biweekly *data reliability* review; quarterly schema roadmap.
- *Inputs:* freshness SLAs, event catalogs, model cards (Section 10.10).
- *Decisions:* schema freezes before peak; telemetry fixes; pipeline priorities.
- *Artifacts: data contract* (fields, latency, quality tests) and runbook for incidents.

WFM & HR/TA/L&D — Lead time and skills as constraints.

- *Cadence:* monthly ramp curves review; quarterly skills roadmap.
- *Inputs:* time-to-hire and time-to-proficiency distributions; training capacity; attrition priors.
- *Decisions:* class sizes/timing; cross-training waves; incentive windows.
- *Artifacts: ramp library* (by LOB/skill) referenced directly in models.

Rituals, not meetings

Range vs. Actuals (weekly, 45 min).   Start with ranges, not stories: show where actuals sat vs. P50/P80; list top three drivers by sensitivity; propose band changes; record decisions with effective dates.

Scenario hour (biweekly, 60 min).   Review two pre-built what-ifs (e.g., absentee spike, campaign over-performance). Each has triggers, actions, and expected impacts. If adopted, link to experiment ID (Section 10.10).

Blameless post-mortem (as needed, 30–45 min).   For any miss beyond control limits: document hypothesis, data, code, assumption diffs, and the change to model/constraint. Publish to the model card.

Shared language and artifacts

- **Glossary.** Single definitions for AHT, occupancy, shrinkage, lift, P50/P80/P95.
- **Constraint register.** Labor law, union rules, business policies—versioned and referenced in optimization (Section 10.8).

- **Decision pack (1–2 pages).** Context, ranges, trade-offs (Pareto), recommendation, triggers, owners.
- **Model cards.** Purpose, assumptions, data windows, failure modes, calibration history (Section 10.10).

Roles at the interfaces (from Section 10.9)

- **OR–WFM Translator.** Turns business constraints into model clauses; turns model output into decision packs; owns glossary/education.
- **Capacity Planning Data Scientist.** Owns distributions, back-tests, scenario sets; publishes model cards.
- **Automation Orchestrator.** Ensures intraday policies honor selected risk bands; feeds telemetry back to models.
- **Business Owners (Finance/Marketing/Ops).** Select risk bands, approve trade-offs, own downstream commitments.

Trust mechanics (applied)

- **Transparency.** Publish assumptions and error bars with every range; link to the model card.
- **Benefit.** Tie each recommendation to a metric the partner owns (e.g., cost band, CSAT, campaign ROI).
- **Control.** Partners choose bands and triggers; models inform, they decide.
- **Risk.** Make residual risk explicit (what happens if we're wrong and by how much).

Anti-patterns (and the replacement)

- *Point-estimate commitments in exec decks* → show bands and triggers.
- *Email-driven last-minute campaign changes* → API with auto capacity feasibility response.
- *Parallel models per function* → one source of truth, many role-based views.
- *Siloed post-mortems* →blameless, cross-functional, published edits to model/constraints.

Outcome

When these contracts, rituals, and artifacts are in place, Level 4 math travels cleanly across the organization: Finance prices risk, Marketing shapes demand within capacity, Ops selects service posture by band, and WFM maintains the living plan. The interpersonal fabric becomes the multiplier that turns models into results—and it is the same fabric Level 5 will rely on for autonomous optimization.

10.12 Technology (T): The Ecosystem Architecture

At Level 4, technology shifts from single-vendor suites to a *composable* ecosystem that connects planning (Section 10.8), continuous processes (Section 10.10), and cross-functional ways of working (Section 10.11). The emphasis moves from deterministic, point-estimate tooling to probabilistic models and event-driven integration.

Where we came from (Levels 1–3, briefly)

- **Level 1.** Spreadsheets, manual handoffs, siloed system exports. Limited visibility and slow response.
- **Level 2.** Integrated WFM suites for forecasting, scheduling, and adherence; gains from centralization, but architectural rigidity and vendor lock-in emerge.
- **Level 3.** Real-time automation layers (e.g., intraday engines) harvest variance and orchestrate work; APIs begin to open, but analytics beyond canned reports often still requires IT.

Level 4: an ecosystem, not a monolith

Level 4 assembles best-of-breed components around shared data contracts and clear decision rights. Four roles dominate (aligned with Section 10.6):

1) Advanced capacity planning (the OR layer). Specialized platforms maintain *living* capacity models: they ingest updated forecasts, business drivers, and operational signals; run scenario sets; and expose ranges with confidence. Example categories include tools that (per vendor materials) combine linear or mixed-integer optimization with simulation and driver correlation. Public, peer-reviewed accuracy claims are limited; treat specific performance numbers as platform claims to be validated in your context.

2) Best-in-breed WFM core. API-first scheduling/forecasting systems remain the system of record for shifts, skills, and adherence. Their job is short- to mid-horizon planning and execution, with clean read/write interfaces for external optimizers and automation.

3) Industrial-strength automation (Level 3 foundation). Intraday engines subscribe to queues, schedules, and agent states to trigger actions (training, coaching, breaks, channel shifts) and to write completions back. At Level 4, these engines also consume risk bands from capacity planning and enforce the selected *service posture* in real time.

4) Modern analytics workbench. Notebook-centric environments (e.g., Jupyter-style) let analysts explore data, run back-tests, and publish model cards and decision packs without IT bottlenecks, under governance.

Integration patterns that make it work

- **Event streaming.** Systems publish state changes (agent state, training complete, campaign go/no-go). Subscribers react; no polling loops.

- **Data contracts.** Versioned schemas (fields, units, latency, quality tests) for forecasts, ranges, constraints, and outcomes. Contracts are owned, tested, and change-controlled.
- **Shared lakehouse.** Operational stores stay local; analytics and model artifacts land in a governed lakehouse for cross-system joins and back-testing.
- **Microservices.** Forecasting, optimization, automation, and reporting are independently deployable services behind stable APIs.

From rules to multi-objective decisions

Level 3 rules answer "if queue healthy, then train." Level 4 weighs competing objectives using OR techniques:

- *Service risk.* Probability that training now pushes later intervals below target.
- *Value.* Which agents gain the most (quality gaps, skill roadmaps).
- *Cost.* Overtime avoidance vs. potential revenue or SLA exposure.
- *Feasibility.* Upcoming meetings, break windows, skill coverage constraints.

Under the hood this can look like: stochastic queue forecasts feeding a small linear (or utility-weighted) program that selects who trains now, who later, and who remains on queue—then pushes the action back to WFM and automation. The objective and constraints are transparent and traceable in the model card (Section 10.10).

Bidirectional intelligence loops

- **Planning → automation.** Capacity models publish bands (P50/P80/P95) and guardrails; intraday execution enforces posture.
- **Automation → planning.** Realized variance (micro-availability, deferrals, acceptance rates) feeds back to recalibrate drivers and buffers.
- **Analytics ↔ all.** Discovery (e.g., handle-time drivers, absentee predictors) becomes new features/constraints in both planning and automation.

Pragmatic vendor evaluation (claim discipline)

When assessing capacity or automation platforms:

- Ask for *proofs in your data*: back-tests, blinded holdouts, and side-by-side pilots.
- Separate *platform claims* from validated results; document assumptions, data windows, and error bands.
- Test integration early (POC on real APIs, real volumes); review security posture (authN/authZ, audit trails, PII handling).
- Favor openness: export of model artifacts, API coverage, and clear SLAs on latency and freshness.

Governance and safety rails

- **Model cards.** Purpose, assumptions, data range, known failure modes, calibration history, owners.

- **Decision packs.** For cross-functional choices (Finance, Marketing, Ops), include ranges, Pareto trade-offs, triggers, and residual risk (Section 10.11).
- **Runbooks.** Rollback paths and safe defaults if feeds fail or latencies exceed thresholds.

Ready for Level 5

Ecosystem architecture (open APIs, events, contracts, model cards) is the substrate Level 5 will use to automate more of the decision loop. The payoff now: faster scenario turns, cleaner handoffs, and models that remain aligned with reality—without ripping out what already works.

10.13 Key Takeaways and the Path to Level 5

Level 4 elevates workforce management from operational discipline to strategic capability. By combining Operations Research, probabilistic thinking, and an ecosystem architecture (Section 10.12), organizations move from intraday variance harvesting (Section 9.13) to planning across multiple plausible futures (Sections 10.2, 10.3 and 10.6). The outcome is not a different spreadsheet—it is a different way of deciding.

Level 4: core lessons

1) From spreadsheets to science.   Single-number plans give way to ranges with stated confidence. Simulation and optimization replace manual scenario tinkering, and models are monitored, calibrated, and versioned (Section 10.10).

2) From platforms to ecosystems.   No single suite suffices. A best-of-breed WFM core, an OR-driven capacity layer, an intraday automation engine, and an analytics workbench interoperate via contracts and events (Sections 10.6 and 10.12).

3) From deterministic to probabilistic.   Plans acknowledge uncertainty explicitly (bands, stress tests, robustness) and link risk posture to business priorities (Section 10.8).

4) From reactive to predictive.   Real-time control remains (Level 3), but is now informed by forward views—drivers, scenarios, and early signals (Sections 10.3 and 10.6).

5) From cost center to strategic asset.   Capacity choices are framed as investments with trade-offs, shared with Finance, Marketing, and Operations via decision packs and model cards (Sections 10.11 and 10.12).

Readiness signals for Level 5

Operational.

- Continuous capacity refresh runs without manual stitch-work; plans include P50, P80, and P95 confidence bands.
- Automation can consume guardrails and enforce a service posture in real time.
- Integration latencies meet agreed SLOs; failover playbooks are in place.

Cultural.

- Teams are comfortable selecting among Pareto-efficient options rather than chasing a single "right" answer.
- Mathematical literacy is present in WFM and visible in cross-functional reviews.
- Governance exists for models: ownership, monitoring, and rollback (Sections 10.10 and 10.12).

Strategic.

- Diminishing returns from manual orchestration; decision cadence outpaces human throughput.
- Leadership endorses human-in-the-loop oversight for algorithmic decisions.

A phased path through Level 4

Phase 1: Build foundation (months 1–6). Establish OR competency (hire or upskill), define data contracts, and run proofs-of-concept on one contained use case (e.g., one line of business capacity). Seek quick wins: weekly automated plan updates, Monte Carlo for peak staffing, and what-if impacts for planned campaigns. Capture ROI with conservative assumptions.

Phase 2: Pilot and learn (months 7–12). Operate side-by-side comparisons against the current process; calibrate models on holdout periods; harden APIs and error handling; document model cards and decision packs; train the audiences (OR practitioners, WFM planners, stakeholders).

Phase 3: Scale and integrate (months 13–24). Roll out across units; deepen Finance/Marketing/Operations touchpoints (Section 10.11); extend to advanced use cases (multi-skill optimization, location mix, M&A scenarios). Establish a change cadence for model retraining, parameter tuning, and post-implementation reviews (Section 10.10).

Level 5 preview: autonomous orchestration

Level 5 builds on Level 4's substrate:

- **AI-driven action.** Systems not only predict but execute routine choices within guardrails; humans supervise exceptions and strategy.
- **Human–digital teaming.** Work routes optimally across people and digital agents based on complexity, urgency, and empathy needs.
- **Self-improving loops.** Models retrain on outcomes; policies adapt within governed bounds.

Action checklist

If you are at Level 3:

1. Identify the highest-friction capacity decisions and define them as optimization problems.

2. Run a POC with your data; insist on back-tests and clear error bands.

3. Invest in baseline literacy (uncertainty, optimization, simulation) across WFM.

If you are early Level 4:

1. Formalize governance (model cards, monitoring, rollback).

2. Integrate OR outputs into existing rituals (budget, campaign, ops reviews).

3. Share early wins with ranges, not single deltas; build trust through transparency.

If you are mature Level 4:

1. Evaluate which decisions can be safely automated end-to-end.

2. Extend the ecosystem beyond the contact center (CRM, QM, knowledge).

3. Pilot advanced methods (e.g., reinforcement learning) under strict guardrails.

Bottom line

Level 4 is not a bigger plan—it is a different planning system. It replaces point estimates with distributions, isolated tools with ecosystems, and ad hoc debate with governed, data-driven choice. With that foundation in place, Level 5's autonomous orchestration becomes an evolution, not a leap.

What to read while you build

Level 4 requires dual fluency: probabilistic thinking to replace brittle point estimates, and systems thinking to design ecosystems that learn. Two books provide this foundation. Start with Meadows to develop the conceptual framework, then move to Hubbard for the quantitative toolkit.

Meadows's *Thinking in Systems*   provides the conceptual architecture for Level 4 ecosystems. Systems fail not from individual components but from how parts interact—feedback loops, delays, unintended consequences. Meadows teaches you to see structures: reinforcing loops that drive growth, balancing loops that create stability, leverage points where small changes yield large effects. Her treatment of system traps describes exactly what happens when WFM tools fight instead of collaborate. This accessible primer brings systems thinking out of equations into practice, shifting your perspective from optimizing pieces to orchestrating wholes.[122]

Hubbard's *How to Measure Anything*   transforms how you approach uncertainty. The core insight: measurement is simply a reduction of uncertainty, not infinite precision. Hubbard shows how Monte Carlo simulation, calibrated estimation, and value-of-information calculations turn "we can't quantify that" into risk-aware ranges that inform decisions. His Applied Information Economics method has been validated across IT portfolios, military logistics, and R&D—exactly where traditional approaches fail. This book makes sophisticated quantitative methods accessible to practitioners, providing the toolkit for Level 4's shift from defending single numbers to communicating distributions.[123]

11 Level 5: Pioneering – Adaptive Orchestration

11.1 Introduction: Beyond the Contact Center

Sarah settled into the executive conference room, two years after Level 4's implementation had transformed capacity planning from Excel marathons into probabilistic science. Her new title—VP of Enterprise Workforce Strategy—reflected a shift the board was still digesting. She was no longer just running contact centers; she was orchestrating work across the enterprise.

"Before we start," CEO Michael Harrison began, "I need to understand something. NorthStar Insurance just announced their 'autonomous contact center.' Cut 60% of agents. Stock jumped 12%. Should we be doing the same?"

Sarah pulled up her dashboard—not just contact center metrics, but enterprise-wide flows. "Three weeks ago, NorthStar's system crashed during renewal season. Their AI couldn't handle complex policy questions. No human fallback. Customers waited hours, social media exploded, stock gave back all gains plus more."

"But they cut costs—"

"They optimized locally and failed globally," Sarah interrupted gently. "Let me show you what we built instead."

The Orchestration Demonstration

Sarah brought up a customer journey from yesterday. "Mrs. Patricia Martinez, age 72, long-time customer. Started on our website researching Medicare supplements. Struggled with the comparison tool—our system detected confusion patterns from her click behavior."

The timeline showed predictive intervention. "Before she called, we knew she'd need help. When she did call, Frank—one of our senior agents specializing in Medicare—was already briefed on her research pattern. Our AI had prepared a personalized comparison based on her existing coverage."

"The call lasted 47 minutes," Sarah continued. "Our AI could have processed the transaction in five. But Frank detected something deeper—recent widowhood affecting her decisions. He didn't just sell a policy. He connected her to our planning services, helped consolidate accounts, and addressed her real need: simplifying finances during a difficult transition."

CFO Margaret Peterson leaned forward. "The financial impact?"

"Immediate transaction: $3,200 annual premium. Lifetime value impact: $67,000 through consolidated products and retained accounts. Plus two referrals from her bridge club. Frank's fully loaded cost for that time: $34."

The Evolution from Department to Enterprise

"This isn't about contact centers anymore," Sarah explained. "It's about orchestrating all work—human, AI, and hybrid—across the enterprise."

She showed how the evolution had progressed:

Level 3: Automated variance harvesting within the contact center
Level 4: Scientific planning with OR and probabilistic models
Level 5: Enterprise orchestration across all functions

"Watch what happens when marketing plans a campaign," Sarah demonstrated.

Marketing entered a new product launch into their system. Instantly, Sarah's orchestration platform responded:

- Predicted 3,400 additional contacts in week one based on similar launches
- Identified skill gaps—only 67% of agents trained on the product
- Calculated optimal human/AI mix for different inquiry types
- Suggested pre-launch micro-training slots using Level 3's variance harvesting
- Estimated revenue impact of different service level targets
- Recommended digital self-service for features, human agents for complex cases

"Marketing used to launch, then we'd scramble," Tom Rodriguez, still on Sarah's team but now Director of Workforce Intelligence, added. "Now we're prepared before they press send."

The Distributed Truth Solution

David Kim, now President of Operations, raised a familiar challenge. "Last year, when I asked for Agent Martinez's fully loaded cost per interaction, it took three days and five spreadsheets."

Sarah smiled. "Ask again."

"What's Patricia Martinez's fully loaded cost per successful Medicare consultation?"

The answer appeared in seconds: $47.23, broken down by:

- Base compensation (HR system)
- Benefits and overhead (Finance)
- Training investment (Learning platform)
- Technology stack (IT)
- Real estate allocation (Facilities)
- Quality and coaching time (WFM)

"We don't own any of this data," Sarah explained. "We orchestrate it. Each system remains the source of truth. We just taught them to talk to each other."

The Human-AI Portfolio

A board member asked the inevitable question: "If AI is so capable, why haven't we reduced headcount?"

Sarah brought up a portfolio view. "We don't choose human or AI. We optimize the mix per interaction, per moment, per customer."

The screen showed dynamic allocation:

- Simple password resets: 100% AI
- Billing inquiries: AI-assisted human (AI retrieves, human explains)
- Technical troubleshooting: AI diagnoses, human implements
- Emotional situations: Human-led with AI providing context
- Complex negotiations: Senior human with AI running scenarios
- Compliance matters: AI ensures accuracy, human makes judgment calls

"Yesterday," Sarah continued, "our system handled 47,000 interactions. AI resolved 31,000 completely autonomously. Humans handled 8,000 high-value or complex cases. The remaining 8,000 were hybrid—AI and human working together. Total cost down 30%. Customer satisfaction up 12%. Employee satisfaction at record highs."

"Why are employees happier if AI is doing more?"

Patricia Washington, now VP of Frontline Experience, answered. "Because they're doing work that matters. No more password resets. No more reading the same script. They solve problems, build relationships, make decisions. They feel like professionals, not robots."

The Predictive Operations Edge

Sarah showed a heat map of the next week. "We don't just react to demand anymore. We see it forming."

The system was tracking:

- Digital behavior patterns suggesting upcoming contact
- Social sentiment about the brand and competitors
- Weather patterns affecting claims probability
- Economic indicators driving financial inquiries
- Marketing spend by channel and message
- Product release schedules and beta feedback

"Tuesday afternoon," Sarah pointed, "we're predicting a spike in investment questions. The Fed announcement plus market volatility. We're already scheduling our certified financial advisors, preparing talking points, and pre-loading relevant disclosures."

The Competitive Reality

Michael pulled up competitor analysis. "Meridian Insurance is implementing something similar. So is Apex Mutual. How do we maintain advantage?"

241

Sarah had been waiting for this. "They can buy the same software. They can hire similar talent. They can't replicate our orchestration culture."

She elaborated:

- "Our feedback loops run in hours, not weeks"
- "Our agents co-design AI improvements—they trust it because they built it"
- "Our systems learn from each other—CRM teaches WFM about customer value, WFM teaches CRM about service cost"
- "Our governance allows experimentation within guardrails—we test 50+ micro-innovations weekly"

"Most importantly," Sarah concluded, "we're not trying to replace humans with AI. We're building something neither could achieve alone."

The Enterprise Intelligence Vision

Sarah returned to her opening theme. "Level 5 isn't about a smarter contact center. It's about WFM principles—optimization, prediction, orchestration—applied everywhere."

She showed ongoing initiatives:

- Claims processing: Orchestrating adjusters, AI assessment, and customer communication
- Underwriting: Balancing automated decisions with human judgment on edge cases
- Sales: Routing leads to the optimal channel/agent/AI based on conversion probability
- Back office: Dynamic work allocation based on skill, availability, and deadline urgency

"Every function is asking the same questions we've been solving for years: How many people? With what skills? When? How do we balance human judgment with AI speed? We don't need to learn their business; we need to teach them our methods."

The Decision Moment

The board had assembled to approve a $50M "Digital Transformation" initiative—essentially trying to catch NorthStar's automation announcement.

Margaret spoke first. "You're saying we don't need to transform. We need to extend what's working?"

"Exactly. We've spent five years building an orchestration capability. Level 1 taught us discipline. Level 2 gave us foundation. Level 3 brought automation. Level 4 added science. Now Level 5 extends all of that beyond the contact center."

Michael stood. "The analyst call is next week. They'll ask about our AI strategy versus competitors going fully autonomous."

Sarah stood as well. "Tell them we're not choosing between humans and AI. We're orchestrating both to create something competitors can't copy—an enterprise that learns, adapts, and improves continuously. While they're figuring out their automation broke, we're already three moves ahead."

Walking Into the Future

As the board approved expanding Sarah's orchestration model enterprise-wide, she thought back to that chaotic Excel spreadsheet at specialty lines six years ago. Each level hadn't replaced what came before—it had extended and amplified it.

Tom caught her after the meeting. "Remember when our biggest problem was Monday morning coverage?"

"Now we're predicting customer needs before they know them," Sarah laughed. "And we're just getting started."

Patricia added, "The agents are already asking what's next. They've seen every level make their work more meaningful. They trust the journey."

Sarah looked at the enterprise dashboard—contact centers, claims, underwriting, sales, all flowing as one system. Not perfectly, not yet. But adapting, learning, improving every hour.

"Level 5 isn't a destination," she told her team. "It's a capability—the ability to orchestrate whatever comes next. AI will evolve. Customer expectations will shift. New channels will emerge. But we've built something that thrives on change instead of fighting it."

As she walked past the contact center floor—agents collaborating with AI, supervisors reviewing predictive insights, the ROC adjusting in real-time—Sarah saw not the end of human work, but its elevation. The future didn't belong to human OR artificial intelligence. It belonged to those who could orchestrate both.

The journey that started with Excel had become enterprise intelligence. And the next movement was about to begin.

11.2 The Enterprise Integration Imperative

For decades, contact centers operated as isolated cost centers, and WFM served as the engine inside that silo—staffing to whatever demand other functions created. That model worked when interactions were simple, channels were few, and change was slow.

Level 5 breaks the silo. The OR modeling, ecosystem integration, and probabilistic planning built in Level 4 position WFM to become an enterprise intelligence function. This is not land-grab; it is reuse of proven capabilities—optimization engines, predictive models, and real-time automation—to answer business questions far beyond staffing.

From Silo to Symphony

Traditional enterprises optimize locally: marketing runs campaigns, finance sets budgets, HR manages hiring, operations pursues efficiency, and the contact center absorbs the consequences. The result is familiar misalignment: viral campaigns without capacity, feature launches that spike support, budget cuts that quietly degrade handle time and CSAT.

Level 5 replaces ad hoc cooperation with orchestration. The same tools that optimized schedules now inform enterprise choices, enabling questions like:

- What is the lifetime value impact of different service levels?
- How do campaign choices cascade through operational cost?
- Which segments drive disproportionate support cost to revenue?
- What is the optimal mix of training investment and self-service?
- How do competitor moves predictably affect contact patterns?

Queueing theory, stochastic simulation, and multi-objective optimization stop being "contact center math" and become shared decision infrastructure.

The Distributed Truth Problem

Enterprise "truth" is spread across systems of record. A simple query—"What is Agent Patricia Martinez's fully loaded cost per interaction?"—requires joining HR (comp, location), WFM (hours, adherence, OT), quality (CSAT, evaluations), learning (skills, proficiency), finance (overhead), real estate (seat cost), and IT (tech stack cost). None is complete; some conflict.

Classic responses try to centralize everything into a warehouse-as-truth. These efforts stumble: replication drift, latency, ownership disputes, another silo.

Level 5 adopts *orchestration without ownership*. The WFM intelligence layer:

- Maps authoritative sources for each element,
- Pulls via APIs at decision time,
- Reconciles conflicts by policy and precedence,
- Enriches with WFM intelligence (e.g., variance patterns) without seizing ownership,
- Publishes insights back to systems, not duplicate data.

As new platforms (e.g., digital worker managers) appear, they are added to the authority map, not bolted into a new monolith.

Second-Order Effects: The Perpetual Pattern

Service technologies reduce simple work and transform the remainder:

- IVR removed basics; AHT rose as agents handled only complex cases.
- Bots deflect routine; escalations arrive pre-frustrated after failed self-service.
- Next-gen AI will heighten the pattern: *capability escalation*, *expectation inflation*, *trust paradoxes*, and *interaction multiplication*.

Level 5 does not try to predict exact shapes of these effects. It senses and adapts:

- Detect shifts in hours, not months,
- Update capacity models automatically,
- Rebalance human/AI/hybrid resources in real time.

The Orchestration Opportunity

Enterprise problems mirror those WFM already solved:

- **Demand uncertainty**: marketing's challenge is WFM's daily work.
- **Resource optimization**: HR's planning mirrors staffing optimization.
- **Real-time adaptation**: operations needs the Level 3/4 engine.
- **Multi-objective balance**: finance's trade-offs match WFM's.

Thus, Level 5 reframes WFM as the enterprise's intelligence layer: connecting distributed data to shared decisions, anticipating second-order effects, and coordinating responses.

This shift is technical *and* cultural. WFM teams expand their remit from "optimize within constraints" to "help set and test the constraints." The sections that follow translate this imperative into workforce models, customer intelligence, and the architecture required to orchestrate at enterprise scale.

11.3 The Adaptive Workforce Framework

Level 5 reframes the human–AI debate as an optimization problem, not a binary choice. Using the same OR and probabilistic methods refined at Level 4, organizations continuously tune the mix of human, automated, and hybrid work based on measured value creation.

Human–AI Collaboration Models

Level 5 recognizes a spectrum of collaboration patterns; the orchestration engine selects among them dynamically.

AI as Tool (Intelligence Amplification). Humans stay in control; AI accelerates judgment:

- **Knowledge enhancement**: instant retrieval and summarization of relevant content.
- **Next–best–action**: context-aware guidance from historical outcomes.
- **Real-time translation**: language support without handoffs.
- **Sentiment detection**: alerts for frustration or confusion.
- **Compliance guardrails**: proactive flagging of potential violations.

Impact is tracked explicitly (e.g., time-to-resolution, CSAT, ramp-time reduction), validating amplification rather than assuming it.

AI as Teammate (Task Specialization). Work is decomposed; AI executes bounded tasks while humans own outcomes:

- Data gathering and validation before engagement.
- Initial triage and routing by complexity/value.
- Auto-documentation and post-contact follow-up.
- 100% quality scanning with exception surfacing.

Boundaries are adjusted by evidence (e.g., if pre-qualification saves AHT but increases customer friction, rebalance questions toward humans).

AI as Orchestrator (Dynamic Allocation). The router becomes resource-agnostic:

- Predictive matching of each interaction to the highest-value handler (human, AI, or hybrid).
- Skill- and capability-based distribution across channels and time zones.
- Continuous rebalancing as queues, availability, or model performance shift.
- Escalation policies that intervene when the probability of success improves with human support.

Quantifying Human Value

Level 5 replaces "human touch" claims with hard, data-linked economics. Define the behaviors that matter, measure their lift on revenue/retention/cost/risk, and route and invest by effect size—not anecdotes.

Revenue impact modeling. Connect interaction handling to financial outcomes:

- **Upsell/cross-sell**: conversion lift for human-led recovery or advice calls.
- **Retention ("save") rates**: human intervention effect for high-LTV cancellations.
- **Downstream cost avoidance**: complex issue resolution avoiding repeat contacts and escalations.
- **Referral creation**: human-resolved complaints generating incremental demand.

Customer lifetime value correlation. Link handler and interaction type to CLV/tenure:

- First-issue resolution by experienced humans correlates with higher CLV and longer tenure.
- Emotional or high-stakes moments show stronger human advantage; routine technical fixes do not.

Emotional labor measurement. Use voice/sentiment analytics and outcomes to value empathy, de-escalation, and trust-building:

- Higher empathy scores associate with lower churn and higher NPS.
- Effective de-escalation reduces complaint and remediation costs.

Complex problem-solving metrics. Capture uniquely human capabilities:

- **Novel-situation resolution**: performance on scenarios outside training data.
- **Context recognition**: detecting life transitions (bereavement, job loss) from subtle cues and adapting goals accordingly.
- **Multi-issue synthesis**: resolving root causes that span policies, products, or life events.
- **Judgment/exception handling**: outcomes where policy, ethics, and risk must be balanced.

These signals drive routing: routine, rule-bound work flows to automation; novel, judgment-intensive, or emotionally charged work flows to humans with the right skill profile.

The Flexibility Imperative

Because capability frontiers shift, the framework prioritizes adaptability over commitment to any static mix.

Build for unknown futures.

- **Modular architecture**: human roles, AI services, and orchestration connect via standard interfaces.
- **Continuous learning loops**: small experiments measure new human–AI configurations; the best persist.
- **Reversible decisions**: fail-fast guardrails; humans reclaim classes of work within hours if outcomes degrade.
- **Portfolio approach**: maintain diverse capabilities instead of single bets.

Elastic workforce composition.

- Core experts for complex/high-value interactions.
- Flexible pools (internal gig/partners) for volume variability.
- Targeted automation where evidence supports parity or superiority.
- Hybrid pods that pair senior agents with AI copilots.
- Ongoing reskilling aligned to emerging demand patterns.

Avoid technology lock-in.

- API-first integration to switch or combine vendors without re-platforming.
- Multi-vendor strategies matched to task domains.
- Proprietary models for differentiators; commercial AI for commodities.
- Scheduled performance reviews against human baselines; retire underperformers.

Scenario planning embedded. Model multiple futures and pre-wire responses:

- *Conservative*: AI progress slows; humans remain primary.
- *Balanced*: AI handles ~60% of interactions; humans specialize.
- *Rapid disruption*: capability leaps shift mix quickly.
- *Hybrid surprise*: novel collaboration patterns emerge.

Outcome

The *Adaptive* workforce framework turns staffing into enterprise orchestration. By selecting the right collaboration model per interaction, quantifying human advantage, and keeping the system flexible, Level 5 organizations maximize value while staying ready for whatever capability frontier arrives next.

11.4 Customer Intelligence and Predictive Operations

Level 5 extends WFM from reacting to demand to *shaping* it. The OR foundations of Level 4 now fuse with enterprise signals so the organization senses need formation, positions resources in advance, and intervenes before customers ask.

From Forecasting to Pre-Contact Sensing

Traditional planning treats arrivals as exogenous. Level 5 connects to the "digital exhaust" that precedes contact and turns it into staffing and routing intent.

Digital behavior signals. Web/app telemetry and digital experience platforms surface patterns that predict near-term contact and type:

- Repeated visits to billing pages within minutes → imminent payment queries.
- Checkout or authentication errors → short-fuse assistance needs.
- Long sessions without completion → frustration-driven outreach.
- First-time use of complex features → onboarding help.
- Form downloads without submission → guidance requests.

These signals drive *specific* preparations (e.g., surge billing-skilled coverage, targeted knowledge surfacing), not generic headcount bumps.

Social sentiment as early warning. Continuous NLP on public channels provides lead-time on volume and intent:

- Complaint velocity → expected spikes and escalation mix.
- Viral mentions → step-changes in contact within hours.
- Competitor incidents → acquisition inquiries.

Detection translates to skill-precise readiness and aligned talking points.

Journey pattern recognition. Real-time journey graphs highlight when self-service is failing:

- Cycling through help articles without resolution.
- Cross-device/channel hopping in tight windows.
- Abandoned flows at known friction points.

Agents receive pre-contact briefs (what was tried, where progress stalled) to start at context, not at zero.

External drivers. Macro and industry signals inform proactive positioning:

- Market volatility → advisory and retention work.
- Weather events → regional claims and logistics.
- Regulatory changes → clarification bursts by segment.

Proactive Resource Positioning

Sensed intent enables intervention at the right moment, via the right channel, with the right capability.

Cart abandonment orchestration. Detect cause, value the opportunity, and select the intervention:

- Price sensitivity → time-delayed incentives.
- Confusion → immediate expert chat/callback with co-browse.
- Comparison shopping → structured product guidance.

Help content intelligence. Dwell and scroll-path analytics reveal confusion points; invitations are *specific* ("Need clarity on the extended return window?"), not generic "Need help?" prompts.

Social response closure. Tie public replies to private resolution:

- Prioritize by viral risk and customer value.
- Acknowledge publicly; route root-cause work to the owning team.
- Track through to fix, not just to response.

Multi-Channel Orchestration

Customers move fluidly; the operation must as well.

Unified view across touchpoints.

- Identity resolution across anonymous/authenticated states.
- Threading of related interactions into a single case history.
- Context preservation during channel switches.

Channel preference prediction.

- Learn per-customer preferences by issue type, time of day, and success history.
- Proactively steer: offer callback to phone-preferring customers stalled in chat; staff tech-forward agents for screen-share–driven calls.

Optimal path selection.

- Assess complexity and customer capability to skip unhelpful steps.
- Incorporate real-time capacity and outcome likelihoods.
- Optimize for *resolution quality* and lifetime value, not speed alone.

Operating Model: Close the Loop

Every prediction and intervention feeds model learning:

- **Signal→Preparation→Outcome**: capture whether preparation matched realized demand.
- Update propensity models (who will contact, about what, via which channel).

- Calibrate staffing and routing rules against financial and experience outcomes.

Result

Customer intelligence plus predictive operations shifts WFM from efficient reaction to proactive value creation. The organization prevents avoidable contacts, accelerates the ones that matter, and meets customers at the right moment with the right mix of human and digital capability—turning the contact center from a cost sink into a strategic lever for growth.

11.5 The Technology Stack Evolution

Level 4 proved the value of an API-first ecosystem inside the contact center. Level 5 extends that fabric across the enterprise and adds intelligence layers that learn, predict, and act. The result is not a replacement of Level 4 components, but their recomposition into a unified decisioning platform.

From Ecosystem to Intelligence Platform

Level 4 as foundation. OR-based capacity planning, real-time automation, advanced analytics, and open APIs persist—now operating as specialized services inside a broader, enterprise scope. The same engines that scheduled agents now allocate work across humans, digital workers, and hybrids; the same automation that harvested intraday variance now coordinates preemptive interventions.

Intelligence layers. Two additions turn an ecosystem into a platform:

- An *orchestration layer* that standardizes how systems communicate, authenticate, and observe one another.
- A *decision layer* that evaluates events against objectives and constraints to choose actions in real time.

Orchestration: Connecting the Enterprise

API/service mesh. A mesh abstracts point-to-point sprawl. Traffic routing, resilience, authn/authz, and telemetry are policy-driven rather than hand-coded per integration.

Unified query facade. A federated API (e.g., GraphQL federation or equivalent) presents business concepts instead of system silos. One request can retrieve "customer value + current intent + open cases" without bespoke joins.

Event backbone. An event bus/streaming layer publishes state changes ("policy updated," "cart abandoned," "queue recovered") so subscribers react within milliseconds. Back-pressure, ordering, and exactly-once semantics are table stakes.

Semantic contracts. A shared business vocabulary and schema registry keep services aligned as they evolve. Data producers own definitions; consumers bind to versions.

Data: From Warehouse to Fabric

Distributed data access. Instead of copying everything into one store, a data fabric virtualizes access to authoritative systems with caching where it helps and lineage where it matters.

Federated governance. Domains (CRM, ERP, HR, CCaaS, LMS) keep stewardship; the platform enforces policy (PII rules, retention, minimization) across queries and streams.

Analytic persistence. Warehouses/lakes still play a role—for history, training data, and heavy analytics—while real-time views come from the fabric. Both are synchronized via governed pipelines.

Decisioning: Real-Time, Multi-Objective

Stream processing. Event processors enrich signals and detect patterns (e.g., high-value customer + repeated billing page views + negative sentiment).

Decision models. Externalized decision tables/graphs let business teams adjust policy without redeploying code (eligibility, priorities, SLAs, guardrails).

Optimization solvers. Linear/constraint solvers select actions under capacity, cost, risk, and experience constraints—at millisecond latencies.

Scenario services. Continuous Monte Carlo/sensitivity checks quantify risk (e.g., service level confidence bands) and feed thresholds back to decision logic.

Closed loop. Outcomes (good/bad) are written to the stream; models and thresholds retrain or recalibrate on actuals.

ML/AI Integration Points

Model serving. A low-latency serving tier exposes models (propensity, churn, handle-time lift, routing suitability) behind stable APIs. Feature stores ensure consistent inputs across training and inference.

Explainability and oversight. Decisions affecting customers or employees carry reasons, confidence, and override options. Drift detection triggers retraining or rollback.

Human-in-the-loop. Default stance: AI recommends; humans supervise. Escalation thresholds route high-stakes or low-confidence cases to people.

Natural Language Interfaces

Conversational access. Stakeholders ask: "What drove yesterday's spike and what's the forecast impact of Campaign A?" The platform composes a cross-system query, runs attribution, and returns narrative + visuals.

Operational controls. Authorized users adjust levers in plain language ("raise hardship coverage by 10 FTE this week if volatility > X") which compile to decision/solver updates with audit.

Autonomy with Guardrails

Policy boundaries. Business policies define allowed ranges (cost ceilings, fairness rules, compliance constraints). Within them, the platform acts autonomously; beyond them, it seeks approval.

Reinforcement learning where safe. Low-risk domains (e.g., micro-timing of training, message variants) learn by experimentation; high-risk domains remain rule/optimization-driven with human review.

Full auditability. Every recommendation, decision, model version, input feature, and outcome is traceable.

Core Integrations (Bidirectional)

CRM (journey intelligence). 360° profiles, relationship graphs, and value scores flow in; resolution quality, effort, and save events flow back to enrich journey models.

ERP (financial impact). Activity-based costs and revenue attribution inform routing and staffing; workforce plans update forecasts and budgets.

HR (workforce capability). Skills, certifications, availability, and development plans shape deployment; performance signals inform learning and talent strategies.

Marketing (demand signals). Campaign calendars and response curves prime capacity; service outcomes feed channel/offer optimization.

Design Principles for Level 5 Readiness

- **Modular & replaceable:** Prefer contracts over tight coupling; assume components will be swapped.
- **Latency aware:** Separate real-time, near-real-time, and batch paths; don't force one tool to do all three.
- **Security by design:** Zero-trust across services, least-privilege tokens, data minimization at query time.
- **Resilience first:** Safe-to-retry actions, retries, circuit breakers, and graceful degradation paths for partial failures.
- **Measure everything:** Decision quality, model lift, constraint violations, and financial impact—not just system uptime.

Outcome

With orchestration, data fabric, and real-time decisioning layered on the Level 4 ecosystem, the technology stack becomes a living platform. It connects to where truth resides, reasons over multiple objectives, acts within guardrails, and learns from outcomes—enabling enterprise-wide workforce orchestration that adapts as fast as customers and markets do.

11.6 Autonomous Operations

Level 5 minimizes manual intervention without sidelining people. Where Levels 1–4 progressively automated decisions, Level 5 systems *learn while operating*: they observe outcomes, adjust policies, and improve continuously—freeing humans to focus on judgment, creativity, and care. Empirical results from field studies echo this pattern: AI that codifies top-performer practices lifts novice performance materially while leaving experts' outcomes largely unchanged. The goal, then, is not replacement but amplification at scale.

Self-Optimizing Systems

Continuous learning loops. Every interaction updates the system's beliefs.

- *Pattern discovery:* Models separate successful from unsuccessful paths (e.g., phrasing that de-escalates anger) and surface guidance in the moment.
- *Strategy evolution:* Safe-to-learn domains use reinforcement learning to test small policy tweaks and converge on better defaults.
- *Knowledge synthesis:* Signals from thousands of agents and journeys accumulate into organization-wide playbooks.
- *Adaptive thresholds:* Targets (quality, risk, timing) recalibrate as demand mix, expectations, or constraints shift.

Automatic rebalancing. Capacity and attention move to where they create the most value.

- *Predictive shifts:* Early signals (social sentiment, web behavior, macro indicators) adjust staffing and skill mix before impacts land.
- *Cross-channel routing:* Work flows to the channel currently resolving fastest/easiest for a given issue, with controlled guardrails.
- *Skill redistribution:* Observed lift (e.g., higher save rates) increases an agent's allocation to similar high-value interactions.

Predictive upkeep. The platform prevents avoidable failures.

- *Burnout prevention:* Fatigue and stress markers trigger workload smoothing, protected time, or targeted coaching.
- *Quality drift alerts:* Emerging defects in process, content, or systems trigger micro-fixes before customers feel them.
- *Tech health:* Degradation is detected early; traffic fails over gracefully with preserved context.

Self-tuning performance.

- *Model retraining:* Drift detectors trigger retrains/rollbacks; canary models prove lift before broad rollout.
- *Parameter search:* Solvers auto-tune routing weights, timeouts, and thresholds to meet multi-objective targets.

- *Waste detection:* Low-ROI training, redundant handoffs, or idle skill pockets are flagged and pruned.

Decision Automation

Human vs. AI vs. hybrid. For each interaction the system evaluates:

- *Complexity & affect:* NLP estimates difficulty and emotion; routine flows to automation, nuanced to people, hybrids when optimal.
- *Value calculus:* Expected value compares options (service outcome, cost, risk, downstream revenue/retention).
- *Capability matching:* Real-time views of human skills and model suitability select the best handler *now*, including brief AI warm-ups before human handoff.
- *Outcome learning:* Routing updates continuously based on realized results.

Dynamic skill matching.

- *Expertise alignment:* Certifications and proven lift guide assignments for technical, retention, or empathy-heavy work.
- *Style compatibility:* Preference and comprehension signals steer customers to communicative "fits."
- *Non-obvious wins:* The system exploits discovered success patterns even when the causal story is incomplete—within fairness guardrails.

Real-time trade-offs.

- *Service vs. cost:* Selects the economically dominant option (e.g., 10-minute callback vs. 30-minute hold) under constraints.
- *Local vs. global:* Balances an individual's experience with fleet-wide performance and SL targets.
- *Now vs. later:* Optimizes for lifetime value, not just today's handle time.

Compliance built in.

- *Regulatory adherence:* Labor, privacy, and industry rules are encoded as hard constraints with automatic audit trails.
- *Policy enforcement:* Shift limits, break protections, credential checks, and escalation rules are non-bypassable.
- *Ethical bounds:* Fairness checks and protected-class safeguards run alongside optimization.

Exception Management

Autonomy hands off gracefully when novelty, stakes, or ambiguity rise.

When to escalate.

- *Novelty:* Out-of-distribution signals route to humans rather than extrapolating.

- *Low confidence:* Recommendations below threshold request approval or alternative input.
- *High stakes:* Large financial, reputational, or precedent-setting choices require human sign-off.

What humans decide.

- *Policy exceptions:* Compassionate, contextual judgments that weigh risk, equity, and long-term trust.
- *Fairness evaluation:* Humans review statistical findings and determine appropriateness in situ.
- *Precedent setting:* Choices that shape norms or future constraints.

Where control resides.

- *Goals:* Humans set objectives and priorities the system optimizes toward.
- *Constraints:* Humans define the guardrails—legal, ethical, brand.
- *Overrides:* Managers can halt, amend, or reverse any autonomous action with full traceability.

Result

Level 5 autonomy handles the repeatable and measurable with superhuman consistency while elevating distinctively human work to where it matters most. Expertise disseminates to every desk; experts are freed for the edge cases and the moments that create durable value. The system and the workforce co-learn, improving each other over time.

11.7 Goals (G): Multi-Stakeholder Optimization

Level 5 redefines success. Earlier levels progressed from basic metrics (Level 1), through AQEE discipline (Level 2), variance harvesting (Level 3), and multi-objective math (Level 4). At Level 5, goals extend beyond the contact center to balance customers, employees, operations, investors, and—where relevant—societal impact. The rigor built at Level 4 now supports enterprise optimization across competing interests.

Enterprise-Wide Objectives

Customer lifetime value (CLV). The core question shifts from "did we answer quickly?" to "did we strengthen the relationship?" Targets span:

- *Relationship depth:* evidence of multi-product adoption, reduced re-contact for the same need.
- *Future value:* potential value uplift, not just current margin.
- *Advocacy:* referral propensity and earned media effects.
- *Trust capital:* resolution credibility and promise-keeping over time.

Routing that prefers an empathetic expert over a faster bot may raise immediate cost but improve CLV; the goal set must recognize that trade.

Employee experience. Employees are not only capacity; they are capabilities that compound.

- *Growth velocity:* time-to-proficiency, skill breadth, internal mobility.
- *Autonomy indices:* schedule flexibility, decision latitude, tool influence.
- *Wellbeing:* sustained workload balance, stress indicators, recovery time.
- *Purpose alignment & recognition:* contribution visibility tied to outcomes.

Operational efficiency—reframed. Efficiency measures the *value* created per unit of effort, not just throughput.

- *Value per interaction:* downstream revenue/retention minus full cost.
- *Learning efficiency:* rate at which models and teams improve.
- *Adaptation velocity:* cycle time from signal to change in production.
- *Resource fluidity:* friction to redeploy people/AI across needs.
- *Waste removal:* time, cognitive load, and emotional "rework."

Strategic flexibility. Optionality is an objective.

- *Capability diversity index:* skill, vendor, and model plurality.
- *Pivot readiness:* tested playbooks for material scenario shifts.
- *Scenario robustness:* stable performance across plausible futures.
- *Learning loop speed:* discovery → decision → deployment cadence.

Innovation enablement. Treat innovation as measurable work, not ambient hope.

- *Experiment velocity & mix:* quantity, quality, and risk-balance of tests.
- *Failure learning rate:* share of "misses" that produce reusable insight.
- *Cross-pollination:* ideas moving across teams and functions.
- *Participation:* percent of workforce contributing implementable changes.

From enablement to evidence.

The innovation enablers just outlined—velocity, learning, cross-pollination, participation—matter when they change outcomes. Figure 11.1 translates those behaviors into a balanced result profile across *CX, EX, Cost, Revenue, Risk*, and *Quality*; the "Before (L2)" and "After (L5)" traces show how orchestration reweights trade-offs in practice.

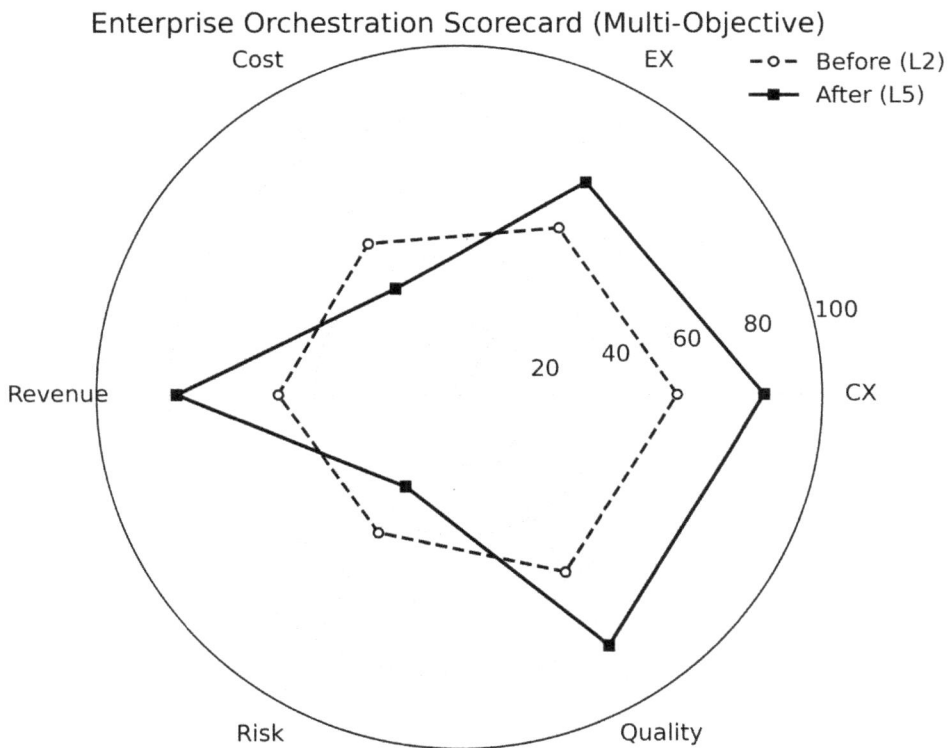

Figure 11.1: Sample Multi-Objective Scorecard

Dynamic Goal Balancing

Fixed hierarchies of goals age quickly. Level 5 systems adjust weights with context.

Real-time priority adjustment.

- *Context-aware weighting:* service incidents raise experience weights; hiring constraints raise wellbeing weights.

- *Stakeholder signals:* complaints, churn risk, burnout markers, and investor guidance shift emphasis automatically.
- *External factors:* macro conditions and regulatory changes update constraints and targets.
- *Feedback loops:* realized outcomes recalibrate future weights.

Preference learning. Optimize based on revealed—not stated—preferences.

- *Customers:* speed vs. thoroughness vs. empathy, by segment and individual.
- *Employees:* observed schedule/task choices and learning paths.
- *Investors:* market reactions to trade-offs (growth, margin, risk).
- *Communities/regulators:* sentiment and compliance responses.

Outcome-based optimization. Measure ends, not proxies.

- *Customer success:* goal attainment and friction removed.
- *Employee fulfillment:* skills realized and careers advanced.
- *Business impact:* value per relationship, not cost per contact.
- *Societal contribution:* tangible improvements tied to operations.

Success Metrics Evolution

Efficiency → effectiveness.

- *L1–L2:* volume and compliance.
- *L3:* stability under variance.
- *L4:* explicit trade-offs.
- *L5:* stakeholder impact.

Cost → value.

- *Traditional:* cost per minute/contact.
- *Transitional:* revenue/save/upsell rates.
- *Level 5:* lifetime value created and relationship multipliers.

Reactive → predictive.

- *Reactive:* SL achieved, issues closed.
- *Proactive:* problems prevented, opportunities captured.
- *Predictive:* future value and capability built.

Implementation Challenges & Practical Responses

Measurement complexity. Intangibles (trust, potential, wellbeing) require:

- proxy metrics and composite indices,
- longitudinal tracking from action to outcome,

- causal designs (A/B, diff-in-diff) to separate signal from noise.

Stakeholder conflicts. When interests clash:

- make trade-offs explicit and transparent,
- enforce minimum thresholds for each group,
- balance over time (who benefits now vs. next),
- look for expansion options that grow total value.

Organizational readiness.

- build progressively through Levels 2–4 capabilities,
- invest in culture that accepts probabilistic goals,
- commit leadership to long-term value,
- ensure the tech stack can run multi-objective optimization in (near) real time.

Bottom Line

Level 5 goals treat workforce management as an enterprise optimization problem: balancing stakeholders dynamically, measuring outcomes rather than activities, and privileging value and learning over narrow efficiency. Done well, the goal system becomes a living contract among customers, employees, the business, and society—and a practical guide for daily decisions at scale.

11.8 Roles (R): The New Workforce Architects

Level 5 completes the role evolution: from operational specialists to enterprise architects who orchestrate human and digital work across the business. Earlier levels built definition (L1), specialization (L2), automation leverage (L3), and mathematical depth (L4). At Level 5, roles expand beyond the contact center to shape enterprise strategy through workforce intelligence.

New Enterprise-Altitude Roles

Chief Workforce Strategist. A senior leader who steers all forms of work—employees, contingent talent, AI agents, and emerging digital workers—as a single portfolio.

- *Portfolio optimization:* balance FTE, gig, BPO, and AI across functions.
- *Capability roadmaps:* anticipate where AI scales, where human skills differentiate, and where hybrid models win.
- *Multi-stakeholder trade-offs:* model customer, employee, financial, and community impacts—not just unit cost.
- *Scenario planning:* maintain resilience across divergent AI and regulatory futures.

AI–Human Collaboration Designer. Designs how people and machines work together.

- *Workflow (re)composition:* decompose processes; assign human/AI/hybrid ownership; recombine with clean handoffs.
- *Team interaction design:* surface recommendations, override paths, and explanation UX that fit human cognition.
- *Hybrid performance metrics:* measure value creation, learning acceleration, and exception quality—not just throughput.
- *Ethical guardrails:* build transparency and dignity into collaboration patterns.

Customer Intelligence Analyst. Moves from descriptive reporting to predictive journey modeling.

- *Journey prediction:* identify pre-contact signals and likely next actions.
- *Cross-channel synthesis:* stitch behavior across web, app, social, and voice.
- *Sentiment trajectory:* detect inflection points where intervention changes outcomes.
- *Value mapping:* connect interaction types and handler choice (human/AI) to CLV.

Workforce Evolution Planner. Ensures readiness for unknown futures.

- *Capability portfolios:* diversify skills, tech, and partners to preserve options.
- *Learning architecture:* shorten time-to-proficiency and reskilling cycles.
- *External ecosystem:* orchestrate education, vendor, and talent-platform links.
- *Weak-signal scanning:* detect emerging skill needs early.

Ethical AI Governor. Operates the governance system for AI in work decisions.

- *Bias monitoring & mitigation:* continuous tests across hiring, routing, and evaluation.
- *Explainability & auditability:* document why and how decisions are made.
- *Regulatory compliance:* translate policy into operational controls.
- *Stakeholder trust:* clear communications to employees and customers.

How Traditional Roles Evolve

WFM Analyst → Enterprise Orchestrator. From interval staffing to cross-business resource orchestration:

- coordinate 50+ channels, multiple geographies, and 20+ worker types,
- optimize human/AI mix in real time with financial and customer constraints,
- align dozens of systems to a single operating picture.

Capacity Planner → Scenario Architect. From seasonal plans to option-rich strategies:

- design responses for extreme events and structural shifts,
- embed automatic plan adaptation to live signals,
- keep optionality (skills, sites, vendors, AI models) intentionally high.

Real-Time Manager → Autonomous System Supervisor. From manual interventions to oversight of self-optimizing platforms:

- monitor model drift and constraint adherence,
- tune policies and thresholds as goals change,
- investigate anomalies for new patterns or risks,
- enforce ethical boundaries.

Building Level 5 Teams

No single profile covers the span. Effective teams blend:

- WFM operators (operational reality),
- data scientists / OR experts (modeling and optimization),
- behavioral scientists (human factors, motivation),
- technologists (AI capabilities and limits),
- business strategists (value linkage),
- ethicists / compliance (guardrails).

Teams work as flexible networks: leadership shifts by problem domain (ethics, workflow design, scaling), not rigid hierarchy.

Career Pathways

Level 5 opens non-linear growth:

- real-time analyst → automation orchestrator → scenario architect → chief workforce strategist,
- scheduler → collaboration designer → enterprise orchestrator,
- QA analyst → customer intelligence analyst → CLV strategist.

Valued capabilities: systems thinking, collaborative problem-solving, comfort with uncertainty, ethical judgment, and continuous learning—alongside technical depth.

Bottom Line

Level 5 roles architect how work happens. They design human–AI systems, govern them responsibly, and align them to enterprise value. In doing so, workforce management completes its shift from back-office function to strategic discipline that shapes how the whole business performs.

11.9 Processes (P): Continuous Evolution

Level 5 completes the process journey: from Level 1 documentation and Level 2 procedure, through Level 3 real-time automation and Level 4 mathematical optimization, to *living* processes that learn, adapt, and orchestrate across the enterprise.

Adaptive Planning: From Prediction to Anticipation

At this level, "planning cycles" dissolve into continuous adaptation streams.

- *Real-time capability assessment:* the system evaluates human skills (including current load and affect), AI skills, and digital workers; it matches capabilities to emerging needs continuously.
- *Proactive orchestration:* a product recall triggers immediate segmentation, tone/need prediction, and resource placement across channels—before the surge arrives.
- *Embedded experimentation:* micro-tests (routing variants, training placements, schedule patterns) run safely by default; winning variants scale automatically, weak ones sunset without ceremony.
- *Rapid pilot deployment:* new AI components launch to low-risk cohorts with auto-created control groups, live KPIs, and rollback paths; scope expands only when thresholds are met.
- *Auto-learning:* models retrain on fresh data; flows, thresholds, and allocations self-adjust within guardrails. Human oversight focuses on goals and constraints, not step-by-step tuning.

Cross-Enterprise Workflows: Beyond Organizational Boundaries

Processes span finance, marketing, product, HR, operations, and service as one system.

- *Unified planning loops:* finance forecast updates re-optimize service levels and hiring plans; campaign calendars adjust journey design and skill coverage automatically.
- *Launch choreography:* as features finalize, the system predicts support mix, generates training from source docs, schedules enablement, and tunes channels for expected intents.
- *Decision-in-context:* per-interaction routing balances CLV impact, resolution likelihood, and cost—drawing on CRM, quality, and financial models in milliseconds.
- *Collaborative optimization:* objectives (service, revenue, EX, brand) are optimized jointly; weights shift with context (e.g., tighten service for strategic segments during a competitive push).

Innovation Pipelines as Standard Process

Innovation is not a side project; it is the operating model.

- *Always-on tech evaluation:* the platform scores new capabilities for fit, risk, integration effort, second-order effects, and projected ROI.
- *Dynamic pilots:* the system selects eligible intents, times, and segments; it instruments outcomes beyond point goals (adjacent impacts, agent effort, downstream volume).

- *Scale/stop criteria:* clear, pre-set gates control expansion; success propagates gradually with health checks, while "no-go" results feed pattern libraries to avoid repeat mistakes.

Self-Improving Architecture

Processes monitor and improve themselves.

- *Meta-metrics:* time-to-adapt, robustness across scenarios, and trade-off quality are tracked alongside traditional KPIs.
- *Living documentation:* procedures update automatically when flows, thresholds, or handoffs change; change history (process genealogy) remains queryable.
- *Institutional memory:* prior experiments, outcomes, and contexts inform future designs, preventing regressions and accelerating iteration.

Human–AI Collaboration Points

Automation is broad; judgment remains human where it adds value.

- *Escalation by design:* novelty detection, low-confidence decisions, high-stakes cases, or wellbeing-sensitive choices trigger human review.
- *Adaptive interfaces:* the system learns which decisions benefit from human input and surfaces the right context at the right moment.
- *Evolving boundary:* as AI matures, some decisions automate; as complexity rises elsewhere, new human checkpoints appear. The mix adjusts continuously.

How to Progress Toward Continuous Evolution

- Shift from static procedures to instrumented processes that *document themselves*.
- Replace periodic improvement cycles with *continuous* experimentation and rollout.
- Orchestrate *enterprise* workflows (finance, marketing, product, HR) rather than contact center silos.
- Embed innovation into BAU with default-safe pilots and clear expansion gates.
- Manage by objectives and guardrails; let systems adapt within those bounds.

At Level 5, processes stop being constraints and become capabilities: they anticipate, orchestrate, and learn—spanning organizational borders while keeping humans focused on decisions that require judgment, empathy, and strategy.

11.10 Interpersonal (I): Enterprise Collaboration

Level 5 represents a step-change in relationships. What began in Level 1 as informal links, tightened through Level 2–3, and broadened via Level 4 cross-functional partnerships becomes *seamless enterprise collaboration*: workforce intelligence flows across business units and even outside the firm, aligning customer outcomes, employee experience, and financial performance.

This is not a sharper version of stakeholder management; it is a different paradigm. Decisions in workforce orchestration ripple instantly across domains—routing choices affect CLV, engagement, cost, and brand—so trust, data, and decision rights must operate at the speed of the business.

C-Suite Partnership: From Support to Strategic Core

At Level 5, workforce strategy sits in the strategy room, not the back office.

- *Direct CEO/COO alignment:* a Chief Workforce Strategist (CWS) partners on questions of market entry, AI adoption posture, and human–AI mix—backed by simulations, risk bounds, and value projections.
- *Board visibility:* discussion centers on scenario robustness, workforce-derived moats, and ethical/brand implications of automation, not unit costs alone.
- *Embedded in planning:* strategic plans are co-authored with workforce intelligence—market intent, talent availability, regulatory constraints, and investment envelopes modeled alongside product and finance.

Cross-Functional Leadership: The End of Silos

Functional boundaries give way to unified operating models.

- *IT co-creation:* WFM and IT jointly design an adaptive platform (APIs, events, model ops). Exploration of new capabilities (e.g., advanced language models) moves through shared labs with safe cohorts, live KPIs, and rapid rollback.
- *HR strategic alignment:* talent intelligence (skills, aspirations, wellbeing) and operations intelligence (demand, outcomes) form one picture. Schedules, roles, and development adapt to life context and capability growth, improving EX and performance together.
- *Finance value partnership:* cost views expand to value-per-interaction, option value, and risk-adjusted returns. Budgeting and risk management run on the same scenarios the orchestration engine uses.
- *Marketing demand collaboration:* shared models link campaigns to service utilization and lifetime value. Flash events auto-trigger skill placement, knowledge updates, and channel posture; service insights feed message refinement.

External Ecosystem: Beyond the Firm

Collaboration extends to vendors, academia, and industry bodies.

- *Vendors as co-innovators:* move from procurement to joint roadmaps, shared telemetry, and value-sharing contract models; combine multiple best-of-breed services behind open interfaces.
- *Academic partnerships:* applied research on human–AI collaboration, multi-objective optimization, and AI ethics informs practice; data- and problem-sharing accelerate both theory and deployment.
- *Industry leadership:* contribute to standards, regulatory pilots, and shared tooling. Publish methods where it lifts the ecosystem while protecting differentiated IP.

Relationship Architecture for Continuous Evolution

Sustained collaboration rests on explicit operating principles:

- *Radical transparency:* default share of intents, metrics, and limits; opaque pockets slow orchestration and erode trust.
- *Mutual value:* governance checks for two-way benefit; win-lose terms decay the network.
- *Continuous learning:* every engagement is instrumented; insights propagate across teams and partners.
- *Ethical foundation:* commitments to fairness, privacy, and worker dignity are encoded as constraints the system cannot violate.
- *Adaptive structure:* networks reconfigure fluidly—leadership shifts to the node with the most relevant insight for the problem at hand.

What "Good" Looks Like at Level 5

- Workforce strategy is a standing item in executive and board agendas, backed by scenario evidence and risk bounds.
- Joint IT–WFM backlog governs platform evolution; pilots ship to production cohorts weekly with automatic guardrails.
- HR and WFM operate a unified talent–work graph; development, scheduling, and routing optimize both EX and outcomes.
- Finance plans on value and options as well as cost; risk and return use the orchestration engine's scenarios.
- External partners contribute to capability roadmaps; co-developed solutions move from lab to scaled use with shared success metrics.

At Level 5, relationships are not merely enablers of optimization—they are the medium through which the organization senses, decides, and adapts. Boundaries between internal and external, human and artificial, operational and strategic fade into a single collaboration fabric that compounds learning and value over time.

11.11 Technology (T): The Autonomous Platform

Level 5 technology is not a bigger suite or tighter integration—it is a *living* platform that learns, adapts, and optimizes across the enterprise. What Levels 2–4 achieved with monoliths, automation, and ecosystems, Level 5 delivers through autonomous, distributed intelligence where human and machine judgment operate as one system.

Distributed Intelligence: Beyond Central Control

Intelligence shifts from a few "smart cores" to many collaborating services, coordinated by events—not handoffs.

- *Microservice orchestration:* Thousands of narrow services (e.g., stress recovery timing, skill-decay prediction, burnout risk) act on streams in parallel, composing emergent responses within milliseconds.
- *Event-driven backbone:* Every state change (campaign launch, policy tweak, anomaly) is an event; services react independently, producing a coordinated outcome via streams and contracts rather than central workflows.
- *Real-time optimization everywhere:* Multi-objective solvers run continuously—routing, scheduling, training, and recovery decisions incorporate CLV, cost, risk, wellbeing, and learning value with live constraints.
- *Federated learning:* Models improve locally while sharing anonymized gradients/patterns across a network, raising industry-wide performance without moving raw data.

AI/ML Integration: From Automation to Intelligence

AI shifts from executing rules to discovering better ones.

- *Predictive models at scale:*
  - *Customer behavior:* Anticipate journey, channel, emotion, and outcome based on digital exhaust, sentiment, lifecycle, and market signals.
  - *Workforce evolution:* Forecast skill trajectories, engagement, burnout likelihood, and best-fit roles; prescribe development actions.
  - *Business impact:* Link workforce decisions to revenue, retention, risk, brand, and total cost to guide value-based choices.
- *Natural language intelligence:* Conversational analytics replaces dashboards; the platform answers "why," proposes "what if," and surfaces unsolicited insights ("I found an emerging pattern in billing chats...").
- *Emotion/intent understanding:* Real-time detection of sentiment, confusion, and unstated needs guides routing, coaching, and recovery.
- *Reinforcement learning:* Always-on micro-experiments optimize policies (routing variants, training formats, schedule shapes); multi-agent learners co-evolve scheduling, routing, and coaching policies toward higher long-term value.

Platform Fabric: Make Change Cheap and Safe

Architecture choices make experimentation routine and reversals painless.

- *Service mesh & API federation:* Uniform discovery, security, and observability; GraphQL/semantic layers expose business concepts over system details.
- *Streaming+state:* Exactly-once streams with replay for post-hoc learning; low-latency state stores for sub-second decisions.
- *Model ops as first-class:* Feature stores, online/offline parity, champion–challenger promotion, and automatic rollback on drift.
- *Guardrails by design:* Policy, regulatory, and ethical constraints enforced as hard limits in every decision path; full audit trails.

Human Interface: Complexity, Hidden; Agency, Preserved

As intelligence grows, interaction gets simpler—and more explanatory.

- *Conversational control:* "Show what matters today," "Simulate 20% more training," "Who risks burnout next month?"—answers include rationale, confidence, and trade-offs.
- *Augmented decisions:* Every choice comes with scenarios, sensitivity, stakeholder impacts, and recommended next steps; people set goals and boundaries, the platform optimizes within them.
- *Adaptive visuals:* Progressive detail, anomaly callouts, and intent-aware views make flows, bottlenecks, and opportunities obvious.

The Living System

The autonomous platform improves itself and the ecosystem around it.

- *Self-improving architecture:* High-value patterns spawn specialized services; underperformers refactor or retire automatically.
- *Autonomous innovation:* The platform proposes new operating policies and proves them on safe cohorts before scaling.
- *Ecosystem evolution:* Federated insights propagate; good ideas spread, bad ones extinguish quickly—raising the frontier for all participants.

Level 5 technology does not replace human judgment; it *amplifies* it—embedding probabilistic reasoning, ethical constraints, and multi-stakeholder value into every decision. The result is a platform that anticipates, learns, and adapts continuously—turning uncertainty into advantage and making the enterprise measurably smarter every day.

11.12 Implementation Journey

Moving from Level 4 to Level 5 is not a tool swap—it is an enterprise reinvention that blends human and machine intelligence into a self-improving operating model. Unlike earlier transitions that a single program could drive, this journey spans years, touches every function, and redefines how value is created.

Maturity Assessment: Start with the Truth

Level 5 only works atop a strong Level 4. Begin with an unvarnished readiness review.

Level 4 Foundation—Verified, Not Assumed

- **Ecosystem depth:** Capacity tools ingest business drivers automatically; automation writes variance back to planning; analytics is self-service; APIs enable live, bidirectional flows.
- **Math in motion:** Probabilistic models inform daily decisions; Monte Carlo underpins risk; multi-objective optimization is operational (not slideware); OR outputs change plans, not just reports.
- **Culture shift:** Variance is viewed as opportunity; silos give way to collaboration; teams think in *ecosystems*, not platforms; employees are partners in optimization.

Enterprise Readiness—Beyond WFM

- **Aligned leadership:** Executives grasp Level 5 as enterprise strategy, not "more automation," and commit through multi-year cycles.
- **Change capacity:** Healthy track record, room on the change calendar, psychological safety for experiments, and fast learning loops.
- **Risk posture:** Patience for probabilistic bets, tolerance for failed pilots, and a bias for learning over certainty.

Technology & Data Groundwork

- **Architecture:** Cloud-*native* (not lifted), event-driven, elastically scalable, zero/low-latency integration; security supports data sovereignty and federated learning.
- **Data:** Clear ownership, quality SLAs, cross-domain models, programmatic access to history, and embedded privacy/ethics.
- **AI/ML:** Production MLOps (feature store, monitoring, rollback), applied experience, and explicit ethical standards.
- **Innovation infra:** Safe sandboxes, cohort/guardrail testing, rapid rollback, and disciplined feedback capture.

Pilot Strategy: Learn Fast, Safely, and Broadly

Design pilots as *learning systems* that deliver value while building muscles you will reuse.

Customer Intelligence Quick Wins

- **Predictive Journey Orchestration:** Track real-time digital behavior, predict next needs, pre-position resources, and close the loop on prediction accuracy. Target outcomes: lower effort, higher FCR/CSAT, fewer preventable contacts.
- **Sentiment-Driven Routing:** Detect emotion across channels; route high-stakes or negative trajectories to empathy specialists; measure lifetime value protection and recovery rates.

Human–AI Augmentation

- **Intelligent Coaching Companion:** In-call suggestions, just-in-time knowledge, and post-call reflection—begin opt-in, "assist" mode only. Track adoption, trust, and capability lift.
- **Predictive Wellness:** Opt-in stress/burnout signals, personalized interventions, and manager nudges—privacy-by-design and transparent models.

Cross-Functional Tests

- **Revenue-Optimized Deployment:** Blend CRM value signals into routing/scheduling; share gains with Sales/Finance; measure incremental revenue and retention.
- **Predictive Capacity Planning:** Wire in marketing calendars, launches, competitive and macro indicators; prove proactive staffing accuracy and cost/risk reduction.

Scaling: From Pilots to Operating System

Avoid "big bang." Scale in waves that compound capability and value.

Capability Waves (illustrative cadence)

- **Wave 1 — Intelligence Foundation (Months 1–6):** Core data/AI fabric, federated learning hooks, conversational analytics.
- **Wave 2 — Predictive Operations (Months 7–12):** Journey prediction, workforce evolution models, omni-channel sentiment, proactive positioning.
- **Wave 3 — Autonomous Optimization (Months 13–18):** Distributed decisioning, reinforcement learners, self-improving processes, ecosystem sharing.
- **Wave 4 — Enterprise Orchestration (Months 19–24):** Cross-functional run-state, full autonomy within guardrails, strategic AI partnerships.

Expansion Pattern

- Start small (one region/site), replicate to similar contexts, adapt for local variance, then bridge to new functions; stand up a Center of Excellence to codify and export patterns.

Continuous Learning: Build a Memory, Not Just Wins

Institutionalize learning so progress compounds.

- **Learning loop architecture:** Structured capture for every pilot, parity focus on failures, searchable repositories, periodic synthesis, and automatic feed-through to roadmaps.

- **Capability progression:** Individuals learn by doing; teams by cross-discipline problem-solving; org by repeated application; ecosystem via federated sharing.

- **Innovation rhythm:** Time-boxed sprints, explicit failure budgets, success defined as *outcomes and insights*, and visible celebrations of learning courage.

Measuring What Matters: Value Over Volume

Evolve metrics to reflect multi-stakeholder, predictive, and learning-driven value.

- **Multi-stakeholder scorecards:** CLV impact; employee capability acceleration and wellbeing; sustainable returns; community benefit; ecosystem contribution.

- **Predictive indicators:** Capability velocity, innovation cycle time, ecosystem health, and durability of competitive advantage.

- **Learning-adjusted returns:** ROI plus option value (flexibility), risk reduction, knowledge creation, and platform effects.

The Imperative

Level 5 is a metamorphosis: from optimized function to autonomous, enterprise-wide intelligence that amplifies human potential. It cannot be outsourced or rushed; it must be *become*. Early movers shape markets; late movers inherit constraints. If Level 4 made you operations-research–driven and ecosystem-ready, Level 5 makes you *Adaptive*—able to anticipate, learn, and reconfigure faster than the world changes. Begin where you can win quickly, learn deliberately, scale methodically, and never stop evolving.

11.13 The Competitive Advantage of Adaptive Orchestration

In the Collaborative Intelligence Era, advantage no longer comes from scale, capital, or tools alone. It comes from *Adaptive Orchestration*—the ability to blend people, processes, data, AI capability, and organizational purpose into a living system that learns and adapts faster than rivals. Level 5 Workforce Management operationalizes that orchestration. Competitors can buy similar software and hire similar talent; they cannot easily replicate the relationships, learning loops, and culture that make the whole outperform the parts.

Strategic Differentiation: Competing in Another Dimension

Predictive vs. Reactive Operations. Level 5 organizations don't discover demand spikes in the morning stand-up—they anticipated them last night and pre-positioned resources accordingly. Signals from launches, sentiment, and digital exhaust flow into predictive models; the platform adjusts schedules, knowledge, and routing in advance. Over time, this anticipation compounds: buffers shrink, service stabilizes, and cost drops—while reactive peers burn 10–15% excess capacity "just in case."

Holistic vs. Siloed Optimization. Traditional shops optimize locally (cost per contact, campaign lift, budget variance). Level 5 optimizes *enterprise value*: routing, training, and scheduling decisions weigh CLV, employee development, brand impact, and risk—thousands of times per second.

- Scheduling balances coverage *and* skill growth/retention.
- Training is placed when near-term productivity loss yields outsized future gains.
- Automation choices factor employee experience, not just throughput.

The result looks unfair from a silo: lower cost, higher CSAT, stronger retention all simultaneously.

Adaptive vs. Rigid Systems. Where legacy processes change by project, Level 5 systems evolve continuously. Microservices add consent capture in hours; channel mix rebalances in days; new human–AI patterns emerge via constant experimentation. Adaptation debt—the lag between change and response—approaches zero.

Sustainable Excellence: Advantages That Compound

Human Value Amplification. As AI absorbs routine work, uniquely human strengths appreciate in value. Level 5 platforms *amplify* empathy, creativity, judgment, and cultural fluency with real-time guidance, knowledge, and insight. You can copy scripts; you cannot copy cultivated judgment at scale. Positive flywheel:

- Amplified agents → exceptional experiences
- Exceptional experiences → loyalty and referrals
- Loyalty → space and resources to develop humans further

Technology Leverage without Dependence. Level 5 is architected for *optionality*: API-first, event-driven, model-agnostic. Benefits:

- Rapid adoption of breakthroughs (weeks, not quarters)
- Vendor independence and negotiating leverage
- Contained downside when bets misfire
- Meta-learning about *how* to adopt technology—an asset itself

Continuous Innovation Capability. Reinforcement learners and guardrailed pilots run perpetually; successful variants scale themselves, failures deposit learning credits. Culture matches system: explicit failure budgets, measured innovation velocity, and recognition for insight creation—so advantage renews faster than rivals can copy.

Future Readiness: Thriving Amid Uncertainty

Multiple-Scenario Preparation. Level 5 embeds options for divergent futures:

- Rapid AI: orchestrate at any human–AI mix
- Plateaued AI: double down on augmentation and human craft
- Tight regulation: excel within constraint via transparent, explainable systems
- Discontinuities: plug-and-play new capabilities through modular architecture

Flexible Architecture Benefits. Distributed, cloud-native fabric yields:

- Geographic agility (talent anywhere)
- Elastic scale (peak without fixed cost drag)
- Capability agility (add/remove microservices without rewrites)
- Business-model agility (monetize intelligence, partner via ecosystems)

Learning Organization Advantages. Level 5 firms appreciate, not depreciate: individuals upskill via AI partnership; teams codify new collaboration patterns; systems learn through federated and local feedback; the company learns to *learn* faster. The gap widens because the leader accelerates with every cycle.

The Adaptive Orchestration Imperative

The Level 5 edge—prediction, holism, adaptability, human amplification, renewable innovation, and future readiness—creates positions competitors cannot easily assail. But it demands vigilance: continued investment, humility, and relentless learning. In this era, standing still is sliding back. Organizations that master *Adaptive Orchestration* won't just win more efficiently—they will redefine the game, compounding value for customers, employees, shareholders, and society while others perfect yesterday's model.

11.14 Key Takeaways and the Future of Work

Level 5—*Adaptive Orchestration*—is more than a technical milestone; it's a new way of conceiving work. The journey from manual chaos to autonomous orchestration replaces "WFM as a cost center" with "WFM as an enterprise intelligence function," blending human judgment and AI into a living system that learns, adapts, and compounds value. Crucially, Level 5 has no finish line: the operating model is *continuous evolution*.

Core Lessons of Level 5: Principles of Orchestration

Integration Without Ownership. Power comes from connecting truths where they already reside (HR, CRM, finance, quality)—not duplicating them. WFM becomes the *intelligence layer* that queries, reconciles, and synthesizes, enabling every function to decide better without centralizing control.

Orchestration Over Control. Leaders set aims and constraints; adaptive systems discover solutions. Rigid plans give way to living frameworks: schedules flex with needs and energy, learning slots appear when variance permits, and deviations are data—not defects.

Human Value in the AI Age. As AI scales consistency and speed, distinctly human strengths appreciate: empathy, creativity, ethical judgment, cultural fluency, and sense-making. Level 5 plans for optimal *human–AI combinations*, and develops human capabilities that grow more valuable as automation expands.

Adaptive Over Predictive. Forecasts matter, but *response velocity* matters more. Level 5 measures adaptation alongside accuracy, designs fluid resources and reversible decisions, and optimizes for option value across uncertain futures.

Enterprise Over Department. Local optima (cost per contact, campaign lift) yield to enterprise value (CLV, employee growth, brand trust, risk). Decisions, metrics, budgets, teams, and incentives are retooled to reflect systemwide effects.

The Path Forward: Navigating Perpetual Evolution

Continuous Evolution Model. Built-in "evolutionary pressure" (parallel algorithms, microexperiments, guardrails) promotes rapid selection and safe failure. Capability *emerges* as microservices, models, and human skills recombine; every action becomes a learning input.

Innovation Readiness. Architectures stay open (APIs, abstraction, modular, event-driven) so breakthroughs plug in via configuration, not rebuild. Cultures normalize experimentation, treat failure as tuition, and cultivate comfort with ambiguity.

Strategic Flexibility. Maintain options that play across scenarios: transferable capabilities, ecosystem partnerships, balanced investment between today's yield and tomorrow's potential, and metrics that evolve with the context.

Human-Centric Technology. Adopt an augmentation philosophy and ethical guardrails: explainability, human override, privacy, fairness, and value alignment. Invest in people—continuous learning, adaptive careers, collaboration-oriented rewards, and meaningful work design.

Final Thoughts: What Endures

WFM as Strategy. At Level 5, WFM shapes strategy, not just schedules. Practitioners must think in systems, speak finance and psychology, and lead cross-functional change.

The Endless Journey. Optimization shifts from single-metric efficiency to multi-stakeholder value, from variance suppression to variance harvest, from perfect prediction to superior adaptation. The work stays interesting—forever.

Building for the Unknowable. Design for technologies, roles, and customer behaviors we can't yet name. Anchor on durable foundations—human needs, rigorous math, shared values—so the organization can flex without breaking.

The Orchestra Plays On

Level 5 organizations don't pick a side (human *or* AI); they conduct the whole. The score is never final—more like evolutionary jazz—yet the principles endure:

- Human potential *amplified* by technology outperforms either alone.
- Value grows when multiple stakeholders win together.
- Adaptation beats precision when the future is fast.
- Orchestration achieves what control cannot.
- Learning velocity compounds advantage.

Welcome to Level 5—the endless frontier of workforce orchestration. The next movement begins now, one decision, one experiment, one improvement at a time.

What to read while you build

Level 5 requires dual mastery: designing effective human-AI collaboration and orchestrating platform ecosystems. Two books provide this foundation. Start with Mollick to understand how humans and AI work together, then move to Cusumano, Gawer, and Yoffie for the strategic architecture that enables enterprise-wide orchestration.

Mollick's *Co-Intelligence* redefines how we work alongside AI. The core insight: AI should be co-worker, co-teacher, and coach—not replacement or threat. Mollick provides four principles for collaboration and introduces centaur (divided labor) versus cyborg (integrated) work patterns that map directly to Level 5's *Adaptive* workforce framework. His methods for quantifying human value—measuring empathy, judgment, and contextual adaptation—provide the evidence base for routing decisions between humans and AI. Published by Portfolio/Penguin (2024), this New York Times bestseller from a Wharton professor brings practical frameworks for preserving what makes humans uniquely valuable while harnessing AI's scaling power.[124]

Cusumano, Gawer, and Yoffie's *The Business of Platforms* provides the strategic architecture for ecosystem orchestration. Drawing on thirty years studying platforms, these MIT, Surrey, and Harvard professors reveal how platforms became the world's most valuable companies through ecosystem effects rather than better products. Their framework distinguishes innovation platforms, transaction platforms, and hybrids—with most successful platforms evolving toward hybrid models. The book explains network effects, platform architecture principles, and governance mechanisms that translate directly to Level 5's API-first design and cross-functional coordination. Published by Harper Business (2019), it transforms "integration without ownership" from philosophy to operational blueprint.[125]

12 The Journey Forward: Synthesis and Pathways

What This Chapter Does

This chapter distills Part II into a practical, level-agnostic guide. It summarizes what changes across the WFM Labs Maturity Model™ and shows how to move from your current state to the next step—whether that means professionalizing foundational practices, introducing real-time automation and variance harvesting, adopting probabilistic planning, or operating an enterprise orchestration layer. The emphasis is action over recap: concise synthesis, a quick placement tool, and concrete pathways framed through GRPIT (Goals, Roles, Processes, Interpersonal, Technology).

How to use it

- Start with Section 12.1 for a one-page maturity snapshot (Levels 1–5 at a glance).
- Use Section 12.2 to self-identify your likely level via a short diagnostic and routing matrix.
- Jump to the relevant pathway in Section 12.3 for time-boxed actions from your starting point.
- Apply the cross-level "moves that matter" in Section 12.4 to harden progress with GRPIT guardrails.
- Align on measurement and safety in Section 12.5 (metrics and governance baselines).
- Close with the one-page checklist in Section 12.6 to lock commitments and cadence.

What it is not

- Not a reprint of Chapters 7–11. Those chapters contain the narratives, examples, and deep dives.
- Not a technology shopping list. Tooling is addressed only where it enables specific capabilities.
- Not a one-size sequence. Progression can be non-linear; the pathways respect different starting points and constraints.

Who this is for

- Executives clarifying outcomes, risk posture, and investment pace.
- WFM leaders operationalizing guardrails and cadence (e.g., *Resource Optimization Center* stewardship).
- Operations, HR, Finance, and Data/Technology partners aligning roles and integration patterns.

Conventions & terminology (aligned with Part II)

- *Variance harvesting*: real-time automation converts safe lulls into value (training, coaching, development) while protecting service.
- *ROC*: the Resource Optimization Center evolves from exception desk to rule steward.
- *Probabilistic planning*: staffing envelopes expressed as P50/P80/P95 with model cards and decision packs.
- *Integration without ownership*: orchestrate truth where it lives via contracts, virtualization, and event streams.
- *Safety & auditability*: autonomy operates with explainability, canary/rollback, decision/model cards, fairness thresholds, and human override.
- Metrics include *AAR* (Automation Acceptance Rate), *VCE* (Variance Capture Efficiency), service-level stability, value (e.g., CLV impact), wellbeing, and governance health.

Outcome

- A single, navigable chapter that connects where you are (Level 1–5) to what to do next, how to measure it, and how to keep it safe—without re-reading the whole of Part II.

12.1 Maturity Snapshot: Levels 1–5 at a Glance

This view summarizes each level of the WFM Labs Maturity Model™ and the practical moves that advance you to the next. Use it with the quick diagnostic in Section 12.2 and the pathways in Section 12.3.

GRPIT key (what we tune at each level): *Goals* (what "good" means), *Roles* (who owns it), *Processes* (cadence and handoffs), *Interpersonal* (norms, trust, governance), *Technology* (systems and data). We use GRPIT as a checklist, not a straitjacket.

Level 1: Initial/Manual

- *Core posture*: spreadsheet-driven, reactive planning; no formal WFM function; informal metrics.
- *Typical pains/risks*: volatile service, opaque capacity, schedule chaos, burnout risks.
- *Next moves (GRPIT)*: **Goals:** publish Service Level (*SL*) / Average Speed of Answer (*ASA*) / *short-abandon* policy, occupancy band, and shrinkage policy; **Roles:** assign a single accountable WFM owner; **Processes:** stand up cadenced forecasting and schedule release; **Interpersonal:** basic norms on adherence and change requests; **Technology:** select a WFM platform and make it the schedule single source of truth (*SSoT*).
- *Ready to progress when*: baseline metrics exist (SL, ASA, adherence); leaders accept posted guardrails; historical data is consistently captured.
- *90-day payoff*: stabilized service, fewer escalations, improved schedule predictability.

Level 2: Foundational

- *Core posture*: structured forecasting & scheduling; siloed roles; intraday is manual.
- *Typical pains/risks*: training cancellations, adherence policing, "human-speed" corrections, limited cross-channel agility.
- *Next moves (GRPIT)*: **Goals:** formalize occupancy bands and shrinkage targets; **Roles:** stand up a *Resource Optimization Center (ROC)*; **Processes:** daily variance loop and a Rule→Trigger→Action catalog; **Interpersonal:** agent control norms (accept/decline/deferral) to build trust; **Technology:** instrument ROC logging and time-to-action.
- *Ready to progress when*: ROC incident data shows repeatable micro-moves; measurable opportunity cost of manual speed.
- *90-day payoff*: preserved development minutes, fewer exceptions, visible business case for automation.

Level 3: Progressive

- *Core posture*: real-time automation; variance harvesting with an auditable rule registry; sub-minute actuation.
- *Typical pains/risks*: tactical focus outweighs horizon planning; rules drift without governance; metrics limited to operations.

- *Next moves (GRPIT)*: **Goals:** add *Service-Level Stability (SLS)*, *Automation Acceptance Rate (AAR)*, and *Variance Capture Efficiency (VCE)*; **Roles:** add an automation strategist; **Processes:** weekly rule tune-ups and decision audits; **Interpersonal:** transparent "why" prompts and preserved human choice; **Technology:** introduce probabilistic inputs (P50/P80/P95), model cards, and a constraint register.
- *Ready to progress when*: telemetry is reliable (AAR/VCE), SL is steady under variance, automation operates within published guardrails.
- *90-day payoff*: more delivered coaching/training with lower planned shrinkage; better wellbeing; steadier SL.

Level 4: Advanced

- *Core posture*: Operations Research (OR)–driven capacity; ecosystem architecture; continuous refresh of staffing envelopes.
- *Typical pains/risks*: coordination overhead; literacy gaps on uncertainty; fragmented decision ownership.
- *Next moves (GRPIT)*: **Goals:** optimize to bands and risk posture (e.g., staff to P80); **Roles:** add a capacity data scientist and an OR–WFM translator; **Processes:** publish envelopes, decision packs, and stress tests; **Interpersonal:** shared outcome ownership with Finance/Marketing/HR; **Technology:** APIs for bands, event streams, and an analytics workbench feeding automation.
- *Ready to progress when*: scenario/decision packs exist; bands drive routing/scheduling; bidirectional telemetry closes the loop.
- *90-day payoff*: tighter budgets vs. outcomes, lower over/under-staffing risk, faster response to drivers.

Level 5: Pioneering

- *Core posture*: enterprise-wide orchestration; *integration without ownership*; guardrailed autonomy with explainability and override.
- *Typical pains/risks*: governance weight; change fatigue; portability/vendor lock-in concerns.
- *Next moves (GRPIT)*: **Goals:** multi-stakeholder value function (customers, employees, P&L, risk); **Roles:** Ethical AI Governor and Enterprise Orchestrator; **Processes:** continuous experiments with error budgets; **Interpersonal:** board-level workforce strategy and transparent safeguards; **Technology:** event backbone, decision services, decision/model cards, and fairness monitors.
- *Ready to progress when*: autonomy charter is live; decision cards/audit trails are complete; objective weights and guardrails are in active use.
- *90-day payoff*: cross-functional value lift (e.g., *Customer Lifetime Value (CLV)*, proactive saves), compounding learning loops, resilient operations.

12.2 Quick Diagnostic: Where Are You Now?

Use this fast, evidence-based self-check to locate your current maturity and surface bottle-necks. For each GRPIT pillar below, select the *highest* statement that has been consistently true for the past 90 days. Record the corresponding level number (1–5) per pillar.

Goals (G)

- **L1** No formal service targets; ad hoc reporting; goals change informally.
- **L2** Published SL/ASA, an occupancy band, and a shrinkage policy; tracked weekly.
- **L3** Add *service-level stability*, *Automation Acceptance Rate* (AAR), and *Variance Capture Efficiency* (VCE); guardrails enforced intraday.
- **L4** Plans expressed as confidence bands (P50/P80/P95) with an explicit risk posture (e.g., staff to P80); decisions packaged with trade-off analysis.
- **L5** Multi-stakeholder value function (customers, employees, P&L, risk) with context-aware weights; autonomy operates within published guardrails.

Roles (R)

- **L1** No accountable WFM owner; scheduling is a side duty.
- **L2** Dedicated forecaster/scheduler/RTA roles; ROC visibility exists.
- **L3** *Automation strategist* in place; ROC stewards a rule registry; analysts author rules.
- **L4** *Capacity Planning Data Scientist* and *OR–WFM Translator* established; cross-functional decision forums.
- **L5** *Chief Workforce Strategist*, *Ethical AI Governor*, and *Enterprise Orchestrator* own objectives, guardrails, and autonomy scope.

Processes (P)

- **L1** Manual forecasts/schedules; exceptions resolved after the fact.
- **L2** Cadenced forecasting and schedule release; intraday adjustments are manual.
- **L3** Rule → Trigger → Action automation handles micro-moves; weekly rule tune-ups; auditable decisions.
- **L4** Continuous refresh of staffing *envelopes*; scenario sets, stress tests, decision packs; planning-to-automation loop closed.
- **L5** Continuous experimentation with error budgets; reinforcement learning where safe; documented pause/rollback and appeal paths.

Interpersonal (I)

- **L1** Manager-driven exceptions; limited schedule transparency.
- **L2** Clear adherence policy; earlier schedules improve predictability.
- **L3** Agent control for accept/defer; prompts explain *why*; supervisors focus more on coaching.
- **L4** Shared outcome ownership with Finance/Marketing/HR; blameless post-mortems update models and policies.

- **L5** Unified decisioning across functions; board-level workforce strategy; transparent safeguards and governance.

Technology (T)

- **L1** Spreadsheets/email as primary tools; fragmented data.
- **L2** WFM platform as schedule SSoT; reporting dashboards; limited integration.
- **L3** Real-time automation layer with sub-minute actuation, bi-directional writes to WFM/LMS, and immutable audits.
- **L4** OR planning layer (simulation/optimization) publishes bands via APIs; event streaming; analytics workbench.
- **L5** Event backbone, decision services, data fabric/virtualization; explainability/fairness monitors; decision/model cards persisted.

How to score

1. For each pillar, record the level (1–5) of the highest consistently true statement.

2. *Current maturity* = median of the five pillar scores.

3. *Drag indicators*: any pillar scoring two or more levels below the median.

4. *Advance readiness*: if at least three pillars score at or above the median and no pillar is below (median–1), you can begin the next-level pathway in Section 12.3.

Interpreting results

- If the median is **L1–L2**, prioritize foundation moves from Section 12.3 and the Level 1/2 playbooks in Chapters 7–8.
- If the median is **L3**, lock in automation governance and telemetry before scaling; prepare probabilistic planning (Section 12.3).
- If the median is **L4**, extend bands into decisioning and codify guardrails (Section 12.4 and Section 12.5) on the path to supervised autonomy.
- If the median is **L5**, focus on portfolio-level experiments, cross-functional value metrics, and governance fitness (Section 12.5 and Section 12.6).

12.3 From Here to Next Level: Minimum Moves & Quick Wins

Use these pathways to advance one level at a time. Each set lists minimum viable moves to unlock the next stage, fast wins (30–60 days), and prerequisites to scale—organized by GRPIT (Goals, Roles, Processes, Interpersonal, Technology). Keep scope tight; prove value in one line of business before broadening.

L1 → L2: Establish Professional Structure

Minimum viable moves

- **G**: Publish SL/ASA targets, an *occupancy band* (e.g., 78–88%), a *shrinkage policy*, and (if applicable) a short-abandon treatment.
- **R**: Name a single accountable WFM owner; stand up basic forecaster/scheduler and RTA responsibilities (can be part-time initially).
- **P**: Cadenced forecasting and schedule release; time-off and exception workflows; daily huddles for variance review.
- **I**: Set clear adherence expectations and schedule lead times; communicate fairness rules (bids, swaps, time-off).
- **T**: Make the WFM platform the schedule *system of record*; retire spreadsheet-as-SSoT; enable ROC-style visibility (real-time dashboards) even if actions remain manual.

Quick wins (30–60 days)

- Earlier, more stable schedules; fewer last-minute changes.
- Visible SL/ASA improvements from eliminating basic over/under-staffing.
- Transparent time-off process reduces frustration and attrition risk.

Prerequisites to scale

- Data hygiene (queues, skills, calendars); baseline metrics for SL, ASA, occupancy, shrinkage.
- Simple change control for forecast/schedule updates.

L2 → L3: Add Real-Time Automation & Variance Harvesting

Minimum viable moves

- **G**: Add *service-level stability*, *Automation Acceptance Rate* (AAR), and *Variance Capture Efficiency* (VCE) to the scorecard; publish guardrails (SL/ASA, occupancy band, shrinkage).
- **R**: Stand up a *Resource Optimization Center (ROC)* as coordination hub; appoint an *automation strategist*; enable analysts to author rules.
- **P**: Create a *rule registry* and weekly tune-up; codify micro-moves: break/lunch protection, end-of-shift smoothing, micro-learning/coaching delivery in safe lulls, VTO/VOT prompts.

- **I:** Give agents *accept/defer* choices where appropriate; explain each action ("why now," "what changed") to build trust.
- **T:** Deploy a real-time automation layer between ACD–WFM–LMS/Comms with *sub-minute actuation*, bi-directional writes to WFM, and immutable audits.

Quick wins (30–60 days)

- Fewer adherence exceptions and overtime via protected breaks/meals.
- 2–3× increase in delivered coaching/training without raising planned shrinkage.
- Faster recovery from spikes; measurable *time-to-stabilize* reduction.

Prerequisites to scale

- Read/write APIs for schedules and activity states; audit storage for decisions.
- Change management plan; agent/supervisor enablement for new prompts and flows.

L3 → L4: Bring Operations Research & Planning Ranges

Minimum viable moves

- **G:** Replace point targets with staffing *envelopes* (P50/P80/P95); choose and publish risk posture (e.g., staff to P80).
- **R:** Add a *Capacity Planning Data Scientist* and an *OR–WFM Translator* to connect policy to models.
- **P:** Continuous refresh of ranges; scenario library and stress tests; *decision packs* that show trade-offs and sensitivities.
- **I:** Joint planning with Finance/Marketing/HR; blameless post-mortems update assumptions and constraints.
- **T:** Stand up an *OR capacity layer* (simulation/optimization) publishing bands via APIs; event streaming for drivers; analytics workbench; *model cards* and a versioned *constraint register*.

Quick wins (30–60 days)

- Budget and hiring plans anchored to ranges, reducing surprise OT/BPO spend.
- Better timing of training and campaigns with band-aware windows.
- Fewer escalations about "accuracy"; decisions framed in risk and options.

Prerequisites to scale

- Data contracts for arrivals, AHT, shrinkage, attrition; sufficient history for calibration.
- Planning–automation feedback loop (bands → guardrails; outcomes → model updates).

L4 → L5: Orchestrate Enterprise-Wide with Guardrailed Autonomy

Minimum viable moves

- **G**: Define a multi-stakeholder *enterprise value function* (customers, employees, P&L, risk) with context-aware weights; publish autonomy scope and guardrails.
- **R**: Establish *Chief Workforce Strategist*, *Ethical AI Governor*, *Enterprise Orchestrator*, *Scenario Architect*, and *AI–Human Collaboration Designer*; formalize MLOps ownership.
- **P**: Continuous experimentation with error budgets; policy engines plus reinforcement learning where safe; pause/rollback and appeal playbooks; *decision/model cards* by default.
- **I**: Unified decision forums across Marketing/Finance/HR/Ops; board-level workforce strategy; transparent safeguards and explainability.
- **T**: Event backbone; stateless *decision services*; data fabric/virtualization (*integration without ownership*); fairness and explainability monitors; lineage and audit at the decision level.

Quick wins (30–60 days)

- Value-/sentiment-aware routing in a scoped segment improves save rates or CLV.
- Human/AI/hybrid assignment reduces handling variance while preserving experience.
- Shorter adaptation latency to external signals (campaigns, outages, social sentiment).

Prerequisites to scale

- Autonomy charter with risk tiering; explainability and fairness thresholds; override paths.
- Shadow/canary deployment patterns; incident response and audit evidence ready.

12.4 Scorecards that Drive Behavior (Measure What Matters)

Scorecards should make better decisions inevitable. Keep them small, outcome-anchored, and level-appropriate. Use ranges and bands rather than single targets, publish who owns which metric, and review on a fixed cadence. Every score on the board must be traceable to decisions, not just activity.

Principles

- **Outcome over activity**: value created for customers, employees, and the business beats counts and compliance.
- **Ranges over points**: report P50/P80/P95 and "within-band" stability, not single numbers.
- **Few, legible, linked**: 3–5 top-line metrics per audience, each with an explicit decision it informs.
- **Closed loop**: metrics write back to planning models and automation guardrails.
- **Anti-Goodhart**: when a metric becomes a target, rotate to the paired counter-metric.

Core Metric Set (by Outcome Domain)

Domain	Metric & Definition	Owner	Cadence
Customer	**CLV Delta**: $\text{CLV}_{post} - \text{CLV}_{pre}$ on treated cohorts; **FCR**; **CES/NPS** by journey	CX / Marketing	M/Q
Employee	**Wellbeing Index** (schedule stability, training delivered/FTE, attrition risk), **Ramp Time** to proficiency	HR / Ops	M
Operations	**Service-Level Stability (SLS)**: % intervals within target band; **Adaptation Latency (AL)**; **Time-to-Stabilize (TTS)**	ROC / Ops	W/M
Financial	**Cost per Resolved Interaction**; **Revenue Protection/Expansion**; **Option Value of Flexibility**	Finance	M/Q
Risk/Gov	**Explainability Coverage**; **Fairness Disparity Ratio**; **Time-to-Rollback**; **Audit Completeness**	Risk / EAIG	M/Q

Operational Metrics that Unlock Levels

- **Automation Acceptance Rate (AAR)**: $\text{AAR} = \dfrac{\text{accepted automated prompts}}{\text{eligible prompts}}$
- **Variance Capture Efficiency (VCE)**: $\text{VCE} = \dfrac{\text{minutes redeployed to value work}}{\text{eligible micro-availability minutes}}$
- **Service-Level Stability (SLS)**: share of intervals where SL and ASA fall within published band
- **Adaptation Latency (AL)**: median time from signal (campaign/outage/sentiment) to effective routing/schedule change
- **Time-to-Stabilize (TTS)**: time from threshold breach to return within service band

- **Schedule Quality Index (SQI)**: composite of schedule lead time, change count, preference match rate

Formulas & Composites

Customer Lifetime Value Impact

$$\Delta \text{CLV} = \frac{1}{|\text{treated}|} \sum_{i \in \text{treated}} \left(\text{CLV}_{i,\text{post}} - \text{CLV}_{i,\text{pre}} \right)$$

Option Value of Flexibility (illustrative)

$$\text{OVF} = \mathbb{E}[C_{\text{static}}] - \mathbb{E}[C_{\text{ranged}}]$$

where C includes OT, BPO spillover, and missed-revenue penalties under scenario weights.

Employee Wellbeing Index (example)

$$\text{EWI} = 0.4 \cdot \text{SchedStability} + 0.3 \cdot \text{GrowthDelivered} + 0.3 \cdot \left(1 - \text{BurnoutRisk} \right)$$

Targets & Bands

- Publish target *bands* (e.g., SL 80/30 with ± tolerance; occupancy 78–88%), and report stability as "% within band."
- Set percentile targets for stochastic metrics (e.g., "$P_{80} \geq$ target for 12 of 13 weeks").
- Pair every metric with a counter-metric to avoid perverse optimization (e.g., AHT with FCR/CLV; adherence with EWI).

Scorecard Evolution by Level

- **Level 1**: SL/ASA, occupancy, adherence, basic shrinkage; introduce SQI.
- **Level 2**: add variance review cadence; publish occupancy band; formalize SQI and training delivered.
- **Level 3**: add AAR, VCE, SCR, SLS, TTS, AL; track focus of supervisor time to coaching.
- **Level 4**: report ranges (P50/P80/P95), scenario robustness, sensitivity; cost bands vs. outcomes.
- **Level 5**: blend value metrics (CLV delta, save rate), adaptability (learning velocity), and governance (explainability, fairness, time-to-rollback).

Minimal Implementation

1. Publish a one-page scorecard per audience (Exec, Ops, ROC) with 3–5 metrics each.

2. Define owners, thresholds, and decision rights for acting on movements.

3. Instrument decision logs so every automated or human lever links to metric deltas.

4. Review weekly for operations, monthly for value/risk; retire one metric when you add one.

12.5 Operating Cadences that Stick

Cadence beats intensity. Small, repeatable forums create the muscle memory that moves you up a level. Keep meetings short, artifacts lightweight, and decision rights explicit. Align each cadence to the horizon it influences and to clear outputs that feed planning models and automation guardrails.

Horizon ⟷ Loop & Owner

Horizon	Loop	Purpose & Outputs	Owner
Intraday (15–60 min)	ROC huddle	Stabilize service; log variance; execute safe micro-moves; update *rule registry*.	ROC Lead
Daily (15 min)	Ops stand-up	Exceptions; backlog; AAR/VCE; TTS; assign fixes.	Ops Manager
Weekly (30–45 min)	Variance review	Patterns from variance log; propose rule tweaks; retire manual workarounds.	ROC + WFM
Weekly (45–60 min)	Scenario forum	Update scenario weights; publish staffing posture by band (P50/P80/P95).	CWS + Finance/Marketing
Monthly (60–90 min)	Governance review	Explainability coverage; fairness; drift; approve guardrails and rollbacks.	EAIG + MLO
Quarterly (90–120 min)	Portfolio review	Outcomes vs. objectives; objective-weight calibration; roadmap commits.	Exec Sponsor + CWS

Minimum Cadence by Level (Level-Up Focus)

- **Level 1 → 2**: Daily ops standup; weekly schedule/forecast check; publish an occupancy band and shrinkage policy; create a single *variance log*. Output: a basic scorecard (SL/ASA, adherence, SQI).
- **Level 2 → 3**: Add ROC intraday huddles and a weekly *variance review*; stand up a *rule registry* and 30-minute *rule tune-up*. Track AAR, VCE, SLS, TTS. Output: codified micro-moves ready for automation.

- **Level 3 → 4**: Launch a weekly *scenario forum*; publish staffing envelopes (P50/P80/P95) and sensitivities; monthly calibration of ranges. Output: machine-consumable bands and guardrails.
- **Level 4 → 5**: Introduce monthly *governance* (explainability, fairness, drift) and quarterly *objective-weight* reviews; embed micro-experiments with promotion/rollback gates. Output: decision services operating under explicit guardrails.
- **Level 5 (sustain)**: Keep the same scaffolding; increase automation of promotion/rollback, and rotate cohorts for fairness checks; publish a quarterly *orchestration report* linking decisions to CLV, risk, and wellbeing.

Agenda Atoms (Time-Boxed)

- **ROC huddle (10–15 min)**: yesterday's SLS/TTS; top 3 incidents; rules that would have helped; today's risks; assignments.
- **Variance review (30 min)**: top repeated patterns; micro-move proposals; AAR/VCE deltas; accept/reject and owner.
- **Scenario forum (45–60 min)**: new signals (campaigns, outages, sentiment); range updates; posture by band; cross-functional impacts.
- **Governance (60–90 min)**: drift, disparity, explainability coverage; rollbacks executed; upcoming model/policy changes; approvals.

Artifacts to Keep Current

- *Variance log* (tagged by driver, interval, impact)
- *Rule registry* (trigger → action, guardrails, audits)
- *Scenario weights* (with rationale and next review)
- *Decision cards* (for automated actions)
- *Model cards* (for governed models)
- *Constraint register* (assumptions, limits, SLAs)

Operating Guardrails

- **Cap ceremony cost**: ≤ 3% of team capacity; cancel when no decision needed.
- **Decide in the room**: every forum ends with owners, due dates, and success criteria.
- **Telemetry or it didn't happen**: no change without a linked metric and log entry.
- **One-in/one-out**: add a meeting only if another is retired or merged.

RACI-Lite for Cadences

Cadence	CWS	EAIG	ROC Lead	MLO
ROC huddle	I	I	A/R	I
Variance review	R	I	A/R	I
Scenario forum	A/R	I	C	C
Governance review	C	A/R	I	R
Portfolio review	A	C	I	C

Abbreviations: CWS = Chief Workforce Strategist; EAIG = Enterprise AI Governance; MLO = Model Lifecycle Owner.

Signals That Cadence is Working

- Fewer ad-hoc escalations; faster TTS; rising AAR/VCE; stable SLS within band.
- Rule registry growth slows while reuse rises; fewer one-off exceptions.
- Scenario weight changes precede—not follow—operational shifts.
- Governance actions (rollbacks, fairness adjustments) occur before incidents escalate.

12.6 Quick-Start Portfolio: Three Pilots with 30/60/90-Day Gates

Start small, learn fast, scale what works. Select one pilot in each lane—*customer value*, *workforce capability*, and *platform/automation*—matched to your current level. Keep scope narrow, run with clear guardrails, and require measurable deltas before scaling.

Level 1 → Level 2: Professionalize the Basics

Pilot	Aim	Primary KPIs
Forecast & shrinkage discipline	Stand up a monthly forecast cadence and publish a shrinkage policy; move off ad hoc spreadsheets.	SL/ASA stability, forecast MAPE by week, shrinkage adherence
Schedule quality uplift	Introduce a schedule quality index (SQI) with preference capture and lead-time targets.	SQI, schedule stability, voluntary time-off fill rate
ROC visibility starter	Launch a daily huddle and a variance log; standardize definitions and tags.	Time-to-stabilize (TTS), incident count by driver, rework rate

Level 2 → Level 3: Add Safe Real-Time Actuation

Pilot	Aim	Primary KPIs
Micro-learning in valleys	Deliver 2–5 minute training during safe lulls with accept/defer options.	Automation Acceptance Rate (AAR), Variance Capture Efficiency (VCE), protected-time retention
Break/lunch protection	Automate small schedule shifts to protect adherence and wellbeing.	SLS band hit-rate, adherence exceptions avoided, TTS
End-of-shift protection & VTO/VOT	Prevent unintended overtime; offer value-aligned VTO/VOT under guardrails.	OT minutes avoided, acceptance mix, employee sentiment

Level 3 → Level 4: Plan With Probabilities

Pilot	Aim	Primary KPIs
Staffing envelopes	Replace point asks with P50/P80/P95 bands for one queue; publish sensitivities.	Envelope hit-rate, cost vs. risk trade-off, variance of SL
Abandonment-aware simulation	Model short-abandon policy and routing to calibrate true service posture.	ASA vs. abandon trade-off curve, customer effort proxy, unit cost
Scenario forum & signals	Establish weekly weight updates tied to campaigns, outages, sentiment.	Scenario weight change lead-time, posture changes enacted, forecast error reduction

Level 4 → Level 5: Orchestrate Across Human/AI/Hybrid

Pilot	Aim	Primary KPIs
Value-based assignment	Route by predicted value and model confidence across human/AI/hybrid.	CLV delta, save rate, escalation quality, override frequency
Decision service & guardrails	Introduce decision cards, explainability, and rollback for one flow.	Explainability coverage, time-to-rollback, fairness disparity within bounds
Cross-functional pre-positioning	Tie marketing spend shifts to WFM posture and finance impact.	Lead-time to posture change, revenue protection, error budget adherence

30/60/90-Day Gate Template (Applies to Any Pilot)

Days 0–30: Ready   Hypothesis and minimal detectable effect defined; cohort and channels scoped; data contracts and owners named; baseline captured; human-in-the-loop path and privacy review complete; rollback path documented; success/fail thresholds signed off.

Days 31–60: Run   Launch with switchback or A/B where feasible; weekly readouts include decision log, incident log, metric deltas, and qualitative feedback; adjust guardrails, not goals; freeze scope creep.

Days 61–90: Decide   Compute effect size with confidence; review operational fit and support load; check fairness and explainability coverage; if thresholds met, scale to the next cohort; otherwise, retire or refactor with documented learning.

Success Thresholds by Pilot Type

Pilot Type	Minimum Success	Guardrails
Micro-learning in valleys	VCE $\geq$ 25%; AAR $\geq$ 70%; no adverse SL drift	SLS within band; opt-out honored; audit trail complete
Break/lunch protection	$\geq$ 50% reduction in adherence exceptions; TTS $\downarrow$ 20%	Max shift per move; daily limit per agent; supervisor visibility
End-of-shift & VTO/VOT	OT minutes $\downarrow$ 30% with neutral CSAT	Equity checks across cohorts; voluntary only
Staffing envelopes	Envelope hit-rate $\geq$ 80% at chosen posture	Published assumptions; monthly calibration
Abandon-aware simulation	Lower unit cost at equal or better effort score	No hidden degradation of critical segments
Value-based assignment	CLV delta > 0 with stable risk metrics	Explainability $\geq$ 95%; override path live; fairness within bounds
Decision service & guardrails	Time-to-rollback $\leq$ 15 min; incident MTTR $\downarrow$ 30%	Decision cards on 100% of auto actions
Cross-functional pre-positioning	Lead-time gain $\geq$ 24 h; measurable revenue protection	Finance sign-off; error budgets enforced

Lightweight Artifacts Required

Pilot charter, data contract, decision cards, model cards (if models used), variance log tags, runbook with pause/rollback, and a single-page KPI pack showing value, risk, and wellbeing impacts.

Common Anti-Patterns to Avoid

Big-bang scope, unmanaged shadow tooling, optimizing only for local KPIs, piloting without a rollback path, and declaring autonomy without explainability or human override.

Join the Community

Move from design to execution in Appendix A, the *WFM Labs Companion—Living Resources*. Find matching templates, calculators, and working examples. Join the operator community to compare guardrails, ask questions, and find the next tool when you hit a constraint.

Appendices

Appendix A

WFM Labs Companion — Living Resources

Why this exists. This book is a playbook; *WFM Labs* is its living companion. We created WFM Labs in January 2023 to continuously test and share next-generation workforce management practices with operators in the field. The community is invitation-based and free for qualified leaders and has grown to more than 1,000 members contributing tools, methods, and case notes.

What is WFM Labs?

WFM Labs is a group of current and former contact center and WFM leaders determined to improve customer and employee experiences by modernizing how service work is planned and run. We prioritize employees first and use automation, simulation, and AI to *orchestrate* outcomes—not merely defend a plan.

Start here

Begin at the main landing page: `https://wfmlabs.org`. From there, you can access the community, wiki documentation, and tools referenced throughout this book. Because these resources evolve, the landing page is the authoritative directory.

What we build (types of resources)

- **Living documentation** that extends book concepts (definitions, maturity model notes, FAQs).
- **Operator tools** (calculators, diagnostics, assessment instruments, planners) aligned to Levels 1–5.
- **Templates & playbooks** for cadences, rule governance, integration contracts, and scorecards.
- **Interactive demonstrations** that illustrate variability, risk bands, and ecosystem behaviors.
- **Research briefs & methods notes** connecting practice to quantitative evidence.
- **Case notes & adoption patterns** from pilots and transformations across industries.
- **Community forums & events** for peer review, troubleshooting, and remixing.

How to engage

1. **Orient:** Read Part I of this book, then visit `https://wfmlabs.org` to locate the current materials mapped to your level.

2. **Instrument:** Use the tools alongside Chapters 8–11 to quantify SL, ASA, AHT, Occupancy, Shrinkage, and risk bands (defined on first use).

3. **Pilot:** Apply the templates and charters to run 30/60/90-day experiments.

4. **Contribute:** Share results, propose changes, or request new tools so the model improves over time.

Governance and transparency

We build in the open. Materials are open to inspect and remix. If you spot an error or omission, raise it on the wiki or in the community; we correct and version updates. The landing page (`https://wfmlabs.org`) is the canonical index, with community access at `https://community.wfmlabs.org`.

Bibliography

[1] Everett M. Rogers. "Categorizing the Adopters of Agricultural Practices". In: *Rural Sociology* 23.4 (1958), pp. 345–354. URL: https://www.legalevolution.org/wp-content/uploads/sites/262/2017/09/Rogers-1958-Rural-Sociology.pdf (visited on 09/25/2025).

[2] Everett M. Rogers. *Diffusion of Innovations*. 5th ed. New York: Free Press, 2003.

[3] Arvind Narayanan and Sayash Kapoor. *AI as Normal Technology: An Alternative to the Vision of AI as a Potential Superintelligence*. Tech. rep. Knight First Amendment Institute at Columbia University, 2025.

[4] Daniel Kokotajlo, Scott Alexander, Thomas Larsen, Eli Lifland, and Romeo Dean. *AI 2027*. Tech. rep. Originally published on AI-2027.com. AI Futures Project, 2025.

[5] Gary N. Smith and Jeffrey Funk. *Destructing the Creative Destruction Myth*. Mind Matters News (Walter Bradley Center for Natural and Artificial Intelligence). Argues Fortune 100 turnover is not evidence of creative destruction; cites increase in average company age from 63 (1955) to 100 (2020). 2021. URL: https://mindmatters.ai/2021/10/destructing-the-creative-destruction-myth/ (visited on 09/25/2025).

[6] Julian Birkinshaw. *Will AI Disrupt Your Business? Key Questions to Ask*. MIT Sloan Management Review (Summer 2025). Diagnostic framework; most incumbents face sustaining AI, not disruption. Reprint #66422. 2025. URL: https://sloanreview.mit.edu/article/will-ai-disrupt-your-business-key-questions-to-ask/ (visited on 09/25/2025).

[7] McKinsey & Company. *The State of AI: Global Survey*. McKinsey & Company. Latest wave reports 78% of organizations using AI in at least one business function; fieldwork July 2024. 2025. URL: https://www.mckinsey.com/capabilities/quantumblack/our-insights/the-state-of-ai (visited on 09/25/2025).

[8] Thomas Kwa et al. *Measuring AI Ability to Complete Long Tasks*. arXiv preprint. 2025. arXiv: 2503.14499 [cs.AI]. URL: https://arxiv.org/abs/2503.14499.

[9] PricewaterhouseCoopers. *2025 Global AI Jobs Barometer*. PwC. Analysis of ~1B job ads across six continents; documents productivity and wage effects in AI-exposed roles. 2025. URL: https://www.pwc.com/gx/en/issues/artificial-intelligence/ai-jobs-barometer.html (visited on 09/25/2025).

[10] Erik Brynjolfsson, Danielle Li, and Lindsey R. Raymond. *Generative AI at Work*. Working Paper 31161. National Bureau of Economic Research, 2023. DOI: 10.3386/w31161. URL: https://www.nber.org/papers/w31161.

[11] Microsoft Corporation and LinkedIn Corporation. *Work Trend Index 2024: AI at Work Is Here. Now Comes the Hard Part*. Tech. rep. Survey of 31,000 knowledge workers across 31 countries. Microsoft, 2024.

[12] Deloitte. *AI is Revolutionizing Work: Employee Value Proposition for the Age of AI*. Tech. rep. Deloitte, 2025.

[13] British Telephones. *GEC Customer Telephone Installations: Birmingham Press and Mail — PABX 4 ACD (1965)*. Historical photo archive and notes. Photographic record of the 1965 GEC PABX 4 ACD installation at Birmingham Press and Mail. 1965. URL: `https://www.britishtelephones.com/gec/custom ers/customers.htm` (visited on 09/25/2025).

[14] A. K. Erlang. "The Theory of Probabilities and Telephone Conversations". In: *Nyt Tidsskrift for Matematik B* 20 (1909). Introduced the traffic equation later known as Erlang-B, modeling call blocking without waiting lines. English translation in Brockmeyer, Halstrøm, and Jensen (1948), Danish Academy of Technical Sciences, pp. 33–39.

[15] A. K. Erlang. "Solution of Some Problems in the Theory of Probabilities of Significance in Automatic Telephone Exchanges". In: *Post Office Electrical Engineers' Journal* 10 (1917). English translation of the 1917 Danish article in *Elektroteknikeren* 13:5–13, pp. 189–197. URL: `https://archive.org/download/solu tion-of-some-problems-in-the-theory-of-probabilitie s-of-significance-in-auto/Solution%20of%20some%20pr oblems%20in%20the%20theory%20of%20probabilities%20o f%20significance%20in%20automatic%20telephones%20ex changes%20POEEJ.pdf` (visited on 09/25/2025).

[16] CCITT. "XIVth Plenary Assembly Proceedings, Montreux, 26–31 October 1946". In: *International Telegraph and Telephone Consultative Committee Proceedings*. Formal adoption of the unit "erlang". 1946, pp. 60–62.

[17] York University School of EECS Museum. *Northern Electric—Nortel Networks Collection*. University museum collection summary. Notes SL-1 as first fully digital business PBX (introduced 1975) and that by 1991 Nortel was the world's largest PBX supplier. 0000. URL: `https://museum.eecs.yorku.ca/collec tions/show/18` (visited on 09/25/2025).

[18] Canadian Encyclopedia. *Northern Telecom*. By 1991 Nortel was the world's largest PBX supplier. 1991.

[19] History.com Editors. "The Rise and Fall of Telephone Operators". In: *History.com* (2020). Documents 88,000 U.S. operators in 1910; 235,000 by 1930.

[20] Science Museum Group. *Enfield Telephone Exchange Switchboard*. Science Museum Collection. Last manual exchange in London switched to automatic on Oct 5, 1960. 1960.

[21] Pipkins, Inc. *Merlang: Erlang C's Sexy Younger Brother*. Company blog. Describes Merlang modifications to handle abandons and multi-skill routing. 2019. URL: `https://www.pipkins.com/2019/12/05/merlang-erlang-c s-sexy-younger-brother/` (visited on 09/25/2025).

[22] Vincent A. Mabert. "Short Interval Forecasting of Emergency Phone Call (911) Work Loads". In: *Journal of Operations Management* 5.3 (1985), pp. 259–271.

[23] Michael L. Andrews and William H. Cunningham. "L.L. Bean Improves Call-Center Forecasting". In: *Interfaces* 25.6 (1995), pp. 1–13.

[24] Charles C. Holt. "Forecasting Trends and Seasonals by Exponentially Weighted Averages". In: *Carnegie Institute of Technology Working Paper* (1957).

[25] Peter R. Winters. "Forecasting Sales by Exponentially Weighted Moving Averages". In: *Management Science* 6.3 (1960), pp. 324–342.

[26] Luigi Bianchi, Jeffrey E. Jarrett, and Rangaraja P. Hanumara. "Improving fore-casting for telemarketing centers by ARIMA modeling with intervention". In: *International Journal of Forecasting* 14.4 (1998), pp. 497–504.

[27] Interactive Intelligence Inc. *Interactive Intelligence Acquires Bay Bridge Decision Technologies*. Tech. rep. Acquisition announcement of Interactive Intelligence acquires Bay Bridge Decision Technologies. DestinationCRM, 2012.

[28] Genesys. *Genesys Completes Acquisition of Interactive Intelligence*. Tech. rep. $1.4 billion acquisition incorporating BayBridge technology into Genesys portfolio. Genesys, 2016.

[29] Forrester Consulting. *The Total Economic Impact™ Of Intradiem: Cost Savings And Business Benefits Enabled By Intradiem*. Tech. rep. A Forrester Total Economic Impact™ Study Commissioned by Intradiem. Forrester Research, Inc., 2022.

[30] OpenAI. *Introducing ChatGPT*. OpenAI Blog. Announcement of ChatGPT, marking the public release of generative AI into mainstream use. 2022.

[31] Aditya Challapally, Chris Pease, and Ramesh Raskar. *The GenAI Divide: State of AI in Business 2025*. Tech. rep. Preliminary findings report; widely cited for the 95% AI pilot failure rate. MIT Project NANDA, 2025. URL: `https://mlq.ai/med ia/quarterly_decks/v0.1_State_of_AI_in_Business_202 5_Report.pdf` (visited on 09/25/2025).

[32] Brett Craig. "Target's Using Artificial Intelligence to Make Your Shopping Experience Even Better". In: *Target Corporate News* (2023). Accessed: January 2025. URL: `https://corporate.target.com/news-features/artic le/2023/12/artificial-intelligence`.

[33] Target Corporation. *Target to Roll Out Transformative GenAI Technology to its Store Team Members Chainwide*. Press Release. 2024. URL: `https://corporate .target.com/press/release/2024/06/target-to-roll-ou t-transformative-genai-technology-to-its-store-team -members-chainwide` (visited on 09/25/2025).

[34] Zhiying Jie, Zhifeng Zheng, and Li Li. "A meta-analysis of Watson for Oncology in clinical application". In: *Scientific Reports* 11.5792 (2021). DOI: `10.1038/s41 598-021-84973-5`.

[35] Casey Ross. "IBM pitched its Watson supercomputer as a revolution in cancer care. It's nowhere close". In: *STAT News* (2017). Accessed: January 2025. URL: `https: //www.statnews.com/2017/09/05/watson-ibm-cancer/`.

[36] Forrester Research. *The 2024 US Customer Experience Index*. Survey of 98,000+ US customers across 223 brands in 13 industries. Customer-obsessed firms show 41% faster revenue growth, 49% faster profit growth, 51% better retention. Forrester Research, 2024. URL: `https://investor.forrester.com/news-releases/news-release-details/forresters-2024-us-c ustomer-experience-index-brands-cx-quality/` (visited on 10/22/2025).

[37] McKinsey & Company. *State of the Consumer 2025: When disruption becomes permanent*. McKinsey Insights. 2025. URL: `https://www.mckinsey.com /industries/consumer-packaged-goods/our-insights/st ate-of-consumer` (visited on 10/22/2025).

[38] McKinsey & Company. *Omnichannel: The path to value*. McKinsey Insights. 2021. URL: https://www.mckinsey.com/capabilities/growth-marketing-and-sales/our-insights/the-survival-guide-to-omnichannel-and-the-path-to-value (visited on 09/25/2025).

[39] McKinsey & Company. *The next frontier of customer engagement: AI-enabled customer service*. McKinsey Insights. Documents 40-50% reduction in service interactions via AI-enabled predictive customer service. 2023. URL: https://www.mckinsey.com/capabilities/operations/our-insights/the-next-frontier-of-customer-engagement-ai-enabled-customer-service (visited on 10/22/2025).

[40] World Economic Forum. *Future of Jobs Report 2025*. Survey of 1,000+ employers representing 14+ million workers. World Economic Forum, 2025. URL: https://www.weforum.org/publications/the-future-of-jobs-report-2025/ (visited on 10/22/2025).

[41] Boston Consulting Group. *Where's the Value in AI?* Documents the 10-20-70 framework for AI transformation. Boston Consulting Group, 2024. URL: https://media-publications.bcg.com/BCG-Wheres-the-Value-in-AI.pdf (visited on 10/22/2025).

[42] McKinsey & Company. *Help your employees find purpose—or watch them leave*. Tech. rep. McKinsey & Company, 2021. URL: https://www.mckinsey.com/capabilities/people-and-organizational-performance/our-insights/help-your-employees-find-purpose-or-watch-them-leave.

[43] S. Lund, A. Madgavkar, J. Manyika, and S. Smit. *The future of work after COVID-19*. Tech. rep. McKinsey Global Institute, 2021.

[44] McKinsey Health Institute. *Thriving workplaces: How employers can improve productivity and change lives*. Tech. rep. McKinsey & Company, 2025.

[45] PwC. *PwC's Global Workforce Hopes and Fears Survey 2024*. Tech. rep. Survey of 56,600 workers across 50 countries; fielded March 2024. PricewaterhouseCoopers, 2024. URL: https://www.pwc.com/gx/en/issues/workforce/hopes-and-fears.html.

[46] Future Forum. *Future Forum Pulse Winter Snapshot: Future Forum Pulse Report Winter 2022–2023*. Research Report. Survey of 10,243 desk workers across the U.S., Australia, France, Germany, Japan, and the U.K., Nov–Dec 2022. Future Forum (Slack, Boston Consulting Group, MillerKnoll, Management Leadership for Tomorrow), 2023. URL: https://futureforum.com/research/future-forum-pulse-winter-2022-2023-snapshot/.

[47] Deloitte. *The Deloitte Global 2024 Gen Z and Millennial Survey*. Survey Report. 22,841 respondents across 44 countries, Nov 2023–Mar 2024. Deloitte Global, 2024. URL: https://www.deloitte.com/global/en/issues/work/content/genz-millennialsurvey.html.

[48] EY. *Belonging Barometer 3.0: Global insights into what matters most, today*. Survey Report. Survey of 5,000+ employed adults from the U.S., U.K., Germany, Singapore, and India, May 2023. Ernst & Young Global Limited, 2023. URL: https://www.ey.com/en_gl/newsroom/2023/09/ey-survey-finds-global-workers-feel-sense-of-belonging-at-their-workpl

aces-yet-most-are-uncomfortable-sharing-all-aspects
-of-their-identities.

[49]   World Health Organization. *WHO guidelines on mental health at work*. Guidelines.
       Geneva: World Health Organization, 2022. URL: https://www.ncbi.nlm
       .nih.gov/books/NBK586364/.

[50]   World Health Organization. *Investing in treatment for depression and anxiety leads
       to fourfold return*. https://www.who.int/news/item/13-04-2
       016-investing-in-treatment-for-depression-and-anxi
       ety-leads-to-fourfold-return. News release; summarizes Lancet
       Psychiatry ROI analysis. 2016.

[51]   Sarah Chapman, Ariel Kangasniemi, Laura Maxwell, and Marie Sereneo. *The ROI in
       workplace mental health programs: Good for people, good for business — A blueprint
       for workplace mental health programs*. Research Report. Deloitte Canada, 2019.
       URL: https://www2.deloitte.com/content/dam/Deloitte/c
       a/Documents/about-deloitte/ca-en-about-blueprint-fo
       r-workplace-mental-health-final-aoda.pdf.

[52]   LinkedIn Learning. *2024 Workplace Learning Report: L&D Powers the AI Future*.
       Tech. rep. Survey of 1,636 L&D/HR professionals and 1,063 learners; retention
       calculated from LinkedIn platform data. LinkedIn Corporation, 2024. URL: http
       s://learning.linkedin.com/content/dam/me/business/e
       n-us/amp/learning-solutions/images/wlr-2024/LinkedI
       n-Workplace-Learning-Report-2024.pdf.

[53]   Sue Cantrell, David Mallon, Shannon Poynton, Kraig Eaton, Jason Flynn, and Nicole
       Scoble-Williams. *2024 Global Human Capital Trends: Thriving Beyond Boundaries —
       Human Performance in a Boundaryless World*. Tech. rep. Survey of 14,000 business
       and HR leaders across 95 countries. Deloitte Insights, 2024. URL: https://ww
       w.deloitte.com/content/dam/insights/articles/2024/g
       lob176836_global-human-capital-trends-2024/DI_Globa
       l-Human-Capital-Trends-2024.pdf.

[54]   Airbnb. *Airbnb is Global and Growing: 4 Million Listings Worldwide*. Company
       newsroom. Announces 4M listings across 191+ countries; more listings than the
       top five hotel chains combined. 2017. URL: https://news.airbnb.com
       /wp-content/uploads/sites/4/2017/08/4-Million-Listi
       ngs-Announcement-1.pdf (visited on 09/25/2025).

[55]   Chiara Farronato and Andrey Fradkin. "How Airbnb has affected the hotel industry".
       In: *U.S. Bureau of Labor Statistics, Beyond the Numbers* (2018). States Airbnb has
       listed more rooms for rent than any hotel chain in the world. URL: https://ww
       w.bls.gov/opub/mlr/2018/beyond-bls/how-airbnb-has-a
       ffected-the-hotel-industry.htm (visited on 09/25/2025).

[56]   TikTok. *Thanks a billion!* Company newsroom. Announces surpassing one billion
       monthly active users globally. 2021. URL: https://newsroom.tiktok.c
       om/en-us/1-billion-people-on-tiktok (visited on 09/25/2025).

[57]   Guinness World Records. *Fastest social media network to reach 1 billion monthly
       active users*. Record entry. Benchmarks TikTok's time-to-1B MAUs versus Face-
       book/Instagram/YouTube. 2021. URL: https://www.guinnessworldr
       ecords.com/world-records/688782-fastest-social-med

`ia-network-to-reach-1-billion-monthly-active-users` (visited on 09/25/2025).

[58] Michael A. Cusumano, Annabelle Gawer, David B. Yoffie, Sarah von Bargen, and Kwesi Acquay. *Is There a "Platform Premium"? An Exploratory Study of Unicorn Business Models and Valuations*. Tech. rep. Platform unicorns valued at $4.3B vs non-platform unicorns at $2.5B (72% premium); sample of 959 unicorns. MIT Sloan School of Management, Harvard Business School, University of Surrey, 2023. URL: `https://questromworld.bu.edu/platformstrategy/wp-content/uploads/sites/49/2023/06/PlatStrat2023_paper_5.pdf`.

[59] Sophia Dodd and Rick Zullo. *The Premium of Platforms: Valuation Insights from the Bessemer Cloud Index*. Equal Ventures, Medium. Platform companies: 8.2× EV/revenue vs traditional SaaS: 3.9× (2.1× premium). 2024. URL: `https://medium.com/@EqualVentures/the-premium-of-platforms-07ef52eac18b`.

[60] Marshall W. Van Alstyne, Geoffrey G. Parker, and Sangeet Paul Choudary. "Pipelines, Platforms, and the New Rules of Strategy". In: *Harvard Business Review* (2016). URL: `https://hbr.org/2016/04/pipelines-platforms-and-the-new-rules-of-strategy`.

[61] GitLab Inc. *Annual Report on Form 10-K*. Approximately 2,375 team members across 60 countries; remote-only; no headquarters. U.S. Securities and Exchange Commission, 2025. URL: `https://www.sec.gov/ix?doc=/Archives/edgar/data/0001653482/000162828025014344/gtlb-20250131.htm`.

[62] CB Insights Research. *State of AI Report: 6 trends shaping the landscape in 2025*. Tech. rep. Report; customer login required. CB Insights, 2025. URL: `https://www.cbinsights.com/research/report/ai-trends-2024/`.

[63] CB Insights Research. *$1B+ Market Map: The world's 1,276 unicorn companies in one infographic*. Tech. rep. Report; customer login required. CB Insights, 2025. URL: `https://www.cbinsights.com/research/report/unicorn-startups-valuations-headcount-investors/`.

[64] European Parliament and Council. *Regulation (EU) 2024/1689 laying down harmonised rules on artificial intelligence*. Tech. rep. EUR-Lex 32024R1689. Prohibited practices provisions enforceable February 2, 2025. Official Journal of the European Union, 2024. URL: `https://eur-lex.europa.eu/eli/reg/2024/1689/oj/eng`.

[65] European Data Protection Board. *EDPB Annual Report 2023*. Tech. rep. Documents €1.97 billion in GDPR fines issued in 2023. European Data Protection Board, 2024. URL: `https://www.edpb.europa.eu/system/files/2024-04/edpb_annual_report_2023_en.pdf`.

[66] UK Supreme Court. *Uber BV v Aslam and others [2021] UKSC 5*. UK Supreme Court judgment. Established five key factors for determining worker status in gig economy. 2021. URL: `https://www.supremecourt.uk/cases/uksc-2019-0029`.

[67] McKinsey & Company. *The consumer-data opportunity and the privacy imperative.* Tech. rep. 87% of consumers would not do business with companies with poor security practices. McKinsey & Company, 2020. URL: `https://www.mckins ey.com/capabilities/risk-and-resilience/our-insight s/the-consumer-data-opportunity-and-the-privacy-imp erative`.

[68] Society for Human Resource Management. *The State of Global Workplace Culture in 2024.* Tech. rep. Survey of 17,234 employed adults from 19 countries. SHRM, 2024. URL: `https://www.shrm.org/content/dam/en/shrm/researc h/the-state-of-global-workplace-culture-2024.pdf`.

[69] Harry Robinson. *Why do most transformations fail? A conversation with Harry Robinson.* McKinsey & Company. McKinsey Transformation Practice leader discussing ~70% failure rate. 2023. URL: `https://www.mckinsey.com/capabil ities/transformation/our-insights/why-do-most-trans formations-fail-a-conversation-with-harry-robinson`.

[70] Alexis Krivkovich, Lareina Yee, Emily Field, Megan McConnell, Hannah Smith, Rachel Thomas, Caroline Fairchild, Priya Fielding-Singh, Mary Noble-Tolla, Gina Cardazone, Hayley Brown, and Marianne Cooper. *Women in the Workplace 2024: The 10th Anniversary Report.* 281 companies; 10M+ employees; 15,000+ surveyed. McKinsey & Company and LeanIn.Org, 2024. URL: `https://www.mckinse y.com/featured-insights/diversity-and-inclusion/wom en-in-the-workplace`.

[71] Amy C. Edmondson and Derrick P. Bransby. "Psychological safety comes of age: Observed themes in an established literature". In: *Annual Review of Organizational Psychology and Organizational Behavior* 10.1 (2023), pp. 55–78. DOI: `10.1146 /annurev-orgpsych-120920-055217`.

[72] International Monetary Fund. *Geoeconomic Fragmentation and Trade: Working Paper No. 2024/122.* Tech. rep. Friend-shoring scenarios could reduce long-term global GDP by 1.8%. International Monetary Fund, 2024.

[73] U.S. Census Bureau. *Top Trading Partners (Goods) — FT-900 Supplemental Exhibit 4.* Monthly goods trade rankings; Mexico ranked #1 in recent periods. 2025. URL: `https://www.census.gov/foreign-trade/statistics/hig hlights/topcm.html` (visited on 10/04/2025).

[74] Daniel M. Ravid, David P. Costanza, and Madison R. Romero. "Generational differences at work? A meta-analysis and qualitative investigation". In: *Journal of Organizational Behavior* 46 (2025), pp. 43–65. DOI: `10.1002/job.2827`.

[75] U.S. Office of Personnel Management. *Federal Workforce Priorities Report 2022.* Tech. rep. Washington, D.C.: U.S. Office of Personnel Management, 2022. URL: `h ttps://www.opm.gov/policy-data-oversight/human-capi tal-management/federal-workforce-priorities-report/`.

[76] U.S. Bureau of Labor Statistics. *Employment Projections—2023-2033.* News Release USDL-24-1776. U.S. Department of Labor, 2024. URL: `https://www.bls.g ov/news.release/archives/ecopro_08292024.htm`.

[77] Future Forum. *Future Forum Pulse Summer Snapshot: New data shows the desire for flexibility has intensified among knowledge workers—and they're willing to walk to get it.* Tech. rep. Future Forum, 2022. URL: `https://futureforum.com /research/future-forum-pulse-summer-snapshot/`.

[78] McKinsey & Company. *Global Energy Perspective 2024*. Tech. rep. Skilled workforce availability as bottleneck for renewables and fossil fuels. McKinsey & Company, 2024. URL: `https://www.mckinsey.com/industries/energy-and-materials/our-insights/global-energy-perspective`.

[79] U.S. Bureau of Labor Statistics. *Wind Turbine Technicians*. Occupational Outlook Handbook. Projected growth (2024–2034); among fastest-growing occupations. 2025. URL: `https://www.bls.gov/ooh/installation-maintenance-and-repair/wind-turbine-technicians.htm` (visited on 09/25/2025).

[80] U.S. Bureau of Labor Statistics. *Employment Projections — 2024–2034*. Tech. rep. Summary release; renewable energy occupations highlighted; combined additions < 20,000 jobs. U.S. Department of Labor, 2025. URL: `https://www.bls.gov/news.release/archives/ecopro_08282025.pdf` (visited on 09/25/2025).

[81] U.S. Bureau of Labor Statistics. *Solar Photovoltaic Installers*. Occupational Outlook Handbook. 2024. URL: `https://www.bls.gov/ooh/construction-and-extraction/solar-photovoltaic-installers.htm` (visited on 09/25/2025).

[82] D. S. Bindeeba, E. K. Tukamushaba, and S. Atuhaire. "From green HRM to sustainable business performance: A two-stage meta-analytic SEM of the mediating role of green innovation". In: *Cogent Business & Management* 12.1 (2025). Meta-analysis of 137 studies across 43 countries. DOI: `10.1080/23311975.2025.2536678`.

[83] Advait Kadolkar, Evelyn Aw, and Sandhya Nair. "Algorithmic management in the platform economy: A systematic review". In: *Journal of Organizational Behavior* (2024). DOI: `10.1002/job.2831`.

[84] Tobias Kretschmer, Aija Leiponen, Melissa Schilling, and Gurneeta Vasudeva. "Platform ecosystems as meta-organizations: Implications for platform strategies". In: *Strategic Management Journal* 43.3 (2022). First published online November 15, 2020. Open access, pp. 405–424. DOI: `10.1002/smj.3250`. URL: `https://sms.onlinelibrary.wiley.com/doi/epdf/10.1002/smj.3250`.

[85] Sunil Gupta and Lauren Barley. *Reinventing Adobe*. Harvard Business School Case 514-066. Revised January 2015. 2014. URL: `https://store.hbr.org/product/reinventing-adobe/514066?sku=514066-PDF-ENG`.

[86] Kara Sprague. "Reborn in the cloud". In: *McKinsey Digital* (2017). Interview with Mark Garrett (CFO) and Dan Cohen (VP Business Operations) discussing Adobe's subscription transformation, recurring revenue growth from 19% to 70%, and $200M operating expense reallocation. URL: `https://www.mckinsey.com/capabilities/mckinsey-digital/our-insights/reborn-in-the-cloud`.

[87] Uber Technologies Inc. *Form 10-K Annual Report*. Fiscal year ended December 31, 2024. Accession No. 0001543151-25-000008. U.S. Securities and Exchange Commission, 2025. URL: `https://www.sec.gov/Archives/edgar/data/1543151/000154315125000008/uber-20241231.htm`.

[88] Siemens AG. *Annual Report 2023*. Fiscal year ended September 30, 2023; discusses data-driven services, IoT-enabled platforms, and service business growth. Siemens AG, 2023. URL: `https://assets.new.siemens.com/siemens/a ssets/api/uuid:be1828a9-2368-4c3b-a85f-f1bcb1f14a59 /Siemens-Annual-Report-2023.pdf`.

[89] Longqi Yang, David Holtz, Sonia Jaffe, Siddharth Suri, Shilpi Sinha, Jeffrey Weston, Connor Joyce, Neha Shah, Kevin Sherman, Brent Hecht, and Jaime Teevan. "The effects of remote work on collaboration among information workers". In: *Nature Human Behaviour* 6 (2022). Published online 09 September 2021, pp. 43–54. DOI: `10.1038/s41562-021-01196-4`. URL: `https://www.nature.co m/articles/s41562-021-01196-4`.

[90] Michael D. Watkins. *The First 90 Days: Critical Success Strategies for New Leaders at All Levels*. Introduces the STARS situations. Boston, MA: Harvard Business School Press, 2003. URL: `https://hbr.org/books/watkins` (visited on 09/25/2025).

[91] James L. Heskett, Thomas O. Jones, Gary W. Loveman, W. Earl Sasser, and Leonard A. Schlesinger. "Putting the Service-Profit Chain to Work". In: *Harvard Business Review* 72.2 (1994). March–April. Reprinted in Harvard Business Review 86, no. 7/8 (July–August 2008), pp. 164–174. URL: `https://hbr.org/2008/07 /putting-the-service-profit-chain-to-work`.

[92] Richard Beckhard. "Optimizing team building efforts". In: *Journal of Contemporary Business* 1.3 (1972). Framework formalized as "GRPI" by Rubin, Plovnick, & Fry (1978). Reprinted in Coghlan & Shani, *Fundamentals of Organization Development*, SAGE, 2010, pp. 23–32.

[93] Harold J. Leavitt. "Applied Organizational Change in Industry: Structural, Technical, and Human Approaches". In: *Handbook of Organizations*. Ed. by James G. March. Leavitt's Diamond: Task, People, Structure, Technology. Chicago, IL: Rand McNally, 1965, pp. 1144–1170.

[94] Robert S. Kaplan and David P. Norton. "The Balanced Scorecard—Measures That Drive Performance". In: *Harvard Business Review* 70.1 (1992), pp. 71–79. URL: `https://hbr.org/2005/07/the-balanced-scorecard-meas ures-that-drive-performance` (visited on 09/25/2025).

[95] Michael E. Porter. "How Competitive Forces Shape Strategy". In: *Harvard Business Review* 57.2 (1979). March–April, pp. 137–145. URL: `https://hbr.org/1 979/03/how-competitive-forces-shape-strategy` (visited on 09/25/2025).

[96] Andrew S. Grove. *High Output Management*. New York, NY: Random House, 1983.

[97] Paul Hersey and Kenneth H. Blanchard. "Life Cycle Theory of Leadership". In: *Training and Development Journal* 23.5 (1969). Later known as Situational Leadership, pp. 26–34.

[98] John P. Kotter. *Leading Change*. Boston, MA: Harvard Business School Press, 1996.

[99] J. Richard Hackman and Greg R. Oldham. "Motivation through the Design of Work: Test of a Theory". In: *Organizational Behavior and Human Performance* 16.2 (1976), pp. 250–279. DOI: `10.1016/0030-5073(76)90016-7`.

[100] Eliyahu M. Goldratt and Jeff Cox. *The Goal: A Process of Ongoing Improvement*. Business novel introducing Theory of Constraints. Great Barrington, MA: North River Press, 1984.

[101] Helmuth von Moltke. *Moltke on the Art of War: Selected Writings*. Ed. by Daniel J. Hughes and Harry Bell. Novato, CA: Presidio Press, 1993. URL: https://archive.org/details/moltkeonartofwar0000molt (visited on 09/25/2025).

[102] Michael J. Gunther. *Auftragstaktik: The Basis for Modern Military Command?* SAMS Monograph. Approved for public release; distribution unlimited. Fort Leavenworth, KS: School of Advanced Military Studies, U.S. Army Command and General Staff College, 2012. URL: https://cgsc.contentdm.oclc.org/digital/api/collection/p4013coll3/id/2963/download (visited on 09/25/2025).

[103] Geoffrey Wawro. *The Franco-Prussian War: The German Conquest of France in 1870–1871*. Cambridge, UK: Cambridge University Press, 2003. DOI: 10.1017/CBO9780511511820. URL: https://www.cambridge.org/core/books/francoprussian-war/6F3211FF365ACE2A217549BE18D8627C (visited on 09/25/2025).

[104] Dwight D. Eisenhower. *Remarks at the National Defense Executive Reserve Conference*. The American Presidency Project. "Plans are worthless, but planning is everything." 1957. URL: https://www.presidency.ucsb.edu/documents/remarks-the-national-defense-executive-reserve-conference (visited on 09/25/2025).

[105] Winston S. Churchill. *A Roving Commission: My Early Life*. New American edition. Chapter 16, "I Leave the Army," pp. 212–213. New York, NY: Charles Scribner's Sons, 1941. URL: https://archive.org/details/rovingcommission00chur (visited on 09/25/2025).

[106] Amazon Web Services. *Intuit Scales Contact Center to Support 20,000 Agents with Amazon Connect*. AWS Case Study. 2023. URL: https://aws.amazon.com/solutions/case-studies/intuit-contact-center-case-study/ (visited on 01/15/2024).

[107] *Marketplace Weekly Enrollment Snapshot: Week 1*. Centers for Medicare & Medicaid Services (CMS) Fact Sheet. Week 1 (Nov 1–6, 2021) includes Marketplace Call Center Volume = 293,511. 2021. URL: https://www.cms.gov/newsroom/fact-sheets/marketplace-weekly-enrollment-snapshot-week-1 (visited on 10/04/2025).

[108] *Marketplace Weekly Enrollment Snapshot: Week 6*. Centers for Medicare & Medicaid Services (CMS) Fact Sheet. Week 6 (Dec 5–15, 2021) includes Marketplace Call Center Volume = 1,299,313. 2021. URL: https://www.cms.gov/newsroom/fact-sheets/marketplace-weekly-enrollment-snapshot-week-6 (visited on 10/04/2025).

[109] Becca Kleinstein, Maurice Obeid, Jessica Kahn, and James Hoey. *Four actions to improve Medicaid contact center performance*. McKinsey & Company. Highlights surging call volumes and operational strain during eligibility events. 2024. URL: https://www.mckinsey.com/industries/public-sector/our-insights/four-actions-to-improve-medicaid-contact-center-performance (visited on 10/04/2025).

[110] U.S. Department of Transportation. *DOT Penalizes Southwest Airlines $140 Million for 2022 Holiday Meltdown*. U.S. Department of Transportation, 2023. URL: `https://www.transportation.gov/briefing-room/dot-penalizes-southwest-airlines-140-million-2022-holiday-meltdown` (visited on 10/04/2025).

[111] Chris Isidore. "Why Southwest is Melting Down". In: *CNN Business* (2022). URL: `https://www.cnn.com/2022/12/27/business/southwest-airlines-service-meltdown/` (visited on 10/04/2025).

[112] Eleanor Bensley, Sergey Khon, David Tan, and Zubin Taraporevala. "Breaking away from the pack in the next normal of retail banking distribution". In: *McKinsey & Company* (2020). Early COVID period: contact center call volumes +29% and waiting times quadrupled; widespread temporary branch closures. URL: `https://www.mckinsey.com/industries/financial-services/our-insights/breaking-away-from-the-pack-in-the-next-normal-of-retail-banking-distribution` (visited on 10/04/2025).

[113] Consumer Financial Protection Bureau. *Consumer Response Annual Report, January 1–December 31, 2020*. Approximately 542,300 complaints in 2020 (54% YoY increase). CFPB, 2021. URL: `https://files.consumerfinance.gov/f/documents/cfpb_2020-consumer-response-annual-report_03-2021.pdf` (visited on 10/04/2025).

[114] Federal Bureau of Investigation. *2020 Internet Crime Report*. 791,790 complaints; 69% increase vs. 2019. FBI Internet Crime Complaint Center (IC3), 2021. URL: `https://www.ic3.gov/AnnualReport/Reports/2020_IC3Report.pdf` (visited on 10/04/2025).

[115] Penny Reynolds. *The Power of One*. 3rd. Nashville, TN: The Call Center School Press, 2005.

[116] Ger Koole. *Call Center Optimization*. Includes online calculators and Excel tools at gerkoole.com/CCO. Amsterdam: MG Books, 2013.

[117] Brad Cleveland. *Contact Center Management on Fast Forward: Succeeding in the New Era of Customer Experience*. 4th. Annapolis, MD: ICMI Press, 2019.

[118] Rob J. Hyndman and George Athanasopoulos. *Forecasting: Principles and Practice*. 3rd. Freely available online with R code examples and datasets. Melbourne, Australia: OTexts, 2021. URL: `https://otexts.com/fpp3`.

[119] John P. Kotter. *Leading Change*. 2nd. Original edition published 1996. Boston, MA: Harvard Business Review Press, 2012, p. 187.

[120] Spencer Johnson. *Who Moved My Cheese? An Amazing Way to Deal with Change in Your Work and in Your Life*. New York, NY: G.P. Putnam's Sons, 1998, p. 96.

[121] Nassim Nicholas Taleb. *Antifragile: Things That Gain from Disorder*. Part of the Incerto series on uncertainty. New York, NY: Random House, 2012, p. 544.

[122] Donella H. Meadows. *Thinking in Systems: A Primer*. Ed. by Diana Wright. Chelsea Green Publishing, 2008.

[123] Douglas W. Hubbard. *How to Measure Anything: Finding the Value of Intangibles in Business*. 3rd. John Wiley & Sons, 2014.

[124] Ethan Mollick. *Co-Intelligence: Living and Working with AI*. Portfolio/Penguin Random House, 2024.

[125]   Michael A. Cusumano, Annabelle Gawer, and David B. Yoffie. *The Business of Platforms: Strategy in the Age of Digital Competition, Innovation, and Power*. Harper Business, 2019.

Glossary

ACD Automatic Call Distributor. Telephony/omnichannel system that routes contacts to agents using skills/policies.

ACW After-Call Work. Post-contact wrap time included in handle time and staffing assumptions.

AHT Average Handle Time. Talk + hold + ACW per contact; a driver of workload and staffing.

AL *Adaptation Latency*. Median time from a material signal (campaign/outage/sentiment) to the effective routing/schedule change.

A/B (test) Experimental design comparing two conditions; often used for pilot rule toggles.

AAR *Automation Acceptance Rate*. Accepted automated prompts ÷ eligible prompts.

ASA Average Speed of Answer. Mean wait time for answered contacts; pairs with SL to show depth of delay.

BPO Business Process Outsourcing; external vendor capacity used under guardrails or envelopes.

BI Business Intelligence; reporting/visualization layer aligned to the single source of truth.

CCaaS Contact Center as a Service; cloud platform providing routing, reporting, and channels.

CES Customer Effort Score; perceived effort to resolve an issue.

CLV Customer Lifetime Value; value contribution over a relationship horizon.

Cohort A defined population segment used for pilots and measurement (e.g., tenure band, skill).

CRM Customer Relationship Management; system of record for customer interactions and attributes.

CSAT Customer Satisfaction; survey-based outcome metric.

Decision Cards Lightweight documentation of automated or human decisions: inputs, owner, guardrails, rollback path.

Bibliography

DES	Discrete-Event Simulation. Event-by-event modeling of queues/skills/policies for planning and policy evaluation.
Envelope (Staffing)	A probability band (e.g., P50/P80/P95) for staffing need; leaders pick a band that matches risk tolerance.
Envelope hit-rate	Share of intervals where realized need falls *within* the chosen band (e.g., P80).
ERP	Enterprise Resource Planning; finance/inventory backbone integrated with WFM decisions.
ETL	Extract–Transform–Load; data pipelines feeding planning and the ROC.
EWI	*Employee Wellbeing Index.* Composite (e.g., schedule stability, growth delivered, burnout risk).
EX	Employee Experience; perceived quality of work environment and systems.
Explainability Coverage	Share of automated decisions with recorded reasons, inputs, and override path.
Fairness Disparity Ratio	Simple fairness lens comparing outcomes across cohorts (e.g., tenure/shift).
Fan Chart	Visual showing a forecast median with widening percentile bands over time.
Feature Store	Managed repository of model features used consistently across training and inference.
FCR	First-Contact Resolution; issue resolved in the first interaction.
Governance Review	Cadence that approves guardrails, rollbacks, and changes to formulas and rule logic.
GRPIT	Goals, Roles, Processes, Interpersonal, Technology. Five-lens structure used in each level's operational profile.
Guardrails	Policy bounds that define safe ranges (e.g., SL floor, occupancy band, fairness limits) for automation and people.
HRIS	Human Resources Information System; authoritative staffing/tenure/attrition data.
Integration Contract	One-pager clarifying inputs/outputs/SLAs between teams/systems for an integration.

ITSM	IT Service Management; incident/ticket framework mirrored in ROC incident handling.
LMS	Learning Management System; source for training content, delivery, and completion data.
LP/MILP	(Mixed-Integer) Linear Programming; optimization methods for schedules/assignments under constraints.
MAPE	Mean Absolute Percentage Error; forecasting accuracy metric (sensitive to small denominators).
Minimal Interval Error Rate	A variance floor for interval forecasts. Approx. $\sqrt{\frac{2}{\pi \cdot FC}} \times$ 100%, where FC is forecasted contacts in the interval.
Model Card	Lightweight model documentation (purpose, data, limits, monitoring).
Model Serving	Low-latency inference tier that exposes models via stable APIs.
Monte Carlo	Sampling-based method to produce distributions (not points) for plans and KPIs.
NPS	Net Promoter Score; "recommend" intent proxy.
Occupancy	Share of agent time engaged on work; manage via bands (e.g., 78–88%).
Option Value of Flexibility (OVF)	Value difference between static and flexible posture under uncertainty.
OT	Overtime; scheduled or incidental work beyond base shift.
Pilot Charter	1-page scope/owners/metrics/rollback for a time-boxed pilot.
Portfolio Review	Quarterly cadence aligning outcomes to objectives; adjusts roadmap and ownership.
Posture (Staffing)	Declared coverage stance (e.g., P80 envelope) given risk tolerance and budget.
Power of One	Nonlinear sensitivity of SL to small staffing changes in tight queues.
RACI-Lite	Roles for cadences: A — Accountable; R — Responsible; C — Consulted; I — Informed. Abbreviations used in this book: CWS, EAIG, ROC Lead, MLO.

Bibliography

CWS

Chief Workforce Strategist. Executive owner for workforce strategy and scorecards; co-owns scenario/portfolio reviews; selects staffing posture by band.

EAIG

Enterprise AI Governance. Cross-functional oversight for explainability, fairness, drift, and rollbacks; chairs the governance review.

ROC Lead

Operational owner of the Resource Optimization Center cadence; chairs daily stand-ups; coordinates intraday moves across skills/sites.

MLO

Model Lifecycle Owner. Accountable for model deployment, monitoring, drift/rollback, and audit evidence; partner to EAIG.

Real-Time Analyst (RTA)

Supervises intraday variance across queues; implements schedule/routing adjustments; manages incident response; and designs/tunes rules and automation with supervisors, WFM, and IT. Present from L2 (reactive) through L3–L5 (increasingly proactive).

Rule→Trigger→Action (R→T→A)

Pattern for automation/playbooks: a rule with a condition and a specific action; *not* the RTA role.

Rule Registry

Versioned inventory of rules with owner, intent, guardrails, metrics, and change history.

Scenario Forum

Weekly review of driver changes and updated weights that feed envelopes and rules.

SCR

Supervisor Coaching Ratio. Share of supervisor time on coaching vs. admin.

Service Level (SL)

Timeliness promise (e.g., 80% in 30s) read at 15–30 minute intervals.

Service-Profit Chain

Link between employee experience, service quality, and financial performance.

Service-Level Stability (SLS)

Share of intervals where SL and ASA are within a published band.

Short-abandon

Policy for ignoring abandons under a small wait threshold in SL math; document threshold.

SSoT

Single Source of Truth; governed, versioned metric/data definitions.

SQI

Schedule Quality Index. Composite of lead time, change count, preference match, and stability.

STaRS	Startup, Turnaround, Realignment, Sustaining Success—context lens for sequencing moves.
TTS	*Time-to-Stabilize*. Time from threshold breach to return within the service band.
VCE	*Variance Capture Efficiency*. Minutes redeployed to value work ÷ eligible micro-availability minutes.
Variance Log	Structured record of incidents, causes, actions, and results that feeds weekly changes.
VOT	Voluntary Overtime; offered under guardrails when understaffed.
VTO	Voluntary Time Off; offered under guardrails when overstaffed.
WAPE	Weighted Absolute Percentage Error; preferred for uneven interval volumes.
WFM	Workforce Management; the loop: forecast → schedule → real-time → learn.
WFM Labs Maturity Model™	Five-level progression (L1–L5) from manual foundations to enterprise orchestration.

www.ingramcontent.com/pod-product-compliance
Lightning Source LLC
Chambersburg PA
CBHW082139210326
41599CB00031B/6034